DAY HIKING

Columbia
River Gorge

DAY HIKING

Columbia
River Gorge

2nd Edition

waterfalls · vistas · state parks
national scenic area

Craig Romano

MOUNTAINEERS
BOOKS

MOUNTAINEERS BOOKS is dedicated to the exploration, preservation, and enjoyment of outdoor and wilderness areas.

1001 SW Klickitat Way, Suite 201, Seattle, WA 98134
800-553-4453, www.mountaineersbooks.org

Printed in China

First edition, 2011. Second edition, 2024.

Design and layout: McKenzie Long, Cardinal Innovative
Cartographer: Pease Press Cartography
All photographs by the author unless credited otherwise
Cover photograph: *Lyle Cherry Orchard (Hike 55)*
Frontispiece: *Balsamroot on the Buck Creek Trail near Monte Carlo (Hike 42)*

Library of Congress Control Number: 2023948042

Mountaineers Books titles may be purchased for corporate, educational, or other promotional sales, and our authors are available for a wide range of events. For information on special discounts or booking an author, contact our customer service at 800-553-4453 or mbooks@mountaineersbooks.org.

Printed on FSC®-certified materials

ISBN (paperback): 978-1-68051-559-6
ISBN (ebook): 978-1-68051-560-2

An independent nonprofit publisher since 1960

Contents

Western Gorge, Oregon

Eastern Gorge, Oregon

Cottonwood Canyon State Park, Oregon

Hike Locator

to Seattle ↑

N

0 ___ 10 ___ 20 MILES
0 ___ 10 ___ 20 KILOMETERS

Kelso

WASHINGTON

MOUNT
SAINT HELENS
NATIONAL
VOLCANIC
MONUMENT

▲ Mount
St Helens

GIFFORD PINCHOT
NATIONAL FOREST

Cascade Range

Pacific Crest Trail

Saint
Helens

Woodland

503

Yacolt

503

Battle
Ground

520

YACOLT
BURN
STATE
FOREST

TRAPPER CREEK
WILDERNESS

28-33

34

1

2

3

24-26

27

38

39

4

7-8

9

38

NATIONAL

6

5

Wind River Hwy

COLUMBIA RIVER GORGE

37

Carson

35

36

Stevenson
Cascade
Locks

87

90

9

VANCOUVER

500

205

16-18

21-23

85

88

89

82-84

86

19-20

13-15

76-80

99-100

Camas

14

140

Washougal

66-68

69

73-75

81

96-97

95

PORTLAND

26

84

10-11

12

70-72

98

Troutdale

62

64

65

Gresham

63

Beaverton

217

Milwaukie

205

Sandy

26

Oregon City

99W

5

OREGON

Pacific Crest Trail

Mount
Hood ▲

35

to Salem

99E

MOUNT HOOD
NATIONAL FOREST

26

Columbia River

30

5

I-5

205

14

Hikes at a Glance

HIKE	DISTANCE IN MILES (ROUNDTRIP)	OVERALL RATING	DIFFICULTY	HIKEABLE ALL YEAR	KID-FRIE
SILVER STAR SCENIC AREA, WASHINGTON					
1. Bells Mountain	6.8	3	3	•	•
2. Summit Springs Trail	5.6	2	3	•	•
3. East Fork Lewis River	8	3	4		
4. Hidden Falls	7.8	2	2	•	•
5. Larch Mountain	5.4	3	2	•	•
6. Silver Star Mountain via Grouse Vista	6.4	4	3		•
7. Silver Star Mountain via North Ridge	4.7	5	3		
8. Starway	10	4	4		
9. Little Baldy	8	5	3		
WESTERN GORGE, WASHINGTON					
10. Columbia River Dike Trail	4.4	2	1	•	
11. Steigerwald Lake NWR	4.2	3	1	•	
12. Cape Horn	7.2	4	3	•	
13. Sams Walker Nature Trail	1.2	3	1	•	
14. Beacon Rock	1.8	5	2	•	
15. River to Rock and Che-che-op-tin Trails	2.9	2	1	•	
16. Hamilton Mountain	7.6	5	4		
17. Hardy Ridge	7.1	3	3		
18. Upper Hardy Creek	6.2	3	3		
19. Strawberry Island	2.7	3	1	•	
20. Fort Cascades Loop	1.2	2	1	•	
21. Gillette Lake and Greenleaf Overlook	5.4/8	2/2	2/3	•	
22. Aldrich Butte	12.4	3	3	•	
23. Table Mountain	15.9	4	5		
24. Wind River Arboretum	1.2	2	1	•	
25. Bunker Hill	4	2	3		
26. Whistle Punk Trail	1.5	2	1		
27. Sedum Point	9	3	3		

DOG-FRIENDLY	WILDFLOWERS	WATERFALLS	OLD-GROWTH	HISTORICAL	WHEELCHAIR ACCESSIBLE	CAR CAMP NEARBY	BACKPACKING
•	•					•	
•						•	
•						•	
•		•				•	
•	•					•	
•	•			•			
	•			•		•	
•	•					•	
•				•	•		
	•			•	•		
	•	•		•			
•	•			•	•	•	
				•		•	
•				•	partially	•	
	•	•		•		•	
•	•					•	
•						•	
•	•			•			
•					•		
•							•
•				•			•
	•						•
				•			
			•	•			
			•	•		•	
	•		•				•

HIKE	DISTANCE IN MILES (ROUNDTRIP)	OVERALL RATING	DIFFICULTY	HIKEABLE ALL YEAR	KID-FRIEN
TRAPPER CREEK WILDERNESS, WASHINGTON					
28. Trapper Creek	10	3	3		•
29. Soda Peaks Lake	10	4	5		
30. Observation Peak via Howe Ridge	12.8	4	5		•
31. Dry Creek	7.8	3	2	•	•
32. Observation Peak via Big Hollow	8.4	3	4		
33. Sister Rocks and Observation Peak	6.6	4	3		•
34. Falls Creek Falls	3.4	5	2		•
EASTERN GORGE, WASHINGTON					
35. Wind Mountain	2.6	3	3		
36. Dog Mountain	6.9	5	4		•
37. Augspurger Mountain	12.8	3	5		
38. Grassy Knoll and Big Huckleberry Mountain	4.0/10.6	5/4	3/4		•
39. Little Huckleberry Mountain	5	3	3		•
40. Buck Creek Falls	2.9	2	2	•	•
41. Nestor Peak	8	3	3		
42. Monte Carlo	10.4	3	4		
43. Monte Cristo	3	4	3		
44. Weldon Wagon Road	4.6	3	3	•	•
45. Willard Springs Trail	3.8	3	1		•
46. Coyote Wall	5.4	4	3	•	
47. Catherine Creek: The Labyrinth	4.2	4	3	•	
48. Catherine Creek: Universal Access Trail	1.2	4	1	•	
49. Catherine Creek: Rowland Ridge	3.5	4	3	•	
50. Catherine Creek: Natural Arch and Tracy Hill	1.9/5.1	3/4	2/3	•	
51. Klickitat Trail: Klickitat River	20.4	3	2	•	
52. Klickitat Trail: Mineral Springs	5.2	3	1	•	
53. Klickitat Trail: Swale Canyon	11.6	3	3		
54. Klickitat River Haul Road	7	3	1	•	
55. Lyle Cherry Orchard	6.8	4	3	•	
56. Stacker Butte	5	4	3		
57. Crawford Oaks	6.6	4	3		
58. Horsethief Butte	1.2	3	2	•	
59. Observatory Hill	2.4	3	2	•	
60. Brooks Memorial State Park	3.4	2	2		
61. Crow Butte	2.2	3	2		

DOG-FRIENDLY	WILDFLOWERS	WATERFALLS	OLD-GROWTH	HISTORICAL	WHEELCHAIR ACCESSIBLE	CAR CAMP NEARBY	BACKPACKING
•			•	•		•	•
•			•			•	•
•	•		•	•		•	•
•			•	•		•	
•	•		•	•		•	•
•	•		•	•			•
•		•	•			•	
			•	•			
•	•			•			
•	•						
•	•			•			•
•	•		•				•
•		•				•	
•	•			•		•	
•	•		•			•	
•	•			•		•	
•	•			•			
•	•		•	•			
	•						
•	•	•					
•	•				•		
•	•						
•	•						
	•						
•	•			•	partially		
•	•			•		•	
•	•			•			
	•			•	partially		
•	•			•			
	•			•		•	
•	•	•		•		•	
	•			•		•	
	•						
•	•					•	
	•			•		•	

HIKE	DISTANCE IN MILES (ROUNDTRIP)	OVERALL RATING	DIFFICULTY	HIKEABLE ALL YEAR	KID-FRIE
WESTERN GORGE, OREGON					
62. Sandy River Delta	3.5	2	1	•	•
63. Oxbow Regional Park	4.2	3	2	•	•
64. Rooster Rock State Park	3.2	2	2	•	•
65. Latourell Falls	2.3	4	2	•	•
66. Bridal Veil Falls	1	2	1	•	•
67. Angels Rest	4.6	5	3	•	•
68. Devils Rest	7.7	3	3	•	•
69. Multnomah Falls–Wahkeena Falls Loop	5.2	5	3	•	•
70. Larch Mountain	14.4	4	4		
71. Franklin Ridge	12.3	3	4		
72. Larch Mountain Crater	6.6	3	3		•
73. Triple Falls	3.6	3	3	•	
74. Ponytail Falls Loop	2.7	4	2	•	•
75. Bell Creek	15.8	4	4		
76. Nesmith Point	10	4	5		
77. Elowah and Upper McCord Creek Falls	2.8	3	2	•	•
78. Wahclella Falls	2.2	4	2	•	•
79. Tooth Rock	1.8	2	1	•	•
80. Wauna Viewpoint	3.6	3	3	•	•
81. Dublin Lake	13.2	2	5		
82. Eagle Creek	12	5	3		
83. Benson Plateau via Ruckel Creek	11.2	3	5		
84. Dry Creek Falls	4.4	3	3	•	
85. Benson Plateau via Pacific Crest Trail	15.6	4	5		
EASTERN GORGE, OREGON					
86. Herman Creek Ancient Cedars	15	4	4		
87. Nick Eaton Ridge	8.3	4	4		
88. North Lake via Wyeth Trail	13	3	5		
89. Mount Defiance	13.2	5	5		
90. Wygant Peak	9.2	3	4		
91. Mitchell Point	2.2	3	3	•	
92. Hood River Waterfront Trail	4.6	3	1	•	
93. Hood River Penstock Flume Pipeline Trail	2.8	3	2	•	
94. Indian Creek Trail (East)	4.2	2	2	•	

DOG-FRIENDLY	WILDFLOWERS	WATERFALLS	OLD-GROWTH	HISTORICAL	WHEELCHAIR ACCESSIBLE	CAR CAMP NEARBY	BACKPACKING
•				•	partially		
			•			•	
•				•			
		•		•	partially		
•	•	•					
•		•	•				
		•		•		•	
•	•	•	•	•		•	•
•	•	•	•			•	•
•	•		•	•			•
		•				•	
		•				•	
•		•	•			•	•
•	•			•		•	•
		•				•	
		•				•	
•				•	partially	•	
•	•					•	
•	•					•	•
		•	•	•		•	•
	•		•			•	•
•		•					•
•	•		•				•
		•	•				•
•	•		•				•
•			•	•		•	•
	•	•	•			•	•
•	•					•	
	•			•		•	
•				•	•		
				•			
•				•			

HIKE	DISTANCE IN MILES (ROUNDTRIP)	OVERALL RATING	DIFFICULTY	HIKEABLE ALL YEAR	KID-FRIEN
95. Punchbowl Falls County Park	2.2	4	2	•	•
96. Wahtum Lake and Chinidere Mountain	4	5	3		•
97. Tomlike Mountain and the Anthill	5.8	5	3		
98. Indian Mountain	9	5	3		•
99. Green Point Mountain	3.2	4	3		•
100. Bear Lake	2.4	3	2		•
101. Mosier Twin Tunnels	9.4	3	2	•	•
102. Mosier Plateau	3	3	2	•	•
103. Memaloose Hills	3.2	3	2		•
104. Rowena Plateau	2.2	3	2	•	•
105. Tom McCall Point	3.6	4	3		•
106. The Dalles Riverfront Trail	14.8	3	1	•	•
107. Deschutes River–Ferry Springs Loop	4.4	4	3	•	•
108. Deschutes River Rail Trail	23	4	3	•	•
109. Columbia River Heritage Trail	4.6	2	2	•	•
110. Lewis and Clark Commemorative Trail	14.6	3	3	•	•
111. Hat Rock	0.9	2	1	•	•
COTTONWOOD CANYON STATE PARK, OREGON					
112. Pinnacles Trail	9.6	4	2	•	•
113. Gooseneck Trail	2.2	4	3	•	
114. Lost Corral	9.2	3	2	•	
115. Hard Stone Trail	3.2	3	2	•	

DOG-FRIENDLY	WILDFLOWERS	WATERFALLS	OLD-GROWTH	HISTORICAL	WHEELCHAIR ACCESSIBLE	CAR CAMP NEARBY	BACKPACKING
		•		•			
•	•		•			•	•
	•		•			•	
•	•		•			•	•
•			•			•	•
•	•			•	•		
•	•	•		•			
•	•						
	•					•	
	•					•	
•	•			•	•		
•	•			•		•	
•	•			•			•
•	•			•			
•				•			
•	•			•	•		
•	•			•		•	
•	•			•		•	
•	•			•		•	
•	•			•		•	

Introduction

The Columbia River Gorge is a one-of-a-kind natural landmark. Nowhere else in America does one of the country's mightiest and longest rivers slice through one of its longest and most dramatic mountain chains—and practically at sea level. And perhaps nowhere else in the Lower 48 are there so many waterfalls, nor is there such a dramatic shift from wet, saturated coastal mountains to arid, sun-kissed flowered bluffs.

Long a major transportation route for First Peoples, explorers, traders, and emigrants, the Gorge played a vital role in the development of the Northwest and the nation. Yet, despite its proximity to a major metropolitan area and its continual use as a busy transportation corridor, it remains remarkably natural. The Gorge would most certainly have become one of America's cherished national parks were it not for the people- and energy-moving infrastructure there. But in 1986, through the insight and hard work of dedicated citizens and maneuvering by enlightened politicians, the bulk of the Columbia River Gorge became a national scenic area, the only one of its kind in the

Wind Mountain and the Columbia River viewed from Indian Point (Hike 87)

country—and a fitting designation for such an important ecological, cultural, and spectacularly beautiful place.

The second edition of *Day Hiking Columbia River Gorge* focuses on the best day hikes within and near the Columbia River Gorge. It includes trails in the Columbia River Gorge National Scenic Area, Silver Star Scenic Area, Trapper Creek Wilderness, and Cottonwood Canyon State Park as well as some select hikes along the Columbia east of the Gorge. Primarily meant to be used for day hiking, there are also hikes suitable for backpacking where it's permissible. Hikers will find trails on both sides of the river, with Oregon and Washington treated nearly equally in coverage. Fantastic hikes stretch from the Gorge's saturated western slopes to its sun-kissed eastern hills, with trails to waterfalls, lakeshores, mountaintops, old-growth forests, islands, shrub-steppe hills and old fire lookout sites. The book explores national forests and wilderness areas, state forests, state parks, county parks, city parks, and national wildlife refuges.

Choose from hikes that are perfect for children, friendly to dogs, and accessible year-round. Explore trails of historical relevance, those of interest to wildflower and waterfall connoisseurs, and locales of note for observing wildlife. They're all included in this packed-with-adventure, 115-hike volume. And nearly all of these hikes are only a 30-minute to 2-hour drive from the Portland–Vancouver metropolitan region. Let's hit the trail!

PERMITS AND REGULATIONS

It's important that you know, understand, and abide by regulations. As our public lands have become increasingly popular, and as both federal and state funding has declined, regulations and permits have become necessary components in managing our natural heritage. To help keep our wilderness areas wild and our trails safe and well-maintained, land managers—especially the National Park Service and US Forest Service—have implemented a sometimes complex set of rules and regulations governing the use of these lands.

Generally, any developed trailheads in western Washington's and western Oregon's national forests fall under the Region 6 (Northwest) Forest Pass program. In order to park legally at these designated national forest trailheads, your vehicle must display a Northwest Forest Pass (usually hung on the rearview mirror). These sell for $5 per day or $30 for an annual pass good throughout Washington and Oregon (which constitute Region 6). The Columbia River Gorge National Scenic Area includes lands within Gifford Pinchot and Mount Hood National Forests requiring passes at several trailheads. These passes can be purchased from National Forest ranger stations, online from Discover Your Northwest, and at select outdoor retailers.

Interagency Passes (which allow for entrance into national parks and wildlife refuges) are also accepted at trailheads requiring a parking pass. Your best bet if you hike a lot in both national parks and forests is to buy an America the Beautiful Pass (an Interagency Pass) for $80. This pass grants you and three other adults (children under 16 are admitted free) in your vehicle access to all federal recreation sites that charge a fee. These include: national parks, national forests, national wildlife refuges, and Bureau of Land Management areas, not only here in Washington and Oregon but also throughout the country. There are also special passes (discounted or free) available for senior

PUBLIC LANDS: WHO'S IN CHARGE?

Almost all of the hikes in this book are on public land. That is, they belong to you and me and the rest of the citizenry. What's confusing, however, is just who exactly is in charge of this public trust. More than a dozen governing agencies manage lands described in this guide.

The agency that oversees the Columbia River Gorge National Scenic Area, where many of the hikes in this guidebook are, is the US Forest Service. A division of the Department of Agriculture, the Forest Service strives to "sustain the health, diversity, and productivity of the nation's forests and grasslands to meet the needs of present and future generations." The agency purports to do this under the doctrine of "multiple-use," in which lands are managed for wildlife preservation and timber harvest, foot traffic and motorbikes. However, supplying timber products, managing wildlife habitat, and developing motorized and nonmotorized recreation options have a tendency to conflict with each other. Some of these uses may not exactly sustain the health of the land either. Several areas administered by the Forest Service have been afforded stringent protections as federal wilderness (see sidebar, "Untrammeled Columbia River Gorge" in the western Oregon section), barring development, roads, and motorized recreation.

The National Park Service, a division of the US Department of the Interior, manages hundreds of thousands of acres of land within the Northwest but very little within the Columbia River Gorge region (Fort Vancouver National Historic Site being an exception). The National Park Service's primary objective is quite different from that of the Forest Service. The agency mandate is "to conserve the scenery and the natural and historic objects and the wild life therein and to provide for the enjoyment of the same in such a manner and by such means as will leave them unimpaired for the enjoyment of future generations." In other words, the primary focus of the National Park Service is preservation.

Other public lands you'll encounter in this book are Washington and Oregon state parks, managed primarily for recreation and preservation. Washington State Department of Natural Resources land, managed mainly for timber harvesting, has pockets of natural-area preserves. National wildlife refuges and state wildlife preserves are managed for wildlife habitat protection and for hunting and fishing. And county parks are managed much like state parks but at a more local level.

It's important that you know what agency manages the land you'll be hiking on, for each has its own fees and rules (like for dogs: generally no in national parks and national wildlife refuges, yes in national forests, and yes but on-leash in state parks). Confusing, yes? But it's our land and we should understand how it's managed for us. And remember that we have a say in how our lands are managed, too, and can let the agencies know whether we like what they're doing or not.

citizens, military members, fourth-grade students, volunteers, and disabled Americans. You can purchase these passes at national park and forest visitors centers as well as many area outdoor retailers. Visit nps.gov/planyourvisit/passes.htm for more information.

Washington State Parks, Department of Natural Resource properties, and Washington Department of Fish and Wildlife properties require a Discover Pass—currently $10 for a day or $30 for an annual pass (good for two vehicles) and available online (discoverpass.wa.gov), at some parks, and at most sporting goods outlets.

Several of Oregon's more popular state parks including some of the parks in the Gorge require a daily parking pass, currently $5 and available at the park. Annual and two-year passes are available for $30 and $50 respectively and can be purchased from most state park offices. Oxbow Regional Park also requires a $5 day-use fee (payable at the park entrance). All required fees and permits are clearly listed in the information block for each hike.

Wilderness Permits

Hikers are required to carry a wilderness permit if entering the Mark O. Hatfield Wilderness in Oregon's Mount Hood National Forest from May 15 through October 15, and if entering the Trapper Creek Wilderness in Washington's Gifford Pinchot National Forest year-round. These permits are free and self-issued at trailheads and wilderness boundaries. Be sure to understand and adhere to all wilderness rules and regulations.

WEATHER

Mountain weather is famously unpredictable, and in the Gorge, with the Columbia River's nearly sea-level passage through the Cascade Range, you can expect all kinds of interesting weather events, from high winds and thunderstorms to ice storms. Weather patterns are radically different in the west and east ends of the Gorge. The west side is influenced by Pacific Ocean currents, creating a more temperate climate with a copious amount of rainfall, heavy from November to April. Summers are generally mild, with extended periods of no or low rainfall. July through early October is usually a delightful time to hike the western region. In the Gorge's east, weather patterns are representative of a continental climate, with cold winters and hot, dry summers. Snowfall is usually light due to the Cascades' rain shadow effect. But higher elevations see ample snowfall, as storm clouds move eastward and are pushed up over the mountains, cooling and releasing their moisture. Heaviest snows usually occur at or near the Cascade Crest.

Plan your hike according to your weather preference. But no matter where you hike in the region, always pack raingear. Being caught in a sudden rain- and windstorm without adequate clothing can lead to hypothermia (loss of body temperature), which is deadly if not immediately treated. Most hikers who die of exposure (hypothermia) do so not in winter but during the milder months when a sudden change of temperature accompanied by winds and rain sneaks up on them. Always carry extra clothing layers, including rain and wind protection.

While snow blankets the high country primarily from November through May, it can

A pair of hikers set out on the PCT on a rainy fall day.

occur any time of year. Be prepared. Lightning is rare along the west slopes but quite common during the summer months in the eastern half of the Gorge. If you hear thunder, waste no time getting off of summits and away from water. Take shelter, but not under big trees or rock ledges. If caught in an electrical storm, crouch down to make minimal contact with the ground and wait for the boomer to pass. Remove your metal-framed pack and ditch the trekking poles!

Other weather-induced hazards you should be aware of are the results of rain and snow episodes. River and creek crossings can be extremely dangerous to traverse after periods of heavy rain or snowmelt. Always use caution and sound judgment when fording. Be aware of snowfields left over from the previous winter's snowpack.

Depending on the severity of the past winter and the weather conditions of the spring and early summer, some trails may not melt out until well into summer or not at all. In addition to treacherous footing and difficulties in routefinding, lingering snowfields can be prone to avalanches or slides. Use caution crossing them.

Finally, strong winds are another concern in the Gorge. Avoid hiking during extreme windy periods, which can fell trees and branches, especially in recent burn areas.

ROAD AND TRAIL CONDITIONS

Trail conditions can change, sometimes very quickly. A heavy storm can cause a river to jump its channel, washing out sections of trail (or access road) in moments. Windstorms can blow down trees by the hundreds, making trails unhikeable. And snow can bury trails well into the summer. Avalanches, landslides, and forest fires can also bring serious damage and obliteration to our trails. The Eagle Creek Fire of 2017 inflicted some serious damage on many of our trails, resulting in indefinite closures and long and costly repairs. Several trails from this book's first edition have been removed from this guide, as their rehabilitation appears unlikely anytime soon.

Lack of adequate funding is also responsible for trail neglect and degradation. Before setting out, be sure you contact the appropriate land manager to check on current trail and road conditions.

On the topic of trail conditions, it's vital to acknowledge the countless volunteers who donate tens of thousands of hours to trail

maintenance each year. The Washington Trails Association (WTA) and Trailkeepers of Oregon (TKO) alone coordinate upwards of two hundred thousand hours of volunteer trail maintenance each year. But there is always a need for more. Our trail system faces ever-increasing threats, including lack of adequate trail funding, inappropriate trail uses, and conflicting land management policies and practices.

As timber harvesting has all but ceased in much of our federal forests, one of the biggest threats to our trails now is access. Many roads once used for hauling timber are also used by hikers to get to trailheads. But many of these roads are no longer being maintained and are becoming downright dangerous to drive, if they're drivable at all. While this author supports the decommissioning of

Recently burned forest on the Big Hollow Trail (Hike 32)

many of the trunk roads that go "nowhere" as both economically and environmentally prudent, I am deeply disturbed by the amount of main trunk roads that are falling into disrepair. Once a road has been closed for several years, the trails radiating from it often receive no maintenance, likely leading them to becoming unhikeable.

With all this in mind, this guide includes trails that are threatened and in danger of becoming unhikeable. These Endangered Trails are marked with a special icon in this book. On the other hand, we've also had some great trail successes in recent years, thanks in large part to the WTA and TKO. These Saved Trails are marked, too, to help show you that individual efforts do make a difference. As you enjoy these Saved Trails, consider becoming involved with the WTA, TKO, or other trails groups (see Appendix II: Conservation and Trails Organizations).

WILDERNESS ETHICS

To ensure the long-term survival of our trails—and more specifically the wild lands they cross—we must embrace and practice sound wilderness ethics. A strong, positive wilderness ethic includes making sure you leave the wilderness as good (or even better) as when you found it. But it goes deeper than simply picking up after ourselves when we go for a hike. We need to ensure that our elected officials and public land managers recognize and respond to our wilderness needs and desires. Get involved with groups and organizations that safeguard, watchdog, and advocate for land protection. And let land managers and public officials know how important protecting lands and trails is to you.

Leave No Trace

All of us who recreate in Washington's and Oregon's natural areas have a moral obligation and responsibility to respect and protect our natural heritage. Everything we do on the planet has an impact—and we should strive to have as minimal of a negative impact as possible. The Leave No Trace Center for Outdoor Ethics is an educational, nonprofit,

WANT TO PROTECT LAND AROUND THE COLUMBIA? BUY IT!

What's the fastest, most surefire, and often least controversial way to protect land? Buy it yourself! That's exactly what land trusts across the country do. A concept that began in Massachusetts in the late 1800s, land trusts today exist in the thousands, from coast to coast, nearly all of them nonprofit organizations whose primary purpose is to buy land and secure development rights in order to protect natural areas, farmland, shorelines, wildlife habitat, and recreational lands. Once the land is secured, trusts usually then transfer it with legally bound stipulations to government agencies to be managed for the public. Many trusts, however, also maintain their own preserves, and most of these are open to the public.

There are several land trusts operating in the Columbia River Gorge region, including the Columbia Land Trust (columbialandtrust.org). Based in Vancouver, Washington, the 3700-member Columbia Land Trust began in 1990 and has been responsible for protecting more than 50,000-acres, including along the Klickitat River, featured in this book. Consider joining them!

apolitical organization that was developed for responsible enjoyment and active stewardship of the outdoors. They have designed a program to help educate outdoor enthusiasts of their recreational impacts and have developed techniques to prevent and minimize such impacts. Their message is framed under seven principles:

1. Plan ahead and prepare
2. Travel and camp on durable surfaces
3. Dispose of waste properly
4. Leave what you find
5. Minimize campfire impacts
6. Respect wildlife
7. Be considerate of others

Visit lnt.org to learn more.

TRAIL ETIQUETTE

We need to be sensitive to other trail users as well. Many of the trails in this book are open to an array of uses. Some are hiker-only, but others allow equestrians and mountain bikers too (a few trails in this book are open to motorbikes). When you encounter other trail users, follow common sense and exercise simple courtesy. With this Golden Rule of Trail Etiquette firmly in mind, here are other things you can do during trail encounters to make everyone's trip more enjoyable:

- **Move off trail.** When meeting other user groups (like bicyclists and horseback riders), the hiker should move off the trail. Hikers are more mobile and flexible than other users, making it easier for them to step off the trail.
- **Make way for horses.** When meeting horseback riders, the hiker should step off the downhill side of the trail unless the terrain makes this difficult or dangerous. Make yourself visible so as not to spook the big beastie, and talk in a normal voice

to the riders. This calms the horses. If hiking with a dog, keep your buddy under control.

- **Stay on trails** and practice minimum impact. Don't cut switchbacks, take shortcuts, or make new trails. If your destination is off trail, stick to snow and rock when possible so as not to damage fragile alpine meadows. Spread out when traveling off trail to minimize the chance of compacting thin soils and crushing delicate plant environments.
- **Obey the rules** specific to the trail you are visiting. Many trails are closed to certain types of use, including mountain bikes and hiking with dogs.
- **Practice responsible dog etiquette.** Hikers who take dogs on the trails should have their dog on a leash or under very strict voice command at all times. And if leashes are required (such as in all state parks) then this does apply to you. Too many dog owners flagrantly disregard this regulation, setting themselves up for tickets, hostile words from fellow hikers, and the possibility of losing the right to bring Fido out on that trail in the future. Remember that many hikers are not fond of dogs on the trail. Respect their right not to be approached by your loveable lab. A well-behaved leashed dog, however, can certainly help warm up these hikers to your buddy. And pack out all dog waste! Those little brown and green bags don't vanish when they're left behind. They are foul and unsightly.
- **Avoid disturbing wildlife.** Observe from a distance, resisting the urge to move closer to wildlife (use your telephoto lens instead). This not only keeps you safer, but it prevents the animal from having to exert itself unnecessarily by fleeing from you.

Trail running on the Blackberry Trail, Deschutes River State Recreation Area (Hike 107)

- **Take only photographs.** Leave all natural things, features, and historic artifacts as you found them for others to enjoy.
- **Never roll rocks off trails or cliffs.** You risk endangering lives below you.
- **Mind the music.** Leave the Bluetooth speakers at home. Wear headphones if you must listen to music on the trail. Blasting music harasses wildlife, is a violation of wilderness ethics, and is an affront on those who come to the woods to seek solace.
- **Pack it in, pack it out.** Anything you pack in must be packed out, even biodegradable items like apple cores and pistachio shells. "Leave only footprints, take only pictures" is a worthy slogan to live by when visiting the wilderness.

And while not every situation is addressed by these rules, you can avoid problems by always remembering to practice *common sense and courtesy.*

WATER

As a general rule, you should treat all backcountry water sources to help prevent contracting giardia (a waterborne parasite) and other aquatic nasties. Assume that all water is contaminated. Treating water can be as simple as boiling it, chemically purifying it (adding tiny iodine tablets), or pumping it through a water filter and purifier.

Cleanup

When washing your hands, rinse off as much as you can in plain water first. If you still feel the need for a soapy wash, collect a pot of water from the lake or stream and move at least 100 feet away. Apply a small amount of biodegradable soap to your hands and lather up. Use a bandanna or towel to wipe away most of the soap and then rinse with the water in the pot.

THE DEFECATION PROCLAMATION
The first rule of backcountry bathroom etiquette says that if an outhouse exists, use it. When privies aren't provided, however, the key factor to consider is location. Choose a site at least 200 feet from water, campsites, and the trail. Dig a cat hole (a trowel comes in handy). Once you're done, bury your waste (and toilet paper, or bag it out) with organic duff and place a "Microbes at Work" sign over it (just kidding about the last one). If you need to go in the snow or an alpine setting where soils are thin, use a blue bag and pack it out. And consider using a blue bag in areas of heavy use where excessive feces has become unsightly and unsanitary.

HUNTING
Hikers should be aware that many of our public lands are opened to hunting. Season dates vary, but generally big game hunting begins in early August and ends in late November. While hiking in areas frequented by hunters, it is best to make yourself visible by donning an orange cap and vest. If hiking with a dog, your buddy should wear an orange vest too. If being around outdoors people schlepping rifles is unnerving to you, stick to hiking in the state parks where hunting is prohibited.

BEARS
The Columbia Gorge and, in particular, places like the Trapper Creek Wilderness and Silver Star Scenic Area harbor healthy populations of black bears, and your chance of eventually seeing one is pretty good. Your encounter will probably involve just catching a glimpse of his bear behind. But occasionally the bruin may actually want to get a look at *you*. In very rare cases a bear may act aggressively, usually during berry failures that cause the bear to be hungry and malnourished or if a sow feels that her cubs are threatened. To avoid an un-*bear*-able encounter, practice bear-aware prudence. Always keep a safe distance. If you encounter a black bear at close range, remain calm, talk in a low manner, do not look it in the eyes, and do not run from it. Hold your arms out to appear as big as possible. Slowly move away upwind from him. The bear may bluff-charge—do not run. If it does attack—fight back using fists, rocks, trekking poles, or bear spray if you are carrying it.

COUGARS
Both Washington and Oregon support healthy populations of the shy and solitary *Puma concolor*. While cougar encounters are extremely rare in the Gorge, they do occur. Cougars are cats—they're curious. They will follow hikers but rarely (almost never) attack adult humans. Minimize contact by not hiking or running alone and by avoiding carrion. If you do encounter a cougar, remember it is looking for prey that can't, or won't, fight back. Do not run, as this may trigger its attack instinct. Stand up and face it. If you appear aggressive, the cougar will probably back down. Wave your arms, trekking poles, or a jacket over your head to appear bigger, and maintain eye contact with it. Pick up children and small dogs, and back away slowly if you can safely do so without taking your eyes off of it. If it attacks, throw things at it. Shout loudly. If it gets close, whack it with your trekking pole, fighting back aggressively.

Rattlesnake warning at Cottonwood Canyon State Park

POISON OAK, TICKS, AND RATTLESNAKES: THE GORGE'S TRIPLE NUISANCE

Compared with other parts of the world that I have hiked in, natural nuisances in the Columbia River Gorge are minimal. But poison oak is pretty ubiquitous, ticks are numerous in early season, and rattlesnakes are fairly common in the Gorge's eastern reaches. Don't be alarmed—just be aware!

Poison oak: Not a member of the elegant *Quercus* (oak) genus but of the sumac family, this shrub thrives in the dry, open (nonpoisonous) oak forests of the eastern Gorge. The leaves and twigs of this plant contain urushiol—a surface oil that causes an allergic reaction in most people who come in contact with it. Symptoms range from mild itching to blistering, and the reaction can last up to two weeks, inflicting some discomfort. In areas rife with poison oak, wear long pants and be sure to wash them after your hike to rid them of any lingering oils. Learn to recognize poison oak by its toothed, lobed, somewhat glossy leaves that grow in compounds of three. Remember, leaves of three, let them be!

Ticks: These pests are a nuisance that you should be far more concerned with. It's their role as a disease vector that raises alarm. Ticks are parasites that live off of the blood of their host. Hikers make great hosts, and ticks will cling to them if given the opportunity. Generally active in the spring (and mainly on the lower slopes of the eastern side of the Cascade Crest), ticks inhabit shrubs and tall grasses. When these plants are brushed up against, the tick is given the opportunity to hitch a ride.

In tick country wear long sleeves and tuck pant legs into socks. Be sure to check yourself, particularly waist and sock lines, after hiking. And if one has fastened itself to you—or your dog—get your tweezers. Gently squeeze its head until it lets go (try not to break its head off, or the tick body may become lodged and infected). Wash and disinfect the bite area. Most ticks in the Northwest do not carry Lyme disease. Still, it's best to monitor the bite. If a rash develops, immediately seek medical help.

Rattlesnakes: There's no need for concern on the wet west side of the Gorge, but in the sunnier eastern reaches, and in particular in lower-elevation dry canyon areas, northern Pacific rattlesnakes may be found. Vipers are as intent on avoiding you as you are them, rattlesnakes generally keep to themselves. But if you get too close, they'll set off an alarm by rattling their tails. Should this happen, walk away, allowing the snake to retreat. Never, ever try to catch, provoke, or pursue one. Rattlesnake bites in Washington and Oregon are extremely rare; deaths by rattlesnake bites even rarer. If bitten, however, remain calm. Wash the bite, immobilize the limb, apply a wet wrap., and seek medical attention immediately.

GEAR

While gear is beyond the scope of this book, it's worth noting a few points here. No hiker should venture far up a trail without being properly equipped. Starting with the feet, a good pair of boots can make all the difference between a wonderful hike and a blistering affair. Every hiker will swear by different brands and types of boots, so your best bet is to be professionally fit and try a bunch out—see what works for you.

For clothing, wear whatever is most comfortable unless it's cotton. When cotton gets wet, it stays wet and lacks any insulation value. In fact, wet cotton sucks away body heat, leaving you susceptible to hypothermia. Think synthetics and layering.

Make sure you have a good well-fitting pack. And while the list of what you pack will vary, there are a few items everyone should have in their packs every trip: the Ten Essentials, developed by The Mountaineers.

The Ten Essentials

1. **Navigation (map and compass):** Carry a topographic map of the area you plan to be in and knowledge of how to read it. Likewise a compass or GPS unit.
2. **Sun protection (sunglasses and sunscreen):** Even on wet days carry sunscreen and sunglasses; you never know when the clouds will lift. At higher elevations your exposure to UV rays is much more intense than at sea level. You can easily burn on snow and near water.
3. **Insulation (extra clothing):** Storms can blow in rapidly. Carry raingear, wind gear, and extra layers.
4. **Illumination (flashlight/headlamp):** Carry extra batteries too.
5. **First-aid supplies:** At the very least, your kit should include bandages, gauze, scissors, tape, tweezers, pain relievers, antiseptics, and perhaps a small manual. Consider first-aid training through a program such as Mountaineering-Oriented First Aid (MOFA).
6. **Fire (firestarter and matches):** Be sure you keep your matches dry. Sealable bags do the trick.
7. **Repair kit and tools (including a knife):** A knife is helpful; a multitool is better. A basic repair kit should include such things as nylon cord, a small roll of duct tape, some 1-inch webbing and extra webbing buckles (to fix broken pack straps), and a small tube of superglue.
8. **Nutrition (extra food):** Always pack in more food than what you need for your hike. Pack energy sports bars for emergency pick-me-ups.
9. **Hydration (extra water):** Carry two full water bottles, unless hiking entirely along a water source. Carry iodine tablets or a filter too.
10. **Emergency shelter:** This can be as simple as a garbage bag or something more efficient, such as a reflective space blanket. A poncho can double as an emergency tarp.

TRAILHEAD CONCERNS

Sadly, the topic of trailhead and trail crime must be addressed. While violent crime is extremely rare, unfortunately, theft and car prowls are far too common at

Flowering ookow along the Weldon Wagon Road (Hike 44)

many trailheads. Our trails are fairly safe places—far safer than most city streets. Common sense and vigilance, however, are still in order. Be aware of your surroundings at all times. Leave your itinerary with someone back home. If something doesn't feel right, it probably isn't. Take action by leaving the place or situation immediately.

Car break-ins, sadly, are a far-too-common occurrence at some of our trailheads. These smash-and-grab episodes are a real concern at many of the Oregon west-side trailheads. Absolutely do not leave anything of value in your vehicle while out hiking. Take your wallet and cell phone with you. Consider taking your registration with you too. Don't leave anything in your car that may appear valuable. A duffle bag on the back seat may contain dirty T-shirts, but a thief may think there's a laptop in it. Save yourself the hassle of returning to a busted window by not giving criminals a reason to clout your car.

If you arrive at a trailhead and someone looks suspicious, don't discount your intuition. Take notes on the person and his or her vehicle. Record the license plate and report the behavior to the authorities. Do not confront the person. Leave and go to another trail.

While most car break-ins are crimes of opportunity by drug addicts looking for loot to support their fix, organized gangs intent on stealing IDs have also been known to target parked cars at trailheads. While some trailheads are regularly targeted, and others rarely if at all, there's no sure way of preventing this from happening to you other than being dropped off at the trailhead or taking the bus (rarely an option either way). But you can make your vehicle less of a target by not leaving anything of value in it. And contact your government officials and demand that law enforcement be a priority on our public lands. We taxpayers have a right to recreate safely in our parks and forests.

CARRYING ON AN OUTDOOR LEGACY

I grew up in rural New Hampshire and was introduced to hiking and the great outdoors at a young age. I grew to admire the men and women responsible for saving and protecting many of our trails and wilderness areas as I became more aware of the often tumultuous history behind the preservation efforts.

When I moved to Washington in 1989, I immediately gained a respect for Harvey Manning and Ira Spring. Through their pioneering 100 Hikes guidebooks, I was introduced to and fell in love with the Washington backcountry. I joined The Mountaineers, the Washington Trails Association, Friends of the Columbia Gorge, and other local trail and conservation organizations so that I could help protect these places and carry on this legacy to future generations.

I believe 100 percent in what Ira Spring termed as "green bonding." We must, in Ira's words, "get people onto trails. They need to bond with the wilderness." This is essential in building public support and funding for trails. When hikers get complacent, trails suffer.

And while I often chuckled at Harvey Manning's tirades and diatribes as he lambasted public officials' shortsighted and misguided land practices, I tacitly agreed with him in many instances. Harvey could be combative and polarizing, risking turning off potential allies. But sometimes you have to raise a little hell to get results.

Consider that many of the trails in this book would have long ago ceased to exist without the phenomenal efforts of people like Ira Spring, Harvey Manning, Louise Marshall, Nancy Russell, and the scores of hikers who joined them pushing for wildland protection, trail funding, and strong environmental stewardship programs.

Write a letter to your member of Congress or state representative asking for better trail funding. Consider joining an organization devoted to wilderness, backcountry trails, or other wild country issues. Organizations like

The Mountaineers, Washington Trails Association, Mazamas, Trailkeepers of Oregon, Friends of the Columbia Gorge, Columbia Land Trust, and countless others leverage individual contributions and efforts to help ensure the future of our trails and the wonderful wilderness legacy we've inherited. Buy a specialty license plate for Washington's national parks or state parks, or an Oregon Crater Lake or salmon plate (benefiting Oregon's state parks), and let everybody on the way to the trailhead see what you value and support.

And while I am well aware of the dilemma of getting too many boots on the ground, I understand that we can't and shouldn't shy people away from our trails, but instead make these people good stewards of the land—defenders of the land—and promoters of healthy lifestyles and good conservation. And perhaps many hikers will also seek less explored places and disperse their use. This book highlights many trails that get very little use—check them out.

There are many challenges facing our trails and wild places. Many outdoors folks

Western fence lizard

view wilderness differently today than in the past. Some want to open up wilderness areas to mountain bikes. People have a lot of gadgets—and they take them into the wilderness. The blasting of speakers and the annoying buzz of drones that violate your privacy and peace of mind are growing affronts that need to be addressed. The explosion of social media has sent mobs of inexperienced hikers into the wilderness—folks lacking knowledge in regard to conservation ethics, wilderness regulations, and wilderness values. Through education, enlightenment, and perhaps a little self-control—we can have quality trail time and a healthy environment with strong wilderness protections. I trust you will do the right thing.

ENJOY THE TRAILS

Most importantly, enjoy the trails in this book. They exist for our enjoyment and for the enjoyment of future generations. We can use them and protect them at the same time if we are careful with our actions as well as forthright with our demands on Congress and state legislators to continue protecting our wild lands.

Democrats, Republicans, Independents, Americans of all walks of life have helped establish and protect our open spaces and wilderness areas. We must see to it that those protections continue and that the last bits of wild land are also preserved for the enjoyment of future generations.

Henry David Thoreau proclaimed, "In wildness is the preservation of the world." And I would like to add, "In wildness is the salvation of our souls, the meaning of life, and the preservation of our humanness." So turn off the gadgets and hit the trail. I've lined up 115 magnificent hikes for you to celebrate nature, life, the incredible landscapes of the Columbia River Gorge, and you. Yes, you—go take a hike, celebrate life, and come back a better and more content person.

And if I'm preaching to the choir, help me then to introduce new disciples to the sacred world of nature. For while we sometimes relish our solitude on the trail, we need more like-minded souls to help us keep what little wildlands remain. Help nature by introducing family members, coworkers, neighbors, children, and politicians to our wonderful trails. I'm convinced that a society that hikes is not only good for our wild and natural places (people will be willing to protect them) but is also good for us (as we live in a healthy and connected way).

Enjoy this book. I've enjoyed writing it. I believe that we can change our world for the better, one hike at a time.

Happy Hiking!

How to Use This Book

This guidebook is designed to be user-friendly by providing clear directions and enough detail to help you explore a region. But I still leave enough room for you to make your own discoveries. I have hiked every mile of trail described in this book, so you can follow my directions and advice with confidence. Conditions do change, however. More on that later in this introduction.

WHAT THE RATINGS MEAN

Each hike starts with detailed trail facts. The **overall rating** of 1 to 5 stars is based on a hike's overall appeal, and the numerical **difficulty score** of 1 to 5 measures how challenging the hike is. These ratings are purely subjective, based on my impressions of each route, but they do follow a formula of sorts.

The **overall rating** is based on scenic beauty, natural wonder, and other unique qualities, such as the potential for solitude and wildlife-viewing opportunities.

***** Unmatched hiking adventure. A bucket list hike!

**** Excellent experience that ranks among the best hikes

*** A great hike that is sure to impress and inspire

** May lack exceptional scenery or unique trail experience but offers a lot of little moments to enjoy

* Worth doing as a refreshing walk, especially if you're in the neighborhood

The **difficulty score** is based on trail length, cumulative elevation gain, steepness, and trail

Grass widows blooming at Catherine Creek (Hike 48)

conditions. Generally, trails that are rated more difficult (4 or 5) are longer and steeper than average. But it's not a simple equation. A short, steep trail over uneven surfaces and ledges may be rated 5, while a long, smooth trail with little elevation gain may be rated 2.

5   Extremely difficult: Excessive elevation gain and/or long distance for a day hike, and possibly rough conditions
4   Difficult: Some steep sections, possibly rough trail or poorly maintained trail
3   Moderate: A good workout but no real problems
2   Moderately easy: Minimal elevation gain or short route with good tread
1   Easy: A relaxing stroll in the woods

OTHER KEY HIKE INFORMATION

Other trail details follow, to help explain these ratings and help you choose a hike:

Round-trip mileage (unless otherwise noted as one-way): While I have measured most of the hikes with GPS and have consulted maps and governing land agencies for all hikes in this book, the distance stated may still not always be exact, but it'll be pretty darn close.

Elevation gain: This is for the *cumulative* difference on the route (and return), meaning not only the difference between the high and low points on the hike but also for all other significant changes in elevation along the way.

LEGEND

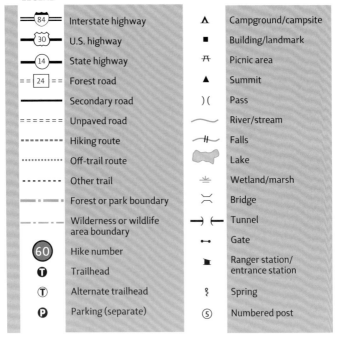

84	Interstate highway
30	U.S. highway
14	State highway
24	Forest road
	Secondary road
	Unpaved road
	Hiking route
	Off-trail route
	Other trail
	Forest or park boundary
	Wilderness or wildlife area boundary
60	Hike number
T	Trailhead
T	Alternate trailhead
P	Parking (separate)

⋀	Campground/campsite
■	Building/landmark
⊼	Picnic area
▲	Summit
) (	Pass
⁓	River/stream
⫲	Falls
	Lake
	Wetland/marsh
	Bridge
→) (←	Tunnel
●—●	Gate
	Ranger station/ entrance station
⸮	Spring
⑤	Numbered post

An icon in the introduction for each hike highlights which routes are kid-friendly.

High point: It's worth noting that not all high points are at the end of the trail—a route may run over a high ridge before dropping to a lake basin, for instance.

Season: Many trails can be enjoyed from the time they lose their winter snowpack right up until they are buried in fresh snow the following fall. But snowpacks vary from year to year, so the hiking season for each trail is an estimate. Contact land managers for current conditions.

Crowds: Here I rate the trail 1 to 5 for crowds, with 1 being a great chance you will be all alone and 5 meaning to expect a popular trail. Some of the trails rated 3 and 4, however, may be only a 1 or 2 on a weekday.

Maps: Hikes in this guidebook typically reference Green Trails maps, which are based on the standard 7.5-minute USGS topographical maps. Green Trails maps are available at most outdoor retailers in the Portland metro area as well as at many National Park Service and US Forest Service visitors centers. I also mention if there's a

useful non-topographic trail map available from an on-site kiosk or agency website.

Contact: Here you'll find each trail's governing agency so that you can contact them to get current trail conditions. Contact information can be found in Appendix I: Land Management Agencies and online.

Notes: Here you'll find whether any permits are required for your visit and specifics on road or trail closures, whether dogs are permitted, and any special hazards or concerns you should be aware of, such as difficult routefinding, river fords, animal concerns, etc. Please note: While some hike descriptions may mention campsites and backpacking options—an overnight permit may be needed (stated if that is the case). Be aware, too, of campfire and group size restrictions especially in national forest, scenic, and wilderness areas.

GPS: Coordinates are provided for each trailhead to help get you to the trail. Coordinates are in the degrees and decimal minutes style derived from WGS84 datum.

A NOTE ABOUT SAFETY

Safety is an important concern in all outdoor activities. No guidebook can alert you to every hazard or anticipate the limitations of every reader. Therefore, the descriptions of roads, trails, routes, and natural features in this book are not representations that a particular place or excursion will be safe for your party. When you follow any of the routes described in this book, you assume responsibility for your own safety. Under normal conditions, such excursions require the usual attention to traffic, road and trail conditions, weather, terrain, the capabilities of your party, and other factors. Keeping informed on current conditions and exercising common sense are the keys to a safe, enjoyable outing.

—Mountaineers Books

Icons and trail introduction: This part of the hike intro is a quick overview of what each trail has to offer, including icons to help you quickly determine the following:

 Kid-friendly

 Dog-friendly (leash may be required)

 Exceptional wildflowers (in season)

 Exceptional or abundant waterfalls

 Exceptional old-growth forest

 Historical significance

 Endangered trail (threatened due to lack of maintenance, motorized encroachment, abandonment, or other detrimental actions)

Saved trail (A formerly threatened or abandoned trail that has been revived and restored)

Getting there: Directions to the trailhead are generally from the nearest large town or geographic location/feature.

On the trail: These route descriptions provide a basic overview of what you might find on your hike, directions to get you to the trailhead, and in some cases additional highlights (Extending Your Trip) beyond the actual trails you'll be exploring.

Opposite: *A rock arch doorway greets hikers on Ed's Trail (Hike 7)*

silver star scenic area, washington

Named for its starlike radiating ridges, 4373-foot Silver Star Mountain straddles Washington's Clark–Skamania county line just 25 miles from Vancouver. Centerpiece of a 10,000-plus-acre roadless area managed by the Gifford Pinchot National Forest and Washington State Department of Natural Resources, the mountain and its environs were heavily forested until 1902, when the nearly 250,000-acre Yacolt Burn consumed most of its timber. With the fire having radically altered the region's environment, the lofty peak and its satellites now harbor some of the finest wildflower meadows in the Cascades. Crisscrossed with old jeep tracks, since closed and converted to trails, the area once the domain of four-wheelers is now welcoming to families and nature enthusiasts who admire outstanding vistas and spectacular floral shows. Home to the threatened Larch Mountain salamander and historical Native American vision quest sites, Silver Star shines with surprises and excellent hiking opportunities.

1 Bells Mountain

RATING/ DIFFICULTY	ROUNDTRIP	ELEV GAIN/ HIGH POINT	SEASON
***/3	6.8 miles	1300 feet/ 1775 feet	Year-round

Crowds: 3; **Maps:** Washington State Department of Natural Resources, Yacolt Burn State Forest map; **Contact:** Washington State DNR, Pacific Cascade Region; **Notes:** Trail open to mountain bikes; **GPS:** N 45° 49.901', W 122° 23.354'

The Bells Mountain Trail is one of several well-built and maintained nonmotorized multiuse trails in the 90,000-acre Yacolt Burn State Forest. It rings out to be explored. While its 8.7 miles make for a great long hike or run, you only need venture a third of the way to

CIRCLING THE GORGE

At the start of the Bells Mountain Trail, an inscribed stone celebrates the designation of 29 miles of the Chinook Trail between Lucia Falls and Bluff Mountain as a national recreation trail. It's a designation that recognizes exemplary trails of local and regional significance. The trail was the brainchild of two longtime Vancouver hiking companions, Don Cannard and Ed Robertson (whom Ed's Trail is named for, Hike 7) back in 1986. In the 1990s the Chinook Trail Association was founded to advocate for the development of a 300-mile, two-state, rim-top loop trail around the Columbia River Gorge.

To make this trail a reality, the volunteer association works closely with the federal, state, and local governments that manage the public lands that the trail crosses. The trail ties together existing trails with new trails. While large contiguous sections currently exist, there are still many gaps and road-walk sections. Many of the original members of the association have passed on or are getting up there in miles and need fresh blood to help make this spectacular long-distance trail a reality. There will be countless day-hiking opportunities, too, on a completed Chinook Trail and its feeder trails. For more information and how you can get involved, visit chinooktrails.org.

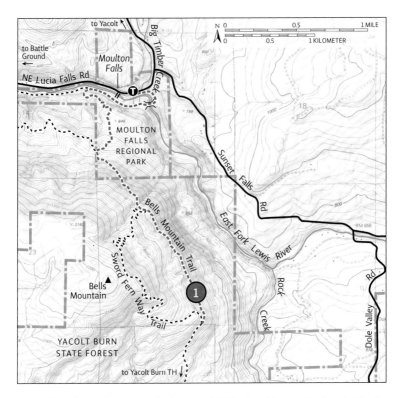

reap its best views. *Hike to a couple of cuts in this working forest and savor sweeping views of Mount St. Helens and Silver Star Mountain.*

GETTING THERE

From Vancouver head north on I-5 to exit 11 (Battle Ground) following State Route 502 east for 5.8 miles to Battle Ground. Turn left onto SR 503 and drive north 5.6 miles, turning right onto Rock Creek Road (which eventually becomes NE Lucia Falls Road). Continue east for 8.1 miles to Moulton Falls Regional Park and parking (elev. 570 ft.).

Additional parking can be found 0.3 mile east. Privy available.

ON THE TRAIL

Starting at the popular Moulton Falls Regional Park, follow the trail east paralleling the road. Cross Big Timber Creek and pass through a picnic area. At 0.2 mile, bear right at a junction with a trail that accesses the upper parking area. Just a little bit farther, come to the well-photographed high-arched bridge (elev. 630 ft.) spanning the East Fork Lewis River at a dramatic chasm. Cross the bridge and, ignoring side trails, continue

Big snags among an understory of vine maples

hiking on a wide trail downriver. Catch some good views of Moulton Falls before coming to the junction (elev. 580 ft.) with the Bells Mountain Trail at 0.7 mile. The main trail continues along the East Fork Lewis River for 2.3 miles (see *Urban Trails: Vancouver, WA*). Now head left on the Bells Mountain Trail. Part of the Chinook Trail (see sidebar, page 38), this work in progress will eventually tie together more than 300 miles of trail on a circuitous route within and near the Columbia River Gorge National Scenic Area.

Leaving the river valley, steadily climb through a luxuriant forest swaddled in mosses and ferns and punctuated with big snags. Bells Mountain is part of the Yacolt Burn State Forest. In 1902, nearly a quarter million acres of the surrounding forest

went up in flames (see sidebar, page 50). In 1929 the Dole Valley Fire consumed another 150,000 acres.

Soon cross a cascading creek and pass a mileage post, the first of many in half-mile increments along the trail. At 1.5 miles, ignore a side trail that leads right. Continue climbing. Cross several creeks (all nicely bridged) and at 1.9 miles, come to an old cut providing the first viewpoint (elev. 1500 ft.). Mount St. Helens hovers above a sea of scrappy green peaks, while directly below is Dole Valley.

Continue farther, returning to forest and crossing a cascading creek. At 2.1 miles, come to a junction with an old road and the northern end of the new Sword Fern Way Trail. Continue straight on an up-and-down course through patches of maturing forest and recovering forest. At 3 miles, come to a junction (elev. 1600 ft.) with the southern end of the Sword Fern Way Trail. Now head right on it through a recent clear-cut, enjoying sweeping views of Silver Star Mountain, Kloochman Butte, and Larch Mountain. At 3.4 miles, come to a logging road (elev. 1775 ft.) and a good place to turn around.

EXTENDING YOUR TRIP

You can continue on the Sword Fern Way Trail, climbing 425 feet and returning back to the Bells Mountain Trail in 2.1 miles. It is entirely forested and is of more interest to mountain bikers with its banked turns and flowy switch-backs. If you can arrange for a car shuttle, continue on the Bells Mountain Trail for another 6.4 miles to its southern terminus at the Yacolt Burn trailhead on DNR road L-1000.

2 Summit Springs Trail

RATING/ DIFFICULTY	ROUNDTRIP	ELEV GAIN/ HIGH POINT	SEASON
**/3	5.6 miles	1760 feet/ 3150 feet	Year-round

Crowds: 1; **Map:** Green Trails Lookout Mountain No. 396; **Contact:** Gifford Pinchot National Forest, Mount St. Helens National Volcanic Monument District; **Notes:** Trail open to mountain bikes and motorcycles; **GPS:** N 45° 48.854 ', W 122° 14.646'

An obscure trail to an old quarry, Summit Spring's best attribute is its loneliness. But solitude aside, the trail traverses an attractive forest decorated with vine maples, bear grass, and huckleberries. And there's a view too—of little-known peaks in this lightly visited corner of the Gifford Pinchot National Forest.

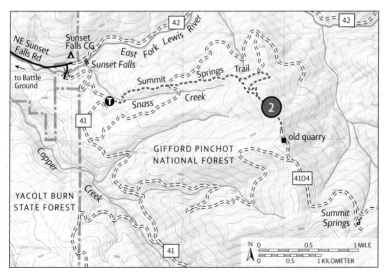

Looking south from the old quarry

GETTING THERE

From Vancouver head north on I-5 to exit 11 (Battle Ground) following State Route 502 east for 5.8 miles to Battle Ground. Turn left onto SR 503 and drive north 5.6 miles turning right onto Rock Creek Road (which eventually becomes NE Lucia Falls Road). Continue east for 8.5 miles and turn right onto NE Sunset Falls Road. Continue for 7.3 miles to the Sunset Falls Campground and turn right onto Forest Road 41. Cross bridge over the East Fork Lewis River and turn left, following rough FR 41 for 0.9 mile to the easy-to-miss trailhead (elev. 1450 ft.) on your left. Continue a few hundred feet to a wide area at a hairpin curve. Park here.

ON THE TRAIL

Locate Summit Springs Trail No. 173 descending from FR 41 and start hiking. Immediately notice the trail's excellent shape despite its light usage. Cross a small creek and keep gently descending. At 0.2 mile cross Snass Creek (elev. 1380 ft.), which might be tricky to negotiate during the wetter months.

The trail now begins to climb paralleling Snass Creek, which flows out of view in a small ravine. The ascent is steady with occasional short, steep bouts. Traverse an even-aged forest recovering from the Yacolt Burn of 1902. Large decaying snags stand out among the younger trees. Vine maples drape over the trail corridor.

At 0.8 mile, cross an old logging road and continue climbing. At 1.6 miles come to a junction. The trail right is an extremely steep shortcut built by mountain bikers. Go left on the official trail and enjoy easy walking traversing a hillside. The way then intersects an old roadbed. Bear right on it and gently ascend through two switchbacks. At 2.4 miles, pass the upper junction with the shortcut trail. The way now gently climbs a ridge crest through thinning forest and patches of bear grass. At 2.8 miles the trail terminates at an old quarry (elev. 3150 ft.) at a forest road spur. Where are the Summit Springs? You can follow the spur 0.2 mile, turn left on FR 4104, and walk 1.3 miles to find them. Better yet—just walk to the top of the quarry and enjoy the good views of nearby McKinley Ridge and over the East Fork Lewis River to Gumboot Mountain, the Tatoosh Hills, and Calamity Peak.

3 East Fork Lewis River

RATING/ DIFFICULTY	ROUNDTRIP	ELEV GAIN/ HIGH POINT	SEASON
***/4	8 miles	1950 feet/ 3530 feet	Mid-July– Sept

Crowds: 1; **Map:** Green Trails Lookout Mountain No. 396; **Contact:** Gifford Pinchot National Forest, Mount St. Helens National Volcanic Monument District; **Notes:** Trail open to mountain bikes and motorcycles. Trail involves two fords of the East Fork Lewis River, safe only during low flows; **GPS:** N 45° 49.423', W 122° 09.905'

Hike along the wild upper reaches of the East Fork Lewis River, and cross it twice. Then climb—steeply at times—out of its lush upper valley. Traverse attractive second-growth forest adorned with vine maples and big snags—legacies of Washington's Big Burn. Then reach an old logging road high on Lookout Mountain and take in excellent views of this quiet and remote corner of the Gifford Pinchot National Forest.

GETTING THERE

From Vancouver head north on I-5 to exit 11 (Battle Ground) following State Route 502 east for 5.8 miles to Battle Ground. Turn left onto SR 503 and drive north 5.6 miles, turning right onto Rock Creek Road (which eventually becomes NE Lucia Falls Road). Continue east for 8.5 miles and turn right onto NE Sunset Falls Road. Continue for

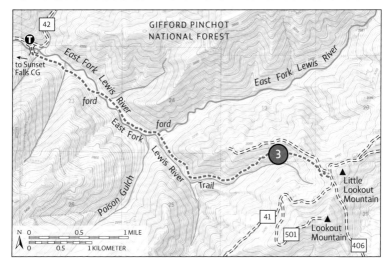

A view into the East Fork Lewis River drainage

7.3 miles to the Sunset Falls Campground. Then continue straight on Forest Road 42 for 5 bumpy, massively potholed miles (high clearance required) to the trailhead (elev. 1850 ft.) on your right at a small turnout.

ON THE TRAIL

East Fork Lewis River Trail No. 139 starts by following a decommissioned road over a big bridge across the river. The Washington Trails Association (WTA) has been working hard to rehabilitate this trail offering a great alternative to the busy nearby Silver Star trails. Sadly, some unenlightened forest users continue to trash the trailhead. Fortunately, they don't venture far up this trail.

Once you're across the bridge, the trail heads east on a gentle grade following along the river—here just a few miles from its headwaters. WTA has done an excellent job restoring tread along the old road, giving it a

real trail look. At 0.5 mile, cross a creek that may wet your boots. At 0.9 mile, come to the first crossing of the river. By late summer you can usually rock hop across the gently flowing waterway. But during rainy periods and other times of the year, it may be difficult to downright dangerous to attempt.

The trail continues now along the north side of the river, offering pleasant near-level walking. Traverse a mature even-aged forest punctuated with big snags attesting to the ancient forest that stood here before the massive Yacolt Burn swept through in 1902. At 1.6 miles come to the second ford of the East Fork Lewis River (elev. 1750 ft.)—this one just above the confluence with the intriguingly named Poison Gulch. Like the first ford, it's a rock hop during low flows.

The trail now continues as single track as you climb out of the valley and traverse steep south-facing slopes. The tread is narrow but generally in decent shape except where it makes a couple of steep ascents. Here motorcycles have damaged the soft tread. Hopefully these sections will be rebuilt in the future. At 2.7 miles cross a small ravine, and then shortly afterward traverse a shale slope granting peekaboo views of Lookout Mountain above.

The way steepens—insanely at times—and passes a few more limited viewpoints. Then after passing a scree slope, the grade mellows as the way passes through a young forest. At 4 miles, reach trail's end (elev. 3530 ft.) at lightly used FR 41. Walk just a couple hundred feet to the right for excellent views down the drainage you just hiked and out to very little-known and hiked summits and ridges.

EXTENDING YOUR TRIP
Turn this hike into a five star by walking FR 41 to the right (west) for 0.7 mile and then taking a left and following FR 501 for 1 mile to the open 4222-foot summit of Lookout Mountain. The lookout has since been replaced by an emergency radio repeater, but the views remain spectacular in every direction. Look out to Mount Hood, the Columbia River Gorge, the Washougal River valley, Silver Star, Mount St. Helens, Mount Adams, the Soda Peaks, and so many more summits.

(4) Hidden Falls

RATING/ DIFFICULTY	ROUNDTRIP	ELEV GAIN/ HIGH POINT	SEASON
**/2	7.8 miles	1400 feet/ 2300 feet	Year-round

Crowds: 1; **Map:** Washington State Department of Natural Resources, Yacolt Burn State Forest map; **Contact:** Washington State DNR,

Pacific Cascade Region; **Notes:** Discover Pass required. Trail open to mountain bikes and horses; **GPS:** N 45° 45.968', W 122° 19.374'

Hike a new trail through old cuts, recent cuts, and mature second growth to a pretty waterfall tucked in a tight ravine. Follow along a babbling creek and catch some views of the prominent basalt outcropping known as Sturgeon Rock. A great choice for a winter hike when Hidden Falls is revealing a lot more crashing water.

Hidden Falls revealed

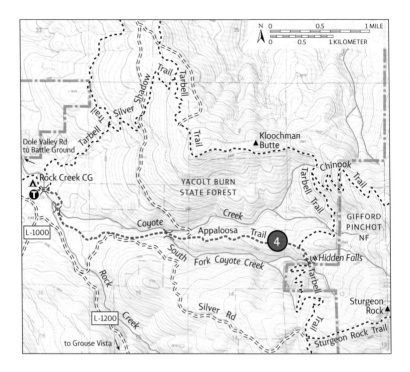

GETTING THERE

From Vancouver head north on I-5 to exit 11 (Battle Ground) following State Route 502 east for 5.8 miles to Battle Ground. Turn left onto SR 503 and drive north 5.6 miles, turning right onto Rock Creek Road (which eventually becomes NE Lucia Falls Road). Continue east for 8.5 miles and turn right (just past Moulton Falls) onto NE Sunset Falls Road. Then proceed for 2 miles and turn right onto NE 312th Avenue, which eventually becomes NE Dole Valley Road. Continue 4.9 miles and turn left into the Rock Creek Campground. Proceed through campground to trailhead (elev. 1100 ft.). Privy available.

ON THE TRAIL

Starting from the inviting Rock Creek Campground, head northeast on the Tarbell Trail and soon cross Rock Creek on a big bridge. Then at 0.1 mile veer right onto the Appaloosa Trail, which was opened in 2021 by Washington State Department of Natural Resources with help from the Washington Trails Association, Back Country Horsemen of Washington, and the Washington Conservation Corps.

The trail makes a quick climb through a recent cut and then descends to cross Coyote Creek on a big bridge at 0.5 mile. The way then follows old logging roads and new tread through stands of trees of various ages. Briefly follow along Rock Creek before following Coyote Creek. At 1.4 miles the way turns left onto a closed logging road and reaches a bridge across Coyote Creek at 1.9 miles.

The way then veers right through tall timber and climbs to a junction with a logging road at 2.2 miles. Turn right and walk the road a short distance before picking up trail again on your right. Climb through a recent cut offering views to Sturgeon Rock cresting above a forested ridgeline. At 2.4 miles, cross the logging road and then soon enter a cool and attractive stand of mature timber. Note that this entire area is an actively managed forest, so that timber may be harvested sometime in the near future. For now, enjoy walking through this very pleasant forest.

At 3.6 miles, come to a junction with the Tarbell Trail (elev. 2300 ft.). Turn right here and switchback down to a cool, lush ravine where a bridge (elev. 2180 ft.) spans the South Fork Coyote Creek just below Hidden Falls at 3.9 miles. The 90-foot falls are quite pretty framed by towering timber. Winter is best for the waterfall show, but in summer this area offers a cool retreat from the heat.

EXTENDING YOUR TRIP

You can make this hike into a long loop by returning northwest on the Tarbell Trail for 3.9 miles. Then turn left onto the Silver Shadow Trail, which brings you back to the Tarbell Trail in 1.8 miles. It is then 1.5 miles left back to your start. Another option is to make a long loop up the Chinook Trail (accessed by hiking north on the Tarbell Trail for 1.6 miles and turning right at the junction), and then hike south over Silver Star and return to the Tarbell Trail via the Sturgeon Rock Trail (old Silver Road). This is an exhilarating and challenging loop that'll tally at 16.5 miles.

(5) Larch Mountain

RATING/ DIFFICULTY	ROUNDTRIP	ELEV GAIN/ HIGH POINT	SEASON
***/2	5.4 miles	1180 feet/ 3496 feet	Year-round

Crowds: 2; **Map:** Washington State Department of Natural Resources, Yacolt Burn State Forest map; **Contact:** Washington State DNR, Pacific Cascade Region; **Notes:** Discover Pass required. Trail open to mountain bikes and horses; **GPS:** N 45° 43.302', W 122° 16.168'

Though this is the highest peak that sits entirely within Clark County, few hikers find their way to its summit. Shadowed by adjacent Silver Star Mountain, Larch lacks that well-loved mountain's sweeping views and dazzling wildflowers—but also its crowds. And while Larch's summit is marred by towers, the way up is pleasant enough with attractive forests, fields of bear grass, and some pretty good views of Silver Star too.

GETTING THERE

From Vancouver head north on I-5 to exit 11 (Battle Ground) following State Route 502 east for 5.8 miles to Battle Ground. Turn left onto SR 503 and drive north 5.6 miles, turning right onto Rock Creek Road (which eventually becomes NE Lucia Falls Road). Continue east for 8.5 miles and turn right (just past Moulton Falls) onto NE Sunset Falls Road. Then proceed for 2 miles and turn right onto NE 312th Avenue, which eventually becomes NE Dole Valley Road. Continue 5.1 miles to junction at pavement's end. Then bear left on DNR L-1200 and drive 5 miles on this generally well-graveled road to trailhead at Grouse Vista (elev. 2375 ft.). Privy available.

ON THE TRAIL

Head west on the Tarbell Trail, which at first follows an old jeep track. The way steadily climbs along a ridge crest. Sounds of industry can be heard on the left, while the soothing sound of nature—particularly babbling Grouse Creek—drifts in on the right. At 0.4 mile, bear left. While most of the way follows old roads, the tread is smooth and mostly free of rocks, unlike Silver Star's old roads.

After a short, steep climb and then a drop, the way skirts an old cut where good views of Mount Hood and Oregon's Larch Mountain can be seen. Just like on that other Larch Mountain, there are no larches on this peak either—early loggers referred to noble firs as larches. At 1 mile, ignore a side trail that heads right. Shortly afterward, bear right. The way should be signed—stay on the Tarbell Trail. At 1.2 miles, in an attractive grove of mature timber, cross Grouse Creek (elev. 2800 ft.) on a big bridge. Then, after passing by shrubby vine maple patches (pretty in fall), emerge at 1.7 miles on a bear-grass-rimmed ridge (elev. 2975 ft.) above a big talus slope and find excellent views of Silver Star Mountain, Mount Adams, Lookout Mountain, Dole Valley, and Mount St. Helens in the distance. This is the highlight of this hike. Feel free to call it quits here.

But if you're summit bound, continue along the pleasant trail lined with ferns and bear grass to a junction (elev. 3300 ft.) at 2.3 miles. Then head left on a rocky path passing a spur on the right to a sprawling bear grass meadow and arrive at the 3496-foot summit, where towers and a road greet you at 2.7 miles. Some fair views to Portland and Vancouver can be had by walking a short way west down a jeep track.

A trail runner negotiates a scree slope on the Tarbell Trail.

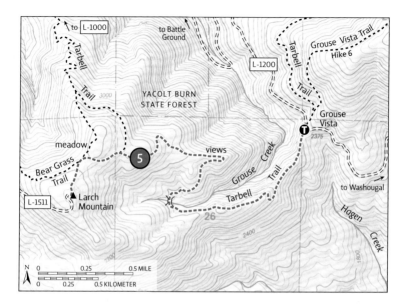

EXTENDING YOUR TRIP

If you can arrange a car shuttle, you can get some variation on the return trip by continuing on the Tarbell Trail northwest. At 0.9 mile past the summit junction, the way steeply descends across a sprawling scree slope granting sweeping views. From there it traverses forests of various ages with a stint alongside Cold Creek before coming to the Yacolt Burn trailhead on DNR Road L-1000 at 4.2 miles from the summit spur junction.

6 Silver Star Mountain via Grouse Vista

RATING/ DIFFICULTY	ROUNDTRIP	ELEV GAIN/ HIGH POINT	SEASON
****/3	6.4 miles	2050 feet/ 4390 feet	May–Nov

Crowds: 4; **Map:** Washington State Department of Natural Resources, Yacolt Burn State Forest map; **Contact:** Washington State DNR, Pacific Cascade Region; Gifford Pinchot National Forest, Mount Adams Ranger District; **Notes:** Discover Pass required. Trail open to mountain bikes and horses; **GPS:** N 45° 43.304', W 122° 16.165'

Follow an old rocky road to one of southwestern Washington's supreme floral gardens. Traverse slopes of mountainside that were scorched clean of greenery more than a century ago, leaving in the flames' wake an alpine wonderland of brilliant blossoms and bountiful berries. Silver Star's open slopes also provide some of the best viewing anywhere, from Mounts Hood, St. Helens, Rainier, and Adams to Portland and the Coast Range—and everything in between.

GETTING THERE

From Vancouver head north on I-5 to exit 11 (Battle Ground) following State Route 502 east for 5.8 miles to Battle Ground. Turn left onto SR 503 and drive north 5.6 miles, turning right onto Rock Creek Road (which eventually becomes NE Lucia Falls Road). Continue east for 8.5 miles and turn right (just past Moulton Falls) onto NE Sunset Falls Road. Then proceed for 2 miles and turn right onto NE 312th Avenue, which eventually becomes NE Dole Valley Road. Continue 5.1 miles to junction at pavement's end. Then bear left on DNR L-1200 and drive 5 miles on this generally well-graveled road to the trailhead at Grouse Vista (elev. 2375 ft.). Privy available.

ON THE TRAIL

The way starts on the Tarbell Trail, a 22.5-mile, multiuse, nonmotorized loop trail. Head east on it, coming to a junction in 0.1 mile. The Tarbell Trail continues left to Hidden Falls and several connecting trails. You want to continue right on the Grouse Vista

BURNING DOWN THE FOREST

On September 11, 1902, the Yacolt Burn, one of the largest forest fires in Washington's history, broke out. The cause of the conflagration was never determined, but loggers burning slash in the Wind River valley may have contributed to it. Fanned by unusually dry winds, the fire quickly spread, darkening the skies and dropping more than half an inch of ash on Portland. Smoke reached Seattle, and many thought that Mount St. Helens or Mount Rainier had erupted. In three days the fire scorched more than 238,000 acres and killed thirty-eight people in Clark, Cowlitz, and Skamania Counties. A forest ranger who had recently been reprimanded for employing a fire crew took no action, fearing he would be disciplined again. Rains eventually put out the blaze.

Consequently, the following year, the Washington State legislature established a state fire warden. In 1910, after the Great Fire scorched more than 3 million acres of Inland Northwest and northern Rockies forest (see Timothy Egan's *The Big Burn*), the US Forest Service under President Taft was transformed into a much larger and organized agency that actively began fire-suppression programs. Almost all of the Silver Star Scenic Area and lands east toward the Wind River valley were touched by the Yacolt Burn of 1902 and still show signs of that epic fire.

On September 2, 2017, a careless teenager illegally set off fireworks along the Eagle Creek Trail on the Oregon side, which started a destructive fire on more than 50,000 acres in the Gorge. Hikers were incensed and devastated over the destruction of old-growth forest and the closing of miles of popular and well-loved trails. Thanks to the tireless work of hundreds of volunteers with the Trailkeepers of Oregon, many of these trails have since been reopened. The burnt forests of the Gorge are slowly recovering. And while fire has always played an integral part in forest succession, the combination of years of fire suppression, a trend of warmer and drier summers, and the disregard of many folks who refuse to honor bans on fires and fireworks calls for reassessment of current fire and recreation management plans.

Hiker on Silver Star's summit with views to Mount St. Helens and Mount Rainier

Trail, which like many of Silver Star's trails was once an old 4x4 road. The Forest Service began closing the mountain to motorized use in the 1960s, completely phasing it out by the 1980s. While the roads generally make good wide trails, they are often steep, occasionally rutted, and contain stretches teeming with loose rocks. They definitely don't make for good running trails. Watch your step, taking care not to twist an ankle.

After you climb steeply for 0.7 mile, the grade eases—and soon forest cover yields to shrubs, then yielding to rocky and flowery open slopes. Bear grass, pentemon, sunflower, paintbrush, lupine, parsley, phlox—the list goes on! June through mid-July are optimal for the blossoms. At 1.4 miles, stay left at a junction (elev. 3300 ft.).

The old road right leads around the back end of 3442-foot Pyramid Rock. Now descend slightly, losing 50 feet to skirt beneath the impressive landmark, crossing a talus slope in the process. The climb then steepens again as you encounter a cool pocket of silver firs. At 2.3 miles reach a junction (elev. 3830 ft.) with the Silver Star Trail. Right heads down the south ridge, a lonely alternative approach. You want to veer left, coming to a four-way junction (elev. 4050 ft.) at 2.8 miles.

Heading left is the old Silver Road (also known as the Sturgeon Rock Trail). Branching right is the Indian Pits Trail. Both of these trails invite exploring (see Extending Your Trip). For Silver Star, continue straight, reaching yet another junction at 2.9 miles.

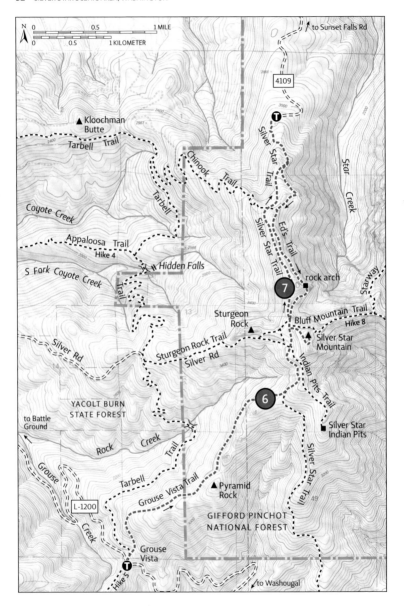

N
0   0.5   1 MILE
0   0.5   1 KILOMETER

to Sunset Falls Rd

4109

▲ Kloochman Butte

Tarbell Trail

Chinook Trail

Coyote Creek

Tarbell

Appaloosa Trail
Hike 4

S Fork Coyote Creek

Trail

Silver Star Trail

Silver Star Trail

Ed's Trail

Star Creek

Stairway

rock arch

7

Hidden Falls

13

Sturgeon Rock ▲

Sturgeon Rock Trail

Silver Rd

Silver Rd

Bluff Mountain Trail
Hike 8

Silver Star Mountain ▲

Indian Pits Trail

14

Silver Rd

YACOLT BURN STATE FOREST

to Battle Ground

6

Silver Star Trail

Silver Star Indian Pits ■

Rock Creek Trail

Grouse Creek

Tarbell

Grouse Vista Trail

L-1200

Pyramid Rock ▲

GIFFORD PINCHOT NATIONAL FOREST

49

Grouse Vista

Hike 5

to Washougal

The Silver Star Trail continues north (see Hike 7). You want to proceed right for 0.3 mile to the 4390-foot summit, once topped by a fire tower. The view is superb! Look north to Mounts Rainier and St. Helens; east to Mount Lookout, Trapper Creek Wilderness, Mount Adams, and Indian Heaven peaks; south to Mount Hood, Mount Jefferson, and the Gorge landmarks Defiance, Larch, Nesmith, and more; and west to the Portland–Vancouver metropolitan area, Saddle Mountain, and Sturgeon Rock rising above a forested ridge. Venture on over to the south summit too for some different perspectives. Then retrace your steps or consider the options below.

EXTENDING YOUR TRIP

From the four-way intersection 2.8 miles from the trailhead, follow the Indian Pits Trail southeast 0.8 mile on an up-and-down course (gaining and losing 500 cumulative feet) to an outstanding arrangement of rock pits once used by young Native Americans for vision quests. When clouds are swirling, the place is ethereal. Enjoy, but don't disturb this important archaeological site.

For a loop, consider following the Sturgeon Rock Trail (old Silver Road) west through forest on a rutted, eroded track at first, then reaching much better tread. At 0.5 mile from the four-way intersection, a primitive side trail heads right to ascend the 4147-foot basalt outcropping Sturgeon Rock (which includes Clark County's highest point). At 1.3 miles, intersect the Tarbell Trail (elev. 3100 ft.). Then head left on this pleasant, generally forested path, crossing several side creeks before crossing Rock Creek near a small cascade on a solid bridge (elev. 2500 ft.) at 2.7 miles. The way then dips and climbs, several times crossing openings that grant views to Pyramid and Sturgeon

Rock and reaching the Grouse Vista Trail at 4.5 miles. Turn right to reach the trailhead in 0.1 mile.

7 Silver Star Mountain via North Ridge

RATING/ DIFFICULTY	LOOP	ELEV GAIN/ HIGH POINT	SEASON
*****/3	4.7 miles	1440 feet/ 4390 feet	June–Nov

Crowds: 3; **Map:** Online Washington Department of Natural Resources; **Contact:** Gifford Pinchot National Forest, Mount Adams Ranger District; **Notes:** Forest Road 4109 is extremely rough and should only be attempted with high-clearance 4x4 vehicles. Eds Trail has two short sections requiring use of hands and is best avoided in wet conditions. Silver Star Trail is also open to mountain bikes and horses; **GPS:** N 45° 46.346', W 122° 14.675'

The shortest hike to Silver Star's stellar summit, this loop uses one of the mountain's old jeep roads (since converted to trail) and a stunning section of the long-distance Chinook Trail. Unfortunately, the access road has become nearly impossible to drive. Starting high, almost immediately saunter across sprawling flower gardens set against a backdrop of snowy, showy volcanoes. En route, pass through a rock arch and a landscape that looks straight out of the Southwest—except for all of the greenery.

GETTING THERE

From Vancouver head north on I-5 to exit 11 (Battle Ground) following State Route 502 east for 5.8 miles to Battle Ground. Turn left onto SR 503 and drive north 5.6 miles, turning right onto Rock Creek Road (which

Looking south along Ed's Trail

eventually becomes NE Lucia Falls Road). Continue east for 8.5 miles and turn right (just past Moulton Falls) onto NE Sunset Falls Road. Then proceed for 2 miles and turn right onto NE 312th Avenue, which eventually becomes NE Dole Valley Road. Continue 2.4 miles and turn left on the (easy to miss) graveled DNR L-1100. Continue for 6.6 miles and turn right onto Forest Road 4109 (4x4 high clearance required). Reach Silver Star trailhead (elev. 3100 ft.) in 2.5 horrendous miles.

ON THE TRAIL

Thankfully, Silver Star's trails are in better shape than several of the roads leading to them. This loop is classic and well loved, but it has declined in use due to the deteriorating condition of the access road. Whether the road will ever be improved is anyone's guess. In the meanwhile, strong hikers can avoid the rough access road and still do this loop by continuing from Silver Star's summit (via Hike 6) and circling back.

If you made it to the trailhead, start by following the route right (the old road left is rocky and eroded), barreling through a tunnel of shrubby vine maple. At 0.4 mile meet up with the old road, and shortly afterward come to a junction (elev. 3450 ft.). You'll be returning on the old road (Silver Star Trail No. 180) on the right—so veer left onto Ed's Trail, named for Edward Robertson, who passed away in 1994, one of the pioneers of the Chinook Trail Association (see sidebar, page 38).

The way travels along the rim of a small canyon streaked with waterfalls early in the season and traverses meadows of brilliant wildflowers and swaying grasses. At 1 mile (elev. 3800 ft.), come to an old jeep track (evidence of past off-road abuses allowed on this special mountain) and the Chinook Trail, coming in from the west. Continue straight on Ed's Trail, now part of the Chinook route. Continue climbing across a landscape that remarkably resembles Arizona or Utah—except it's too green!

Skirt above, around, and beneath ledges and knobs, traversing slopes that are increasingly steep. At 1.5 miles pass through the trail's highlight landmark, a rock arch that strangely looks like two rock transformer robots butting heads. Next, a short but very steep section of trail must be negotiated, requiring the use of hands. Just beyond, another short scramble awaits. It's best to avoid this trail in wet conditions. Now enjoy excellent views of Silver Star as you descend 85 feet before gently climbing to meet a major junction at 2.1 miles. The trail veering southeast is the Bluff Mountain Trail (Hikes 8 and 9). The primitive trail veering southwest is a shortcut to the Silver Road Trail (Sturgeon Rock Trail). Head left up the old road and reach a giant cairn and junction at 2.2 miles.

At this junction, straight heads to the Indian Pits and Grouse Vista Trails (Hike 6). You want to head left to reach Silver Star's 4390-foot summit at 2.5 miles. Savor sweeping views of volcanoes Mounts Hood, Rainier, St. Helens, Adams, and Jefferson plus a plethora of minor but equally beautiful peaks and ridges.

Then retrace your steps 0.3 mile back to the cairn junction and follow the Silver Star Trail (the old road) right on a gentle descent (after a short 75-foot climb) through meadows of brilliant wildflowers. This route isn't

as rocky as the old roads coming up from the south. Pass the Chinook Trail at 3.8 miles and reach the beginning of Eds Trail at 4.3 miles. Your vehicle is 0.4 mile downhill from here.

8 Starway

RATING/ DIFFICULTY	ROUNDTRIP	ELEV GAIN/ HIGH POINT	SEASON
****/4	10 miles	2100 feet/ 3977 feet	June–Nov

Crowds: 1; **Map:** Online Washington Department of Natural Resources; **Contact:** Washington Department of Natural Resources, Pacific Cascade Region; Gifford Pinchot National Forest, Mount Adams Ranger District; **Notes:** Discover Pass required. Trail to Silver Star open to mountain bikes and horses; **GPS:** N 45° 43.304' W 122° 16.165'

Stand on a lonely ridge above a steep canyon savoring sweeping views of Silver Star before you and several iconic Pacific Northwest volcanoes on the horizons. Come in early summer and be dazzled by wildflowers and cascading creeks. The Starway is a lonely and difficult trail with terrible road access. But the best part can be reached by strong hikers going up and over Silver Star (and back). The extra effort is worth the solitude in this popular area.

GETTING THERE
From Vancouver head north on I-5 to exit 11 (Battle Ground) following State Route 502 east for 5.8 miles to Battle Ground. Turn left onto SR 503 and drive north 5.6 miles, turning right onto Rock Creek Road (which eventually becomes NE Lucia Falls Road). Continue east for 8.5 miles and turn right (just past Moulton Falls) onto NE Sunset Falls Road. Then proceed for 2 miles and turn

right onto NE 312th Avenue, which eventually becomes NE Dole Valley Road. Continue 5.1 miles to junction at pavement's end. Then bear left on DNR L-1200 and drive 5 miles on this generally well-graveled road to the trailhead at Grouse Vista (elev. 2375 ft.). Privy available.

ON THE TRAIL

Lightly traveled, the Starway Trail begins at the Copper Creek trailhead as an old road that once serviced a series of mines. From there it brutally climbs via a cat track and sans switchbacks up a steep and forested ridge before reaching a 3977-foot open summit. Accessed via Forest Road 41, this notoriously bad road can only be driven by folks with high-clearance 4x4 vehicles. But if you're willing to hike up and over Silver Star

Silver Star as seen from the Starway

as described next, you can hike the best part of the Starway, enjoy solitude, and not sacrifice your vehicle on the way to the trailhead.

From the Grouse Vista trailhead head northeast on the Tarbell Trail. In 0.1 mile veer right on the Grouse Vista Trail and follow this old and rocky road (see Hike 6) coming to a cairned junction (elev. 4100 ft.) at 2.9 miles. Then continue straight, slightly descending on the Silver Star Trail, which is an old road, to reach another junction at 3 miles. Take your first right here onto the Bluff Mountain Trail (Hike 9).

Now on a slight ascent, traverse below the summit block of Silver Star across scree and through forest. Then descend across an open flowered bowl. Views south into Oregon are excellent. The way then continues descending across a narrow catwalk and skirting below cliffs and steep knolls. It's a dramatic landscape softened by swaying flowers and bear grass. At 3.9 miles, just after a couple of short ups and downs, reach a junction (elev. 3750 ft.).

Now head left on the Starway Trail, steeply descending through groves of mature silver fir. At 4.2 miles reach a narrow saddle (elev. 3460 ft.) above a small grassy wetland depression. Then travel along a narrow ridge crest before avoiding a cliff face and steeply climbing increasingly open slopes. The way is a little brushy, but the tread is defined. Make a sharp turn left and then one right as you crest the ridge. Now pass through a forest grove and, on flowered slopes, climb steeply one more time. At just shy of 5 miles, before reaching a small scree slope, step left off the trail—careful not to trample delicate vegetation—and attain a 3977-foot high-point knoll.

Now enjoy excellent views to Lookout Mountain, Bluff Mountain, Little Baldy,

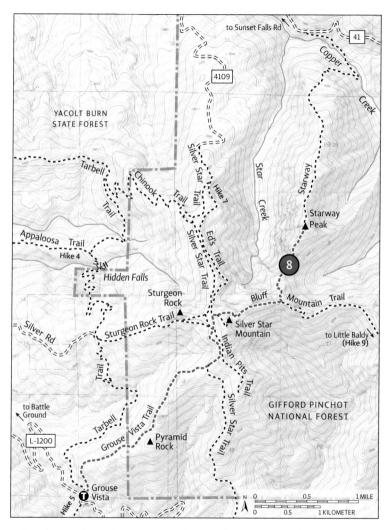

and a lineup of familiar snow-topped volcanoes. Be mesmerized, too, with the wonderful close-up view of Silver Star Mountain and the deep canyon between it and where you stand. In early summer, residual snowfields feed scores of crashing silvery cascades into Star Creek way below. From here, it's best to head back the way you came, although the Starway continues north, dropping off the knoll and traversing attractive forest and meadow patches for 0.6 mile along the ridge before insanely descending to the Copper Creek trailhead in 2.5 miles.

Crowds: 1; **Maps:** Green Trails Lookout Mountain No. 396, Bridal Veil No. 428; **Contact:** Gifford Pinchot National Forest, Mount Adams Ranger District; **Notes:** Forest Road 41 requires high-clearance 4x4 vehicle; **GPS:** N 45° 46.803', W 122° 10.019'

⑨ Little Baldy

RATING/ DIFFICULTY	ROUNDTRIP	ELEV GAIN/ HIGH POINT	SEASON
*****/3	8 miles	1600 feet/ 3940 feet	Jun–Nov

Follow this lofty route over high ridges, through old-growth forest, and across open slopes awash in wildflower splendor and exploding with views reaching in every direction. The most breathtaking way to reach Silver

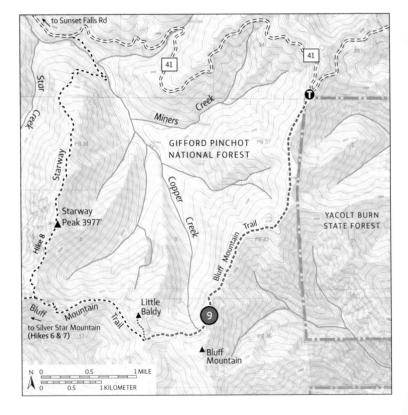

Copper Creek Drainage and Mount Rainier in the distance

Star—stopping short at the pyramidal heap of talus—Little Baldy will deliver plenty of satisfaction. Thanks to the Washington Trails Association, the trail is in excellent shape. Unfortunately, the access road is not, restricting access to this topnotch trail.

GETTING THERE

From Vancouver head north on I-5 to exit 11 (Battle Ground) following State Route 502 east for 5.8 miles to Battle Ground. Turn left onto SR 503 and drive north 5.6 miles turning right onto Rock Creek Road (which eventually becomes NE Lucia Falls Road). Continue east for 8.5 miles and turn right (just past Moulton Falls) onto NE Sunset Falls Road. Follow this paved road for 7.3 miles to the Sunset Falls Campground. Turn right onto Forest Road 41, proceeding through the campground to a bridge over the East Fork Lewis River. Turn left and follow the potholed, rutted, and very rough FR 41 for 9 miles to a high saddle. The unsigned trailhead is on the right (elev. 3540 ft.).

ON THE TRAIL

As soon as you get out of your vehicle, the views begin. Look east to Lookout Mountain and west to Silver Star Mountain, and trace the ridgeline you'll be hiking across. Now start hiking Bluff Mountain Trail No. 172, following an old jeep track, across the century-plus-old Yacolt Burn, which devastated timber stocks but replaced them with fields of flowers.

Crest a small knoll and look south to Oregon's Larch Mountain, Benson Plateau, and Nesmith Point. In early summer the flowers are profuse: paintbrushes, star tulips, harebells, tiger lilies, avalanche lilies, lupines, penstemons, bistorts, wooly sunflowers, and bear grass. Especially bear grass—it lines the way, dancing in the nearly perpetual breezes.

Continue along the rolling ridge, slightly climbing and dropping. At 1.5 miles reach a 3675-foot knoll and begin descending. Look for deer and coyote tracks in the soft and rocky roadbed. Deer are profuse in the Silver Star area. At 2.2 miles the old road ends. Bear right, continuing on trail now and dropping, coming to a gap (elev. 3100 ft.) swathed in huckleberry bushes at 2.4 miles.

Now resume climbing, crossing a scree slope before rounding cliffs that grant good views of Little Baldy and the Copper Creek watershed. Snow patches linger here in early summer. At 3 miles, come to a swath of mature forest—a real rarity in the Silver Star highlands. Cross a seasonal creek and continue ascending, traversing yet another scree slope. At 3.4 miles reach a gap (elev. 3600 ft.) shrouded in an even-aged stand of silver fir. Continue climbing, skirting around the rocky summit of Little Baldy. At 3.8 miles, just before the trail crosses the massive scree slopes on the peak's western face, head right and carefully pick a route along the steep ridgeline, reaching Little Baldy's 3940-foot rocky summit in about 0.2 mile.

Juniper and penstemon carpet the peak while a few Native American vision pits pock the high rocky slopes. The view is stupendous! North to Mounts St. Helens and Rainier. East to Lookout and Adams. South to Bluff, Hood, and Portland below. And west to the radiating flowery ridges of Silver Star. Stay long and savor it.

EXTENDING YOUR TRIP

You can continue following the Bluff Mountain Trail through some spectacular open country, traversing scree and fields of bear grass. In 1.1 miles the way teeters above steep ledges, granting excellent views north and east. At 1.5 miles, come to the Starway Trail. From here it's 1.3 miles to Silver Star's summit (see Hikes 6 and 7).

Opposite: *Lupines add a purple touch to the Sams Walker Nature Trail (Hike 13).*

western gorge, washington

Classic scenery and dramatic landscapes are what you'll experience in the Columbia River Gorge, a deep canyon cut by the West's mightiest river through one of its most rugged mountain chains. With a southern exposure, many of Washington's mountain trails melt out earlier than Oregon's. The wildflower shows on this side of the Columbia rival the Oregon side's waterfalls for stunning beauty. Many of the trails here are easily reached by State Route 14, the old Evergreen Highway, offering a scenic and more relaxed drive than Oregon's I-84. At the center of the Gorge in Washington State sits charming Stevenson, home to the excellent Columbia Gorge Interpretive Center Museum and a great base from which to explore. Beacon Rock State Park offers family-friendly camping, and Vancouver's wide array of amenities are less than an hour away from most of these trails.

10 Columbia River Dike Trail

RATING/ DIFFICULTY	ROUNDTRIP	ELEV GAIN/ HIGH POINT	SEASON
**/1	4.4 miles	Negligible/ 20 feet	Year-round

Crowds: 4; Map: Online cityofvancouver.us/parksrecculture/page/parks-trails; Contact: Port of Camas-Washougal; Notes: Wheelchair accessible. Dogs permitted on leash; GPS: N 45° 34.081', W 122° 20.365'

Hike along the Columbia River near the mouth of the Gorge, passing through Captain William Clark Regional Park, where Lewis and Clark and the Corps of Discovery spent six days securing provisions for their return journey back east. Check out an old steamboat dock and the sandy shores of Cottonwood Beach. And enjoy excellent views of Mount Hood looming over the river.

Wide open views of the Columbia River

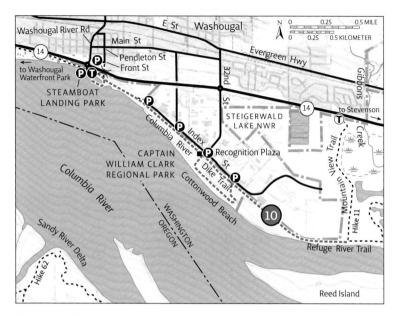

GETTING THERE

From Vancouver head east on State Route 14 for 16 miles, turning right at the roundabout at milepost 16 onto 15th Street into Steamboat Landing Park. Privy available. Alternative trailheads and parking can be accessed from Front Street and along Index Street.

ON THE TRAIL

The trail immediately heads east along the Columbia River on an extensive dike. But before heading upriver, check out the floating dock for an excellent view up and down the river. Here, too, see well-weathered pilings, remains of an old dock that once serviced steam paddlewheel boats from the 1880s until 1916.

You can follow the dock back to the main trail for a small loop. Now follow the Columbia River Dike Trail (also known as the Lewis and Clark Heritage Trail) east. Immediately come to a junction with a trail leading left under SR 14 to Washougal's historic downtown (and alternative trailhead at Front Street). Continue straight, passing observation decks and interpretive displays. At 1 mile come to Recognition Plaza in the Captain William Clark Regional Park, complete with its replica dug-out canoes and plaques recognizing donors who helped make this wonderful park a reality.

Continue straight on the Columbia River Dike Trail or head right for a slightly longer loop option that delivers you to lovely Cottonwood Beach. Here, visit where Lewis and Clark camped for six days from March 31 to April 6, 1806, on their return trip east. From this campsite Captain Clark led by a native guide "discovered" the Multnomah (later to be named Willamette) River. Earlier, the

Corps of Discovery had missed it both traveling up and down the Columbia.

Cottonwood's sandy beaches can usually be walked for over a mile. And while it is located 125 miles inland from the Pacific Ocean, the river here is still tidal, its water levels fluctuating throughout the day.

The Cottonwood Beach loop trail rejoins the Columbia River Dike Trail 0.25 mile east of Recognition Plaza. Continue hiking upriver, entering the Steigerwald Lake National Wildlife Refuge after another 0.3 mile. The trail then traverses a more pastoral landscape across former farmlands and under rows of giant cottonwoods. At 2.2 miles from the trailhead, come to the junction with the Mountain View Trail (Hike 11). Turn around here or consider extending your hike (below).

EXTENDING YOUR TRIP

You can continue east on the dike on the now-named Refuge River Trail for 2.1 miles

to its end at gated private property. Enjoy excellent views of Crown Point and Mount Hood across the river and Reed Island in the river. Five-hundred-acre Reed Island is protected as a Washington state park offering excellent camping, wildlife observing, and hiking. You'll need your own watercraft to get there.

You can also head west from Steamboat Landing on a new paved trail for 1.1 miles to the lovely Washougal Waterfront Park (see *Urban Trails: Vancouver, WA*).

11 Steigerwald Lake National Wildlife Refuge

RATING/ DIFFICULTY	ROUNDTRIP	ELEV GAIN/ HIGH POINT	SEASON
***/1	4.2 miles	Negligible/ 50 feet	Year-round

Crowds: 4; **Maps:** At refuge trail or online; **Contact:** Steigerwald Lake National Wildlife Refuge; **Notes:** Wheelchair accessible. Dogs

GETTING TO THE "CORPS" OF DISCOVERY

Take to the trails and parks along the shores of the Columbia River and you will be bombarded not only with beautiful scenery but also with memorials, interpretive displays, and artifacts commemorating the Lewis and Clark expedition, called the Corps of Discovery. Departing St. Louis, Missouri, in the spring of 1804, Meriwether Lewis and William Clark, accompanied by a black slave named York, the fur trapper Toussaint Charbonneau, and his young Shoshone wife Sacagawea and their infant son, led the party of thirty-three across the continent to the Pacific and back. Commissioned by President Thomas Jefferson, the expedition's mission was to explore the newly acquired Louisiana Purchase.

They first entered what would become Washington State in the autumn of 1805, following the Snake River to the Columbia and then to that huge river's mouth on the Pacific, where they wintered at Fort Clatsop in what would later become Oregon. They returned along the Columbia in the spring of 1806, further exploring the river, its tributaries, and its environs. Their findings would later encourage American settlement, leading to the Oregon Country becoming US soil in 1846. As you hike the shores of the Columbia, take time to learn more about these fascinating explorers and their most amazing journey.

One of two decorative art doorways at Steigerwald Lake National Wildlife Refuge

prohibited on all trails except Refuge River Trail accessible via Cottonwood Beach in Washougal. Entrance open sunrise to sunset and controlled by a gate. Section of Gibbons Creek Wildlife Art Trail closed Oct.–Apr. for wildlife protection; **GPS:** N 45° 34.279', W 122° 19.217'

Hike along a new levy above restored wetlands to the Columbia River. Then loop through a rich riparian world of wetland meadows, sloughs, cottonwood breaks, and shallow lakes that teem with birds and other critters. Steigerwald Lake National Wildlife Refuge occupies former farmland, now protected wildlife habitat at the extreme western edge of the Columbia River Gorge National Scenic Area. Here, urban yields to rural, bluffs overshadow a floodplain, and a multitude of avian residents pass through, mate, nest, and reside.

GETTING THERE

From Vancouver, head east on State Route 14 for 18 miles, turning right into a large parking area just before entering the Columbia River Gorge National Scenic Area. Privy available.

ON THE TRAIL

The 1000-plus-acre Steigerwald Lake National Wildlife Refuge was created in 1987 from mostly old farmland to help offset riparian habitat loss from the construction of the Bonneville Dam. In 2020 refuge officials began the Steigerwald Reconnection Project to reconfigure the refuge's levees and reconnect floodplain habitat to the Columbia

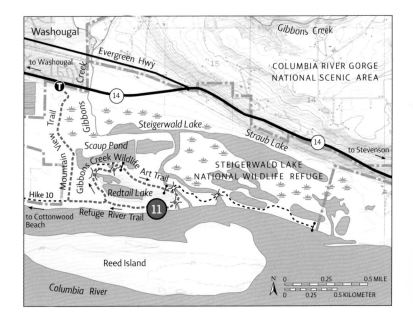

River. This project also resulted in reconfiguring the refuge's trails.

Start your hike on the Mountain View Trail, which follows along a new levee. Aside from enjoying excellent views of the surrounding mountains sloping down to the Columbia River Gorge, take in sweeping views of Steigerwald Lake. Notice, too, all of the reconfiguring that has happened that, over the years, will take on a more natural appearance as the new vegetation becomes more established. The refuge is a birdwatching hotspot due to its location near the mouth of the Columbia River Gorge, the lowest gap through the Cascade Mountains, allowing birds more associated with the east side of the Cascades to occasionally stray here. Look for kingbirds, phoebes, nighthawks, Lewis's woodpeckers, and burrowing owls. There should be plenty of herons, geese, goldfinches, ducks, eagles, and kingfishers on hand as well.

At 1 mile come to the Refuge River Trail, which runs along a levee on the Columbia River. Right heads to Cottonwood Beach (Hike 10) and Washougal. Leashed dogs, bikes, and running are allowed on this trail. Head left and come to a junction at 1.3 miles. You'll be returning right so head left on the Gibbons Creek Wildlife Art Trail, a delightful path with commissioned pieces of art along the way. Skirt Redtail Lake, a shallow body of water usually supporting a heavy concentration of birds. The trail continues over an attractive boardwalk. It then bends east along a cottonwood-lined slough and crosses it, coming to a junction at 1.7 miles.

The trail left dead-ends in 0.1 mile. It's a remnant of the original trail. Head right passing through an attractive doorway if you're here between May 1 and September 30 (closed October through April to protect wintering birds). If the trail is closed, retrace your steps—if not, continue hiking, traveling along rows of Sitka roses and Gibbons Creek. At 2.2 miles pass through another decorative doorway and come to a junction with the Refuge River Trail.

Now head right, passing through tree and thicket groves between Redtail Lake and the Columbia River until you return to a familiar junction at 2.9 miles. Continue straight 0.3 mile and turn right, returning to the trailhead at 4.2 miles.

EXTENDING YOUR TRIP

At the second door on Gibbons Creek Wildlife Art Trail, head left on the Refuge River Trail, crossing Gibbons Creek and a channel and winding through open former pastureland. Views are excellent of Reed Island in the Columbia River and Oregon's Vista House at the mouth of the Gorge. At 1.2 miles the trail ends at gated private property.

12 Cape Horn

RATING/ DIFFICULTY	LOOP	ELEV GAIN/ HIGH POINT	SEASON
****/3	7.2 miles	1650 feet/ 1330 feet	Year-round

Crowds: 4; **Map:** Green Trails Columbia River Gorge West 428S; **Contact:** Columbia River Gorge National Scenic Area; **Notes:** Dogs permitted on leash (but not recommended); Lower Loop is closed Feb. 1–July 15 to protect nesting peregrine falcons; **GPS:** N 45° 35.363', W 122° 10.721'

The Columbia River from the lower viewpoint

ACTING TO SAVE THE GORGE

Establishing the Columbia River Gorge National Scenic Area was not without its controversies. But with strong backing from both sides of the political aisle, from then-current and former governors of both Washington and Oregon, from all four of the states' US senators, and from nearly all members of Congress from both states, President Ronald Reagan signed the act into law on November 17, 1986. It established a national scenic area, the second of its kind, "to protect and enhance the scenic, natural, cultural and recreational resources of the Columbia River Gorge; and to protect and support the economy of the area by encouraging growth to occur in urban areas and allowing future economic development consistent with resource protection."

The national scenic area is managed in partnership by both states, six counties, the US Forest Service, and the Columbia River Gorge Commission, which is funded equally by the two states and is composed of twelve volunteers appointed by the counties and states. No small feat considering that the area consists of 292,500 acres of public and private lands spanning a distance more than 80 miles. A lifelong dream for many who cherish the natural, cultural, historical, and scenic significance of this great place, without this landmark act, surely the Gorge would have been relentlessly developed and subdivided during the boom years that followed. There are still interests who would like to see the act weakened—even abandoned— but watchdog organizations like Friends of the Columbia Gorge (see sidebar, "Befriending the Gorge" in the western Oregon section) work hard to make sure that doesn't happen.

Soak up stunning non-stop views of river, mountains, and valley from one of the most prominent landmarks in the Columbia River Gorge. Round Cape Horn on this loop, passing precipitous ledges, hilltop pastures, a spectacular waterfall, and contorted oak- and fir-cloaked basalt cliffs looming over the Columbia.

GETTING THERE

From Vancouver, follow State Route 14 east for 26 miles, turning left onto Salmon Falls Road. Then immediately turn right into a Park and Ride lot, and park. The trail begins on the west side of Salmon Falls Road (elev. 535 ft.). Privy available.

ON THE TRAIL

Cape Horn Trail No. 4418 was built almost entirely by volunteers and has evolved into one of the Gorge's best loved trails. Cross Salmon Falls Road and enter mature forest saved from development by the Columbia Land Trust (see sidebar, "Want to Protect Land Around the Columbia? Buy It!" in the introduction) and immediately reach a junction. Bear right (you'll be returning left) and drop into a lush draw crossing a creek. Then begin switchbacking up an increasingly steep ridge to Pioneer Point. The way bends left, traveling under a tunnel of greenery and skirting a powerline swath, granting good views of Silver Star Mountain.

At 1.3 miles bear left at a junction (the way right is a bypass for horses) coming to the first of two ledge-top viewpoints on 1300-plus-foot Pioneer Point that provide sweeping views across the Columbia out to Oregon. Exercise caution and keep children and dogs close by, or use the bypass trail if

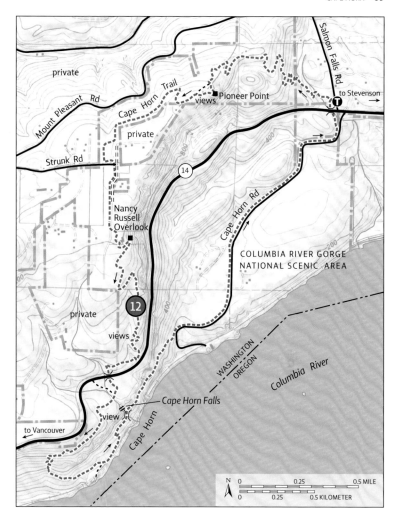

skittish of heights. Then climb to a second viewpoint and meet up with the bypass trail.

Head left along the ridge before switching back and descending to an old woods road. The trail then follows the old road, gently ascending in quiet forest and coming to Strunk Road at 2.3 miles. Cross the road and continue on trail to the left (do not walk across field), soon coming to another old road where you'll turn right. Then begin a long gentle descent passing an old home site and, at 2.7 miles, coming to the Nancy Russell Overlook, honoring the founder of the Friends of the Columbia Gorge who purchased this spectacular parcel later transferred to the US Forest Service. This is a good spot to turn around if the lower loop is closed.

Otherwise, continue on the loop, heading back into forest. Slowly descending, reach a spectacular viewpoint above SR 14. This is the classic Cape Horn view that motorists get. You'll have it here with far less company.

The trail continues descending through mature forest, passing some big trees. The tread here can become slick mud during wet periods—making trekking poles a good accompaniment. Cross a creek on a footbridge then cross beneath SR 14 via a pedestrian tunnel. At 3.9 miles reach a junction (elev. 675 ft.). Right leads to a trailhead and parking on SR 14. Left leads via stairs to an excellent overlook of Cape Horn Falls.

The main trail darts into a small ravine to cross a creek before coming to a junction (closed beyond from February 1 to July 15) at 4.2 miles. The spur left drops down to a viewpoint high on a basalt cliff framed by wind-contorted firs. The main trail then switchbacks downward before heading east across 200-plus-foot high-river bluff tops and traversing the base of a large scree slope. The tread can be rough and rocky in places.

At 5 miles come to a stunning cliffside view (use caution) of Cigar Rock, a narrow basaltic pinnacle. Winds can be fierce here. The trail then climbs across a large scree slope adorned with mosses and ferns before reaching a big bridge at the base of gorgeous Cape Horn Falls. Cross the bridge and descend on a rough path coming to paved Cape Horn Road (elev. 190 ft.) at 5.9 miles.

Then head left and begin walking up this quiet country road, respecting private property postings.

Be sure to look west and up for good views of Cape Horn and the highway viaduct. At 7 miles leave the road left for trail and pass through a pedestrian tunnel under SR 14. Then bear right at the junction to return to the trailhead at 7.2 miles.

13 Sams Walker Nature Trail

RATING/ DIFFICULTY	ROUNDTRIP	ELEV GAIN/ HIGH POINT	SEASON
***/1	1.2 miles	Negligible/ 50 feet	Year-round

Crowds: 1; **Map:** Green Trails Columbia River Gorge West 428S; **Contact:** Columbia River Gorge National Scenic Area; **Notes:** NW Forest Pass or Interagency Pass required. Dogs permitted on leash. Wheelchair accessible; **GPS:** N 45° 36.708' W 122° 03.109'

One of the quieter trails in the Columbia River Gorge, Sams Walker is perfect for a leisurely morning or evening stroll. Wander along this nearly level, barrier-free trail through attractive oak and ash forest and riverside fields, listening to birdsong and watching for deer.

GETTING THERE
From Vancouver, follow State Route 14 east for 33 miles, turning right (just before the Skamania General Store) onto Skamania Landing Road. After 0.3 mile come to the trailhead on your right (elev. 40 ft.). Privy available.

ON THE TRAIL
While Sams Walker Trail No. 4402 is short, it's long on delights. Young children will

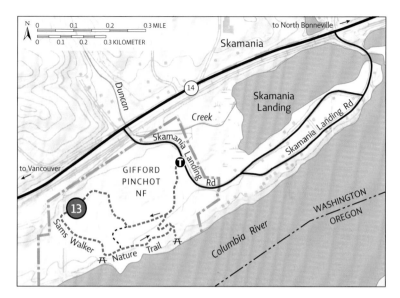

especially like it. Take time to read the attractive interpretive plaques along the way. Then pause, reflect, and absorb. In springtime, Sams Walker is alive with floral bouquets and avian symphonies. In early summer, it's abuzz with mosquitoes! Come fall, stately oak, ash, and maple add streaks of gold to this emerald easel.

Rife with history as well as wildlife, this natural area was home to Native peoples before it was homesteaded by German immigrants in the 1880s. Later, the Sams family raised fourteen children here on their dairy farm (and an eponymous Walker married into the Sams family, hence the trail's name).

The trail starts as a wide swath across an old farm field now sprouting lupines and

Interpretive panel along Sams Walker Nature Trail

other native vegetation. Enjoy good views of Oregon's Nesmith Point directly south across the Columbia. March across the field and look back at Hardy Ridge, Archer Mountain, and Hamilton Mountain. In 0.2 mile the trail splits. Go right—you'll be returning from the left. At 0.3 mile the trail splits again. Unless you want to shorten this loop (and why would you do that?), continue to the right, soon entering a mature forest of hardwoods and cedars. Emerge back in pasture that has been replanted with native vegetation and reach a picnic area on a bluff above the Columbia. When foliage is thin, Horsetail Falls can be seen across the grand river.

Continue on the loop, ignoring the short-cut leading left, and traverse a grove of cottonwoods, oaks, and ashes. Come to a junction with a short spur leading right to a picnic table set among some giant cotton-woods. The loop continues left passing some big oaks, and perhaps a rabbit or deer or two. Return to the first junction and head right for the trailhead. Note that this beautiful area almost became a subdivision before being secured for preservation.

EXTENDING YOUR TRIP

Three miles to the west, visit the Saint Cloud picnic area (NW Forest Pass required) and take to its 0.4 mile of barrier-free orchard-weaving trails.

14 Beacon Rock

RATING/ DIFFICULTY	ROUNDTRIP	ELEV GAIN/ HIGH POINT	SEASON
*****/2	1.8 miles	600 feet/ 848 feet	Year-round

Crowds: 5; **Map:** Green Trails Columbia River Gorge West 428S; **Contact:** Beacon Rock State Park; **Notes:** Discover Pass required.

Dogs permitted on leash (but not recommended). Trail frequently closed during winter storms; **GPS:** N 45° 37.730', W 122° 01.285'

Follow a twisting trail of ramps and stairways to the top of the largest basaltic monolith in the Northwest. Then take in breathtaking views of the Columbia River and its striking gorge from this 848-foot core of an ancient volcano. Named by Lewis and Clark in 1805, the rock was bought by wealthy engineer and amateur botanist Henry J. Biddle in 1915, and he constructed this marvel of a trail. After his death, his children gave the rock to the state for a new park in 1935.

GETTING THERE

From Vancouver, follow State Route 14 east for 35 miles to Beacon Rock State Park (1.8 miles east of Skamania). The trail begins on the south side of the highway, just past the campground entrance (elev. 250 ft.). Privy available.

ON THE TRAIL

The trail starts at the base of the imposing landmark. Follow the wide and well-trodden path through old growth around the western base of the basaltic behemoth. Then commence climbing on a trail that is truly one of the engineering marvels of the hiking world. By way of a series of dangling catwalks and stairways and switchbacking ramps, the sturdy trail ascends the rock's sheer face. Iron railings provide safety, but keep small children close by. Constructed from 1915 to 1918 by Biddle and his buddy Charles Johnson, and later reinforced by the Civilian Conservation Corps, the trail truly is a marvelous feat.

After twisting and turning and switch-backing fifty-three times, the trail ends on

The Beacon Rock Trail is an engineering marvel.

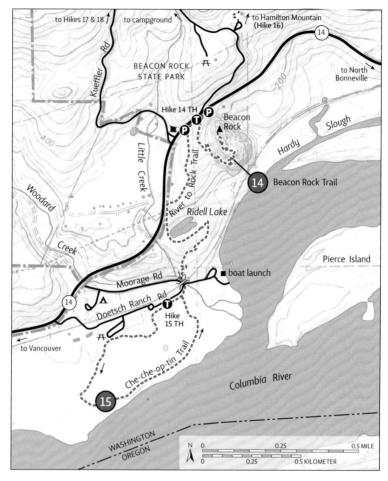

to Hikes 17 & 18
to campground
to Hamilton Mountain (Hike 16)
14
Kueffler Rd
BEACON ROCK STATE PARK
to North Bonneville
200
Hike 14 TH
T P
P
Beacon Rock
Slough
Little Creek
River to Rock Trail
Hardy
400
14 Beacon Rock Trail
Woodard
Ridell Lake
Creek
Pierce Island
Moorage Rd
boat launch
14
Doetsch Ranch Rd
T
Hike 15 TH
to Vancouver
Che-che-op-tin Trail
Columbia River
15
WASHINGTON
OREGON
N 0   0.25   0.5 MILE
0   0.25   0.5 KILOMETER

top of the rock at 0.9 mile. Views along the way are breathtaking, taking in the Bonneville Dam in the east all the way to Crown Point in the west. Watch trains chug and boats putter below. Imagine Lewis and Clark plying the river before you more than 200 years ago. It was they who named the rock back on October 31, 1805. And it was here at Beacon Rock that they first noticed tidal influences in the river. Yet, nearly 150 miles inland from the Pacific, it would still be some time before they exclaimed, "Ocean in view!" The airy viewing loft can be quite crowded on a sunny summer day, so be prepared to share.

EXTENDING YOUR TRIP

Combine with the River to Rock Trail and Che-che-op-tin Trail (Hike 15).

15 River to Rock and Che-che-op-tin Trails

RATING/ DIFFICULTY	ROUNDTRIP	ELEV GAIN/ HIGH POINT	SEASON
**/1	2.9 miles	280 feet/ 250 feet	Year-round

Crowds: 2; **Map:** Green Trails Columbia River Gorge West 428S; **Contact:** Beacon Rock State Park; **Notes:** Discover Pass required. Dogs permitted on leash. Che-che-op-tin Trail is ADA accessible; **GPS:** N 45° 37.185', W 122° 01.602'

Explore the quiet corner of Beacon Rock State Park by taking to these two easy, family-friendly trails in the Doetsch Ranch day-use area. Walk on a paved path around a meadow that once bustled with cattle. Then amble up the park's newest trail skirting a small pond at the base of imposing Beacon Rock.

GETTING THERE

From Vancouver, follow State Route 14 east for 34 miles and turn right onto Doetsch Ranch Road (signed for boat launch) in Beacon Rock State Park. Continue for 0.2 mile and turn right into a large parking area and trailhead (elev. 40 ft.). Privy and picnic tables available.

ON THE TRAIL

Start by following the paved 1.2-mile Che-che-op-tin loop trail counter clock-wise. First Peoples referred to Beacon Rock as Che-che-op-tin, which means "the navel of the world." It was Lewis and Clark who first paddled through this area in October of 1805 naming it Beaten Rock and then Beacon Rock. *Beaten*—it is the remaining core of an ancient volcano, and *Beacon*—it has served as an important landmark for centuries.

The Che-Che-op-tin Trail loops around an old cattle ranch.

Leisurely walk the trail circling a large meadow that served as a cattle ranch operated by the Doetsch family (who arrived from Kansas in 1894) from 1920 until 1987, when it became part of Beacon Rock State Park. The way passes by some large oaks—then some large cottonwoods along the river. Take in good views of Beacon Rock, Hardy Ridge, and Aldrich Butte.

When the trail approaches Doetsch Ranch Road, don't head left to return to your vehicle yet. Instead, walk the road right a short distance and then head left on Moorage Road. Immediately upon passing under railroad tracks, head right on the 0.75 mile River to Rock Trail. Cross Woodard Creek on a bridge and head up some stone steps, passing the remains of a small stone building, an old orchard, big firs, and thickets of invasive Himalayan blackberry.

Gently climbing, catch some river views through the brush before coming upon tiny Ridell Lake, which may be dry by late summer. Enjoy good close-up views of imposing Beacon Rock before continuing on the trail. After crossing a powerline right-of-way, the trail climbs through a fir forest. Crest a small ridge and come to the trail's northern trailhead near the Beacon Rock trailhead. Tack on a trip up Beacon Rock (Hike 14), or return to your start for a quiet 2.9-mile hike.

16 Hamilton Mountain

RATING/ DIFFICULTY	ROUNDTRIP	ELEV GAIN/ HIGH POINT	SEASON
*****/4	7.6 miles	2100 feet/ 2438 feet	Apr–Nov

Crowds: 5; **Map:** Green Trails Columbia River Gorge West 428S; **Contact:** Beacon Rock State Park; **Notes:** Discover Pass required.

Dogs permitted on leash; **GPS:** N 45° 37.951', W 122° 01.213'

One of the most popular destinations on the Washington side of the Gorge, Hamilton Mountain lives up to its hype, delivering breathtaking views, dazzling wildflowers, and a pair of dramatic waterfalls. Amble below, along, and above basaltic cliffs, gazing out at the dramatic gorge spread before you. And delight in the trails and bridges leading you to all of this, the showy legacies of the 1930s-era Civilian Conservation Corps (CCC).

GETTING THERE

From Vancouver, follow State Route 14 east for 35 miles to Beacon Rock State Park (1.8 miles east of Skamania). Just after the park headquarters, turn left toward the campground and reach the trailhead in 0.3 mile (elev. 475 ft.). Privy available. Additional parking is available at the nearby picnic area. Parking is limited at both spots—arrive early.

ON THE TRAIL

While Beacon Rock is the crown jewel of the 4458-acre state park that shares its name, attracting scads of admirers, Hamilton Mountain is where the real hiking action is in the park. But don't expect solitude here either. The trail starts at a lovely picnic area graced with structures built by the CCC. Beacon Rock is one of over 800 state parks nationally that was developed and enhanced by President Franklin D. Roosevelt's "Tree Army" during the Great Depression.

Enter a grove of large firs and immediately start climbing. At 0.4 mile, in a powerline swath, bear right at a junction with a trail leading to the campground. Continue climbing through attractive forest that's

Rodney Falls

decorated by snowy-white Pacific dogwood bouquets in spring and garnished with golden vine maple leaves in autumn.

At 1.1 miles, come to a junction (elev. 960 ft.) with the Hardy Falls Viewpoint spur. Affording not the best vista, the spur drops steeply 50 feet to a platform above the falls. Better waterfall viewings wait ahead, so carry on 0.1 mile to another junction. Left leads to Rodney Falls, an impressive 50-foot cascade that thunders through a tight chasm into a punchbowl basin named the Pool of Winds. Pool of Mist is more appropriate—and you'll realize why soon enough!

After literally soaking in the view, continue on your way to Hamilton, dropping 50 feet to cross Hardy Creek on a hardy bridge. Then, steeply climb to reach a junction (elev. 1100 ft.) with the Hardy Creek Trail at 1.4 miles. You'll be returning from the left, so proceed right, steadily climbing, switchbacking beneath and around steep ledges and cliffs, views expanding at each turn. Beacon Rock and the Bonneville Dam lie directly below. Mount Hood peeks above Oregon's steep and impressive Gorge Face. Look to the west too for a good view of Archer Mountain and a series of cinder cones scattered across the landscape. In late spring and early summer, paintbrush, phlox, larkspur, and other flowers decorate Hamilton's steep slopes.

At 3.2 miles crest Hamilton's 2438-foot summit, where a sign erroneously says 2480 feet. Brush obscures viewing to the south and west, but views are good to the east, especially to impressive Table Mountain.

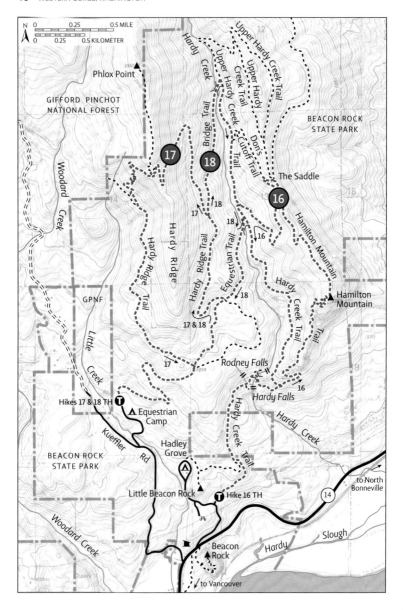

N
0   0.25   0.5 MILE
0   0.25   0.5 KILOMETER

Phlox Point

GIFFORD PINCHOT
NATIONAL FOREST

Upper Hardy Creek Trail

Hardy Creek

Upper Hardy Creek Trail

Upper Hardy Creek Trail

Upper Hardy Creek

Don's Cutoff Trail

Bridge Trail

BEACON ROCK
STATE PARK

The Saddle

17

18

16

18

17

18

18

16

Hamilton Mountain

Woodard Creek

Hardy Ridge Trail

Hardy Ridge

Hardy Ridge Trail

Equestrian Trail

Hardy Creek Trail

Trail

Hamilton Mountain

GPNF

18

17 & 18

17

Rodney Falls

16

Hardy Falls

Hikes 17 & 18 TH

Equestrian
Camp

Little Creek

Kueffler Rd

Hardy Creek Trail

Hardy Creek

Hadley
Grove

BEACON ROCK
STATE PARK

Little Beacon Rock

Hike 16 TH

to North
Bonneville

14

Woodard Creek

Beacon
Rock

Hardy

Slough

to Vancouver

Now, continue along Hamilton's north ridge, enjoying excellent views of Hardy Ridge. At 3.9 miles emerge on an open flat basaltic saddle (elev. 2100 ft.), perfect for lunchtime and staring into the distance.

At 4.1 miles reach a junction with an old fire road. Follow it to the left, slowly descending through forest, passing Don's Cutoff (an alternative route—turn left at its terminus), and reaching the Upper Hardy Creek Trail (elev. 1500 ft.) at 5 miles. Continue left, and after 0.1 mile veer left onto the Hardy Creek Trail. The trail leading right connects to the West and East Hardy Ridge Trails (Hike 17 and an alternative approach).

Now paralleling Hardy Creek, gently descend through lush forest, occasionally passing remnant burnt snags. At 6.2 miles arrive back on the Hamilton Mountain Trail. Turn right and retrace familiar ground 1.4 miles back to the trailhead.

EXTENDING YOUR TRIP

For a slight variation on the return, take the campground spur trail for 0.4 mile to the Little Beacon Rock Trail. Follow this nice path through pika-hopping talus for 0.2 mile to the mini monolith, Little Beacon Rock. Return to the main trail or turn left, hiking 0.2 mile through Hadley Grove (named for park's first superintendent) to the campground set in old-growth forest. Then follow the road 0.5 mile back to your vehicle.

17 Hardy Ridge

RATING/ DIFFICULTY	ROUNDTRIP	ELEV GAIN/ HIGH POINT	SEASON
***/3	7.1 miles	1800 feet/ 2550 feet	Apr–Nov

Crowds: 3; **Map:** Green Trails Columbia River Gorge West 428S; **Contact:** Beacon Rock

State Park; **Notes:** Discover Pass required. Dogs permitted on leash. Part of loop open to horses and bikes; **GPS:** N 45° 38.473', W 122° 01.930'

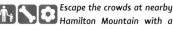 *Escape the crowds at nearby Hamilton Mountain with a loop nearly as invigorating up and over Hardy Ridge. Wander old fire roads and new tread through thick forest to Hardy's flower gardens and basalt outcroppings. And enjoy good views of Oregon peaks and the Columbia River.*

GETTING THERE

From Vancouver, follow State Route 14 east for 35 miles to Beacon Rock State Park (1.8 miles east of Skamania). Just before park headquarters, turn left onto Kueffler Road and proceed for 1 mile. Turn right (signed "Equestrian Trailhead"), coming to picnic grounds, an equestrian campground, and the trailhead in 0.3 mile (elev. 750 ft.). Privy available.

ON THE TRAIL

Starting on the Equestrian Trail—an old fire road (closed to vehicles), wind your way up a hillside of deciduous trees that resemble an eastern hardwood forest. At 1.2 miles come to a four-way junction (elev. 1350 ft.). You'll be returning on the trail to the left. The trail to the right makes a 1-mile loop back to the main trail. Continue straight, and at 1.8 miles come to another four-way junction (elev. 1550 ft.). To the right is the previously mentioned loop trail; straight ahead, the main trail (Equestrian Trail) continues 0.5 mile to Hardy Creek (Hike 18) and connects with the Hamilton Mountain loop (Hike 16). Bear left on the Hardy Ridge Trail.

After a short climb, pass through a cool stretch of forest and arrive at another junction

Spring wildflowers along Hardy Ridge

(elev. 1800 ft.) at 2.7 miles. Here the Bridge Trail (Hike 18) veers right for Hardy Creek. Continue straight. At 3.2 miles the way leaves old road for a single-track hiker-only trail. In cool hemlock forest, switchback up steep slopes and come to a junction (elev. 2550 ft.) among flowered outcroppings and great views at 3.9 miles. The trail to the right is an unofficial path along Hardy Ridge. Scorched of its tree cover from the 1902 Yacolt Burn, the ridge is shrouded with low-lying shrubs and flowering plants. Consider wandering up it 0.2 mile to a 2700-foot knoll for stunning views of the Columbia River, Larch Mountain, Nesmith Point, and Hamilton Mountain. Admire the floral arrangements in early summer. The path continues another 0.5 mile to 2957-foot Phlox Point.

From the junction, the Hardy Ridge loop continues west, now gradually descending and passing more fine viewing and flower gardens. At 4.3 miles the trail emerges onto an old road before descending on switchbacks and reaching another old road at 4.7 miles. Now head left, continuing on an easy grade that may be sporting high grasses (check for ticks), and return to the first four-way junction at 5.9 miles. Turn right and return to your vehicle in 1.2 miles.

EXTENDING YOUR TRIP

Combine with the Bridge Trail for a longer loop via the Upper Hardy Creek Trail (Hike 18).

18 Upper Hardy Creek

RATING/ DIFFICULTY	ROUNDTRIP	ELEV GAIN/ HIGH POINT	SEASON
***/3	6.2 miles	1300 feet/ 1800 feet	Apr–Nov

Crowds: 2; **Map:** Green Trails Columbia River Gorge West 428S; **Contact:** Beacon Rock

State Park; **Notes:** Discover Pass required. Dogs permitted on leash. Trail open to horses and bikes; **GPS:** N 45° 38.473', W 122° 01.930'

Beyond Beacon Rock State Park's Hamilton Mountain and Hardy Ridge is a whole network of trails that see light use. Trade the views and crowds of the park's popular peaks for a chance to walk in solitude. Let tumbling Hardy Creek serenade you with its melodic water music. And let the surrounding deep forest cleanse you of your outside worries.

GETTING THERE

From Vancouver, follow State Route 14 east for 35 miles to Beacon Rock State Park (1.8 miles east of Skamania). Just before the park headquarters, turn left onto Kueffler Road and proceed for 1 mile. Turn right (signed "Equestrian Trailhead"), coming to picnic grounds, an equestrian campground, and the trailhead in 0.3 mile (elev. 750 ft.). Privy available.

ON THE TRAIL

Starting on the Equestrian Trail—an old fire road (closed to vehicles)—wind your way up a hillside coming to a four-way junction at 1.2 miles (elev. 1350 ft.). The way left heads to Hardy Ridge (Hike 17). The trail to the right makes a 1-mile loop back to the main trail, offering a longer option. Continue straight, and at 1.8 miles come to another four-way junction (elev. 1550 ft.). To the right is the previously mentioned loop trail. You'll be returning on the main trail (Equestrian Trail) straight ahead. So head left on the Hardy Ridge Trail, and after a short climb, arrive at another junction (elev. 1800 ft.) at 2.7 miles.

Now veer right on the Bridge Trail, soon coming to a small cascading creek. Admire the rock drainage work and general construction of this lovely trail built

Bridge over Hardy Creek after a snow

by the Washington Trails Association. The trail continues through lush forest, slowly descending toward Hardy Creek. It then begins a slow ascent, coming to a big bridge spanning tumbling Hardy Creek. Continue on and reach a junction (elev. 1800 ft.) with the Upper Hardy Creek Trail at 3.6 miles.

Now head right on this old woods-road-turned-trail, traversing thick woods alongside the crashing creek. At 4 miles come to a junction (elev. 1700 ft.) with Dons Cutoff, which offers an alternative approach to the Saddle on the Hamilton Mountain loop (Hike 16). Continue straight, soon passing a privy and reaching a junction (elev. 1500 ft.) with the Equestrian Trail at 4.4 miles. Left heads to Hamilton Mountain—you want to go right. Soon pass the Hardy Creek Trail and cross Hardy Creek, then slowly ascend to reach a familiar four-way junction at 5 miles. Go straight and follow the Equestrian Trail 1.2 miles back to the trailhead.

EXTENDING YOUR TRIP

Make your loop longer by heading left on the Upper Hardy Creek Trail from the Bridge Trail junction. The trail continues north on an old woods road and slowly climbs out of the creek drainage. At about 0.7 mile, as the trail turns south, it splits. Go either way (left is slightly longer), as they meet up again on a 2300-foot forested ridge. Then continue hiking through pleasant forest, reaching a junction with the Equestrian Trail near the Saddle (elev. 2100 ft.) at 1.7 miles from the Bridge Trail junction. Enjoy some excellent views before returning right on the Equestrian Trail, from where it is 3.3 miles back to the trailhead.

You can also hike 0.5 mile up the hiker-only Dons Cutoff, traversing a slope of young uniform forest to reach the Equestrian Trail just below the Saddle. Make a quick jaunt to the Saddle and then return to the trailhead via the Equestrian Trail.

⑲ Strawberry Island

RATING/ DIFFICULTY	LOOP	ELEV GAIN/ HIGH POINT	SEASON
***/1	2.7 miles	140 feet/ 170 feet	Year-round

Crowds: 2; **Map:** Green Trails Columbia River Gorge West 428S; **Contact:** Bonneville Trails Foundation; **Notes:** Dogs permitted on leash; **GPS:** N 45° 38.018', W 121° 58.731'

Wide-open lawns of swaying grasses provide stunning views of towering surrounding peaks. Let me take you down to Strawberry Island's fields, where the scenery is quite real! Retrace the footsteps of Lewis and Clark along a wildlife-rich slough and open bluff above the Columbia River, across what the intrepid explorers called Strawberry Island. And while the island is no longer an island and is now known as Hamilton, wild strawberries still grow profusely upon it.

GETTING THERE

From Vancouver follow State Route 14 east for 37 miles, turning right on the North Bonneville access road. (From Portland, follow I-84 east to exit 44 at Cascade Locks and take the Bridge of the Gods—$3+ toll—to SR 14. Turn left and drive 4 miles west, turning left into North Bonneville.) Then, immediately turn right onto Cascade Drive. After 0.4 mile, turn left onto Portage Drive, coming to the trailhead (elev. 35 ft.) at ballfields in 0.2 mile.

ON THE TRAIL

Several miles of excellent trails traverse Strawberry Island, connecting with North Bonneville's Heritage Trails, the Fort Cascades Trail, and the Hamilton Island fishing areas. The loop described here is a great introduction to this excellent kid- and dog-friendly trail system. With more than 12 miles of trails, you'll have plenty of options to lengthen or shorten your hike.

From the trailhead, immediately come to a four-way intersection. You can head straight on the Viewpoint Trail and reach the island's high point and viewing area in 0.25 mile. But I suggest heading right on the Strawberry Loop instead and taking your time getting there. On a level path (that can get wet and muddy during the winter) walk across meadows edged by giant cottonwoods. At 0.6 mile come to a junction. Continue right along Hamilton Creek, entering thickets of blackberries and singing blackbirds.

At 0.8 mile take a 0.1-mile spur right to Clark's Viewpoint on the western tip of Strawberry Island. Here, take in views of Ives and Pierce Islands, both remnants of the Bonneville landslide that blocked the Columbia (see sidebar, "The Gods Must Be Angry"). Return to the junction and continue right on the loop, now heading east along the Columbia, enjoying excellent views of Munra and Nesmith Points across the river. Watch for rabbits dining on grasses and bald eagles hoping to dine on rabbits! At 1.2 miles come to a junction. The trail right leads 0.5 mile along the Columbia to the fishing access road, an alternative starting point (privy available). Head left, coming to another junction at 1.3 miles. The trail left leads 0.1 mile back to the loop section you previously hiked. Bear right and climb a wide-open grassy bluff, enjoying views of Beacon Rock, Hamilton Mountain, Aldrich Butte, Table Mountain, and a wall of Oregon peaks and ridges. At 1.4 miles come to another junction. Continue straight, cresting the bluff and enjoying even wider views. The Strawberry Loop that continues to the right is equally scenic, with excellent river views.

At 1.8 miles come to a junction, a set of benches and great views at the height (elev. 170 ft.) of the crest. The trail right leads 0.15

Excellent views of the mountains facing the Gorge

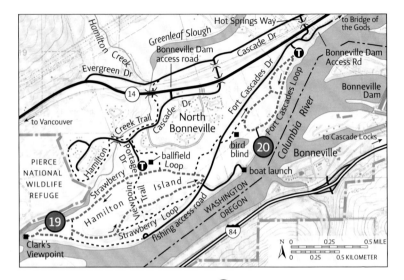

mile to the Strawberry Loop. The Viewpoint Trail to the left leads 0.25 mile back to the trailhead. Continue straight on a wide, double-track trail, enjoying Columbia River breezes and vistas up the Gorge as you slowly descend to a junction with the Strawberry Loop at the fishing access road (no trailhead parking here) at 2.2 miles. Now head left, coming to a junction at 2.3 miles. The trail right leads to a bluff with good views before connecting with the Fort Cascades Loop (Hike 20).

Continue hiking straight, skirting a handful of houses and coming to a junction with one of the paved paths heading into North Bonneville. At 2.7 miles return to the trailhead.

EXTENDING YOUR TRIP

Consider an easy stroll on the 2-mile paved Hamilton Creek Trail, or combine this hike with the Fort Cascades Loop.

20 Fort Cascades Loop

RATING/ DIFFICULTY	LOOP	ELEV GAIN/ HIGH POINT	SEASON
**/1	1.2 miles	50 feet/ 70 feet	Year-round

Crowds: 1; **Maps:** Green Trails Columbia River Gorge West 428S, interpretive map from onsite kiosk; **Contact:** US Army Corps of Engineers, Bonneville Lock and Dam; **Notes:** Dogs permitted on leash. Wheelchair accessible; **GPS:** N 45° 38.661', W 121° 57.481'

Take this short and easy trail for a trip through Pacific Northwest history. While this riverbank locale just downstream from the Bonneville Dam now consists merely of a quiet young forest of oak and fir, it once boasted a town, military post, railroad, and a flurry of human activity. Floods in the late 1800s and then the construction of the dam in 1938 changed all of that. Grab an interpretive brochure at the trailhead and wander back in time.

GETTING THERE

From Vancouver, follow State Route 14 east for 38 miles and turn right on the Bonneville Dam access road (directly across from Hot Springs Way 1 mile east of North Bonneville town access). (From Portland, follow I-84 east to exit 44 at Cascade Locks and take the Bridge of the Gods—$3+ toll—to SR 14. Turn left and drive 3 miles west, turning left onto dam access road.) In 0.1 mile turn right at the stop sign, onto Fort Cascades Drive (the fishing access road), and proceed another 0.1 mile to Fort Cascades Historic Site (elev. 60 ft.). Privy available.

ON THE TRAIL

Start by stopping at the kiosk and reading the fine displays on this area's past exploration, transportation, settlement, military, and fishing history. While traces remain of these past pursuits, it's the change wrought by the Bonneville Dam that is most pronounced here. The Cascades of the Columbia, a once formidable obstacle for travel along the river, no longer exist—having been harnessed for power and corralled for flood prevention.

Grab an interpretive brochure and begin hiking to the fourteen stops along the loop. At 0.1 mile the trail splits—head left, dropping down along the river and enjoying good views while learning about the flood of 1894. Pass a junction with a shortcut that heads right and a viewpoint spur that heads left. Soon come to the old Cascades townsite. Settled in 1850 while Washington was a territory, Cascades served as the Skamania county seat until 1893. A year later, the flood put a permanent end to the town.

Pass a petroglyph replica and continue through quiet forest to a meadow providing excellent views of Munra Point across the river. The trail then loops back, coming to a junction at 0.7 mile. The trail left continues 0.25 mile past a fish-monitoring station to a bird blind beside a marsh. It also connects to North Bonneville's trail system (Hike 19), leading around Hamilton Island (now a peninsula). The loop continues right for another 0.5 mile, passing more historical relics, including parts of a narrow-gauge railway and an 1861 gravestone for Thomas McNatt, one of the early settlers of Cascades.

Remnants of a narrow gauge railroad

21 Gillette Lake and Greenleaf Overlook

RATING/ DIFFICULTY	ROUNDTRIP	ELEV GAIN/ HIGH POINT	SEASON
**/2	5.4 miles	800 feet/ 450 feet	Year-round

RATING/ DIFFICULTY	ROUNDTRIP	ELEV GAIN/ HIGH POINT	SEASON
**/3	8 miles	1240 feet/ 650 feet	Year-round

Crowds: 3/1; **Map:** Green Trails Columbia River Gorge West 428S; **Contact:** Columbia River Gorge National Scenic Area; **Notes:** NW Forest Pass or Interagency Pass required; **GPS:** N 45° 39.028', W 121° 55.988'

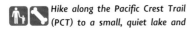 *Hike along the Pacific Crest Trail (PCT) to a small, quiet lake and* a small ledge granting some good views. Here, about 700 years ago, large portions of nearby Greenleaf and Table Mountains slid off, depositing jumbled boulders and creating varying depressions, some of which eventually became lakes. The massive landslide even blocked the Columbia River's passage (see sidebar, "The Gods Must Be Angry"). Travel through this hummocky landscape, appreciating the sheer force of nature.

GETTING THERE

From Vancouver, follow State Route 14 east for 39 miles to the Bonneville trailhead, located on the left (elev. 130 ft.). (From Portland, follow I-84 east to exit 44 at Cascade Locks and take the Bridge of the Gods—$3+ toll—to SR 14. Turn left and drive 2 miles

Table Mountain adds a dramatic backdrop to Gillette Lake.

west to the trailhead, located on your right.) Privy and picnic tables available.

ON THE TRAIL

From the large trailhead area, follow Tamanous Trail No. 27, coming to the PCT (elev. 300 ft.) at 0.6 mile. Named after the Great Spirit of several Northwest tribes, Tamanous is a delightful trail through attractive forest, especially during autumn. At the PCT junction, the way right travels 1.4 miles to the Bridge of the Gods, skirting a couple of residences and paralleling the highway. The way left, your route, travels up and down over small ridges and passes and by many small pools and ponds. If you walk this way in autumn, when the area pools are refilling from heavy rains, you'll need to watch your step: hundreds of rough-skinned newts will be migrating to pools and ponds to begin breeding. Unlike their higher-altitude brethren who mate during the summer, these temperate valley-residing newts breed during the winter.

Pass through an old cut, and at 1.2 miles cross an old logging road. Reenter mature timber and emerge in another cut at 2.1 miles. At 2.4 miles cross a service road and powerline swath. Then start descending across a talus slope, enjoying views of Table Mountain above and Gillette Lake below. At 2.7 miles reach a series of campsites near a stream. Locate a path heading left and follow it a short distance to Gillette Lake (elev. 300 ft.), its northern shore graced with cascaras and its eastern shore decorated with talus. The lake is a popular swim hole for locals and PCT thru hikers alike.

For the Greenleaf Overlook, avoid confusing side trails and continue north on the PCT, crossing Gillette's feeder creek on a footlog. Enter another old cut, and cross another old logging road. Then resume hiking in attractive forest. Look for Pacific dogwood, easier to notice in spring with its showy blossoms. Pass small Greenleaf Pond on the left, home to invasive bull frogs and native Pacific (Western) pond turtles, a species threatened with extirpation in Washington State. Shortly afterward, drop into a cool ravine, crossing Greenleaf Creek on a wide and sturdy bridge.

Then resume climbing, coming to the Greenleaf Overlook (elev. 650 ft.), a mossy outlook set among tall firs at 4 miles. Enjoy nice views of the Bonneville Dam and the imposing emerald flank of steep Oregon ridges behind it.

EXTENDING YOUR TRIP

You can keep hiking the PCT north to trails leading to excellent viewpoints on Aldrich Butte (Hike 22) and Table Mountain (Hike 23).

22 Aldrich Butte

RATING/ DIFFICULTY	ROUNDTRIP	ELEV GAIN/ HIGH POINT	SEASON
***/3	12.4 miles	1900 feet/ 1141 feet	Year-round

Crowds: 2; **Map:** Green Trails Columbia River Gorge West 428S; **Contact:** Columbia River Gorge National Scenic Area; **Notes:** NW Forest Pass or Interagency Pass required; **GPS:** N 45° 39.028', W 121° 55.988'

The views from Aldrich Butte are "dam" good. So dam good that the US military constructed a defense post here during World War II to watch over the Bonneville Dam below. A foundation and remnants of a gun mount are all that remain—and of course those fine views too. Survey Table Mountain, Hamilton Mountain, Tanner Butte,

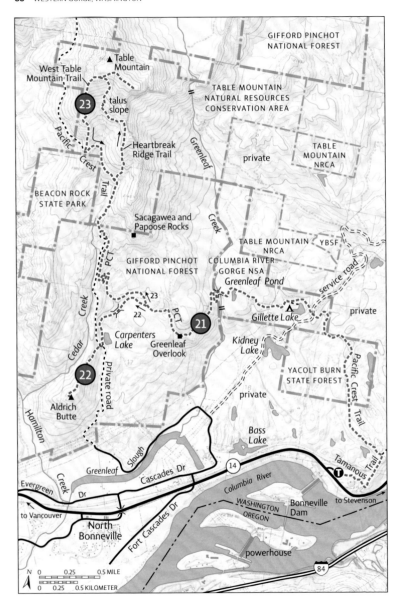

GIFFORD PINCHOT
NATIONAL FOREST

West Table
Mountain Trail

▲ Table
Mountain

talus
slope

23

Pacific

Crest

Heartbreak
Ridge Trail

TABLE MOUNTAIN
NATURAL RESOURCES
CONSERVATION AREA

Greenleaf

private

TABLE
MOUNTAIN
NRCA

BEACON ROCK
STATE PARK

Trail

Sacagawea and
Papoose Rocks

Creek

PCT

GIFFORD PINCHOT
NATIONAL FOREST

TABLE MOUNTAIN
NRCA

YBSF

service road

COLUMBIA RIVER
GORGE NSA

Greenleaf Pond

23

22

PCT

21

Gillette Lake

private

Cedar

Creek

Carpenters
Lake

Greenleaf
Overlook

Kidney
Lake

17

22

private road

16

YACOLT BURN
STATE FOREST

Aldrich
Butte

private

Bass
Lake

Pacific Crest Trail

Hamilton

Slough

Greenleaf

Cascades Dr

Tamanous Trail

T

Evergreen

Creek

Dr

14

Columbia River

WASHINGTON
OREGON

Bonneville
Dam

to Stevenson

to Vancouver

North
Bonneville

Fort Cascades Dr

powerhouse

84

N   0   0.25   0.5 MILE

0   0.25   0.5 KILOMETER

Bonneville Dam and mountains in Oregon along the Columbia River Gorge

the Greenleaf Slough, and Hamilton Island from this oft-overlooked landmark in the heart of the Gorge.

GETTING THERE

From Vancouver, follow State Route 14 east for 39 miles to the Bonneville trailhead, located on the left (elev. 130 ft.). (From Portland, follow I-84 east to exit 44 at Cascade Locks and take the Bridge of the Gods—$3+ toll—to SR 14. Turn left and drive 2 miles west to the trailhead, located on your right.) Privy and picnic tables available.

ON THE TRAIL

Getting to this small butte overlooking North Bonneville used to be a short hike. But the old route crossed private property, and the current landowners revoked the easement. Now the hike is three times as long, making Aldrich Butte a far less visited destination. Embrace the solitude as you drudge along.

From the Bonneville trailhead follow Tamanous Trail No. 27, coming to the Pacific Crest Trail (elev. 300 ft.) at 0.6 mile. Then head left, traveling up and down over small

ridges and passing by many small pools and ponds. Pass through old cuts and cross logging roads. After crossing a service road and powerline swath, start descending, reaching a stream and a path heading left to Gillette Lake (Hike 21) at 2.7 miles.

Then continue north on the PCT, crossing the creek on a footlog. After passing through another old cut and crossing another old road, enter attractive forest. Pass small Greenleaf Pond shortly afterward, drop into a cool ravine, and cross Greenleaf Creek on a sturdy bridge.

Then resume climbing coming to the Greenleaf Overlook (Hike 21) at 4 miles. Continue gently climbing, coming to a junction with an old woods road (elev. 840 ft.) at 4.7 miles. The route to the right leads to Table Mountain (Hike 23). You will head left (signed "Carpenters Lake") on the old-road-turned-trail. The way is brushy (watch for nettles) and muddy at times, but the going is easy with a long, gradual descent. Cross a bridge over a creek and soon afterward skirt Carpenters Lake, a marshy haven for birds and insects.

At 5.5 miles come to a junction (elev. 685 ft.). Now follow an old road right and climb to another junction (elev. 780 ft.) at 5.6 miles. The road-trail right returns to the PCT in 1.2 miles. You want to continue left on the old road and steeply climb. At 5.8 miles, pass an unmarked side trail to Cedar Mountain (be sure to have a map if you explore this and other unmarked trails and roads in the area). At 6.2 miles reach Aldrich Butte's 1141-foot summit.

Trees have reclaimed the butte, growing within and around an old foundation and gun mount. But the views are still good, particularly from just below the summit. Locate Dog and Wind Mountains, Tanner Butte, and Munra Point directly across the river. Of course, there's also a great view of the Bonneville Dam and the city of North Bonneville. Aldrich's sun-kissed openings also harbor some oaks and a few showy flowers, including arrowleaf balsamroot, which is pushing its western range here in the heart of the Gorge.

23 Table Mountain

RATING/ DIFFICULTY	ROUNDTRIP	ELEV GAIN/ HIGH POINT	SEASON
****/5	15.9 miles	4300 feet/ 3400 feet	May–Nov

Crowds: 3; **Map:** Green Trails Columbia River Gorge West 428S; **Contact:** Washington State Department of Natural Resources, Pacific Cascade Region; **Notes:** NW Forest Pass or Interagency Pass required. Dogs prohibited on Table Mountain. Hike is extremely difficult and involves scrambling up a talus slope. Stay on designated trails to avoid disturbing endangered plants; **GPS:** N 45° 39.028', W 121° 55.988'

An iconic peak within the Gorge, Table Mountain gave birth to the original *Bridge of the Gods hundreds of years ago when half of it slid off in a massive landslide, damming the Columbia River. But what's left of Table is impressive too: sheer cliffs, mystical rock formations, and a tabletop draped in alpine flowers, including several endangered ones. To be seated at this table, however, requires physical prowess and competence with negotiating rocky and steep terrain. Really steep! This is one of the toughest hikes in this book.*

GETTING THERE
From Vancouver, follow State Route 14 east for 39 miles to the Bonneville trailhead, located on the left (elev. 130 ft.). (From Portland, follow I-84 east to exit 44 at Cascade Locks and take the Bridge of the Gods—$3+ toll—to SR 14. Turn left and drive 2 miles west to the trailhead, located on your right.) Privy and picnic tables available.

ON THE TRAIL
Getting to Table Mountain used to be a lot shorter and easier (but never easy). But the old route crossed private property, and the current landowners revoked the easement. Now the hike is much longer and out of reach for many day hikers. This is a tough hike and should not be taken lightly.

From the Bonneville trailhead follow Tamanous Trail No. 27, coming to the Pacific Crest Trail (PCT, elev. 300 ft.) at 0.6 mile. Then head left, traveling up and down over small ridges and passing by many small pools and ponds. Pass through old cuts, and cross logging roads. After crossing a service road and powerline swath, start descending, reaching a stream and a path heading left to Gillette Lake (Hike 21) at 2.7 miles.

Then continue north on the PCT, crossing the creek on a footlog. After passing through

Dramatic view of Mount Hood rising above the Bonneville Dam

another old cut and crossing another old road, enter attractive forest. Pass small Greenleaf Pond shortly afterward, drop into a cool ravine, and cross Greenleaf Creek on a sturdy bridge.

Then resume climbing, passing the Greenleaf Overlook (Hike 21) at 4 miles and reaching a junction with an old woods road (elev. 840 ft.) at 4.7 miles. The way left leads to Aldrich Butte (Hike 22). You want to continue straight, crossing a small creek and traversing a grove of big firs. The route then parallels the creek before switchbacking

and reaching an old road (elev. 1450 ft.) at 6 miles. The old road on the left is part of the old approach and can be followed for 1 mile to the Aldrich Road Trail.

Here the PCT continues left—but it's brushy, as most hikers continue straight on the paralleling old road. So head that way, merging with the PCT at 6.2 miles and continuing on good trail. At 6.5 miles cross a spring-fed creek, a popular rehydrating spot for PCT thru hikers. Just beyond, come to a junction and a kiosk introducing you to the Washington State Department of Natural

THE GODS MUST BE ANGRY

One of the more attractive and well-known man-made structures in the Columbia River Gorge is the Bridge of the Gods, built in 1926 and spanning a narrow section of the river near Stevenson, Washington, and Cascade Locks, Oregon. But much more intriguing is the natural bridge that the gods built many years prior.

Somewhere between AD 1000 and 1700 (geologists aren't sure of the exact date), a huge landslide occurred. Massive amounts of Table Mountain and Greenleaf Peak slid off, covering more than 5.5 square miles of the valley below and blocking the Columbia River. This natural dam, more than 200 feet high and 3.5 miles long, impounded the river and formed a lake 35 miles long. Eventually, the river broke through it. Area First Peoples recount the event with numerous legends and stories.

One such, told by the Klickitat people, explains that two brothers named Pahto and Wy'east were quarreling over land in the valley. Their father, the great chief Tyhee Saghalie, shot two great arrows in opposite directions across the river, indicating where the sons would settle. In the process, the great arrows formed a bridge, allowing the family to periodically congregate. But eventually, peace was lost when the two sons fell in love with Loowit. They violently fought over her, causing the bridge to fall apart and creating the Cascade Rapids (since buried by the construction of the Bonneville Dam). Saghalie punished all three by turning them into great mountains: Mount Adams (Pahto), Mount Hood (Wy'east), and Mount St. Helens (Loowit).

But Loowit had the last word in 1980 when she blew her top!

Resources' 2837-acre Table Mountain Natural Resources Conservation Area.

Here, at an elevation of 1800 feet, you have roughly gained 2060 feet of elevation over a course of 6.5 miles. You will gain the next 1600 feet in 1.2 miles. While the trail is steep, it's not exposed. But it can be dangerous, with its route up loose talus and rocky tread. Avoid in bad weather and snow. Bring trekking poles and wear good gripping shoes.

Now head right on the user-built Heartbreak (more like lung-buster) Ridge Trail, climbing at an insanely ridiculous grade straight up. At 7 miles, reach a saddle (elev. 2500 ft.) beneath the impressive face of the mountain and teetering above a sheer drop-off above a jumbled pile of landslide debris.

The trail then drops 80 feet through wind-contorted firs and maples before commencing up a series of tight switchbacks. At an elevation of 2700 feet, reach the base of a large talus slope. The trail goes straight up it. Rock hop (stick to the left of the slope) for 300 vertical feet. Then resume on tread at the top of the talus and angle left, back into forest, reaching a junction (elev. 3200 ft.) at 7.6 miles.

You'll be returning on the left, but first the summit awaits 0.3 mile to the right. After a short brushy and eroded stretch, emerge just below Table's 3400-foot summit. Then continue on a slight descent across flowered meadows to a vertigo-inducing, heart-pounding viewpoint (use caution) directly above sheer 1000-foot-plus cliffs at the face of the mountain. What a view! Hamilton Mountain, Benson Plateau, Chinidere Mountain, Mount Defiance, Eagle Creek valley, the Columbia River, and above it all, Mount Hood! Look north and east, too, to Mounts Adams, Rainier, and St. Helens as well as Greenleaf Peak, and the Soda Lake Peaks. Take time to smell the flowers (but stay on the trail). Can you locate Howell's daisy? Endemic to the Gorge, the largest population of this threatened species is found on Table.

Now retrace your steps 0.3 mile back to the previous junction. Then continue straight on the West Table Mountain Trail, steeply (insanely at times) descending along an open ridge (with good views northwest to Lookout and Silver Star Mountains) and the edge of cliffs. Loose rock makes the descent difficult in spots and easy to twist an ankle or slide out.

At 8.9 miles reach the PCT (elev. 2000 ft.). You survived! Now head left on excellent tread and reach the Heartbreak Ridge Trail junction at 9.4 miles. Continue straight for 6.5 familiar miles back to the trailhead!

24 Wind River Arboretum

RATING/ DIFFICULTY	ROUNDTRIP	ELEV GAIN/ HIGH POINT	SEASON
**/1	1.2 miles	200 feet/ 1230 feet	Year-round

Crowds: 2; **Map:** Green Trails Wind River No. 397; **Contact:** Gifford Pinchot National Forest, Mount Adams Ranger District; **Notes:** Respect historic buildings and privacy of any guests staying at them; **GPS:** N 45° 47.906', W 121° 56.004'

Wander through plots of trees, both native and introduced, in the oldest arboretum in the Pacific Northwest. Located in the Wind River Historic District—which includes a nursery, experiment station, and several historic buildings—the Arboretum Trail was nearly lost to history. But thanks to a dedicated group of volunteers, this short but intriguing trail is once again available.

A grove of giant sequoias, better adapted to the Sierra Nevada than to the Cascades

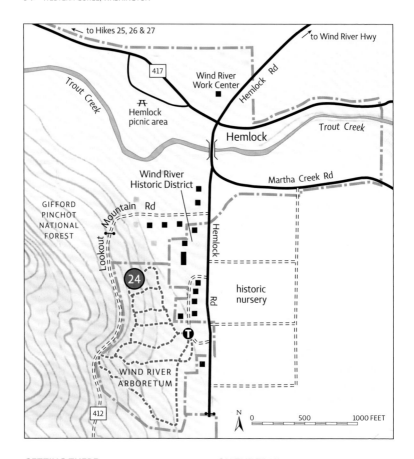

GETTING THERE

From Stevenson, head east on State Route 14 for 3.2 miles, turning north at the traffic circle onto Wind River Highway. Then drive 8.6 miles and turn left onto Hemlock Road. Continue on Hemlock Road (passing the Wind River Work Center) and entering the Wind River Historic District coming to the trailhead in 1.6 miles (elev. 1150 ft.).

ON THE TRAIL

When pioneering forest research scientist Thornton T. Munger arrived in the Pacific Northwest fresh out of the Yale Forest School in 1908, he immediately went to work studying the region's Douglas firs. In 1912 he established the Wind River Arboretum, studying whether many non-native trees from the world's temperate zones were suitable to grow in the region. The area had recently been heavily impacted by the Yacolt Burn, and reforestation efforts where in process.

Walk the Arboretum Trail, which is actually a series of many short trails weaving through the various experimental plots that Munger established. Stroll among redwoods, pines, junipers, firs, hemlocks, cedars, and more. Many of the species have not survived or are struggling. The sequoias, however, took to the area fairly well. Walk the periphery trail and then zigzag through the plots.

In the last few decades, the arboretum suffered many years of neglect. Fortunately, a group of volunteers recently formed the Wind River Trust with the intent to rehabilitate many of the area's historic structures, including the arboretum. They cleared the arboretum's trails and put in place new signage, making this place a delight to visit once again. After your walk through the arboretum, consider heading through the historic district too—just respect the privacy of individuals staying or working at some of the structures.

And after you wrap up your hike among the arboretum's scores of species, you'll easily see what Munger concluded about his research plots—that native trees grow best in the region.

25 Bunker Hill

RATING/ DIFFICULTY	ROUNDTRIP	ELEV GAIN/ HIGH POINT	SEASON
**/3	4 miles	1250 feet/ 2383 feet	Mar–Dec

Crowds: 1; **Map:** Green Trails Wind River No. 397; **Contact:** Gifford Pinchot National Forest, Mount Adams Ranger District; **Notes:** NW

Forest Pass or Interagency Pass required; **GPS:** N 45° 48.459', W 121° 56.428'

There's nothing revolutionary about this Bunker Hill, and you won't need to battle for it either—it'll all be yours. Named by two settlers for the famous site in Boston, this little peak—an igneous volcanic plug—once served as a fire lookout. The tower is long gone and the trees have grown in, obstructing any viewing. But some ledges just below the summit grant some excellent views of the valley below.

GETTING THERE

From Stevenson, head east on State Route 14 for 3.2 miles, turning north at the traffic circle onto Wind River Highway. Then drive 8.6 miles and turn left onto Hemlock Road. After 1.2 miles (just beyond the Wind River Work Center), turn right onto Forest Road 43. Proceed for 0.7 mile and turn right onto FR 417. Continue for 0.3 mile passing the Pacific Crest Trail (PCT, no parking) to a large parking area for the Whistle Punk Trail (elev. 1150 ft.). Privy available.

ON THE TRAIL

Walk the road 0.2 mile back to the PCT, following along a fence line of a now unused section of the Wind River Nursery. Decades of budget cuts and dwindling staff have reduced much of this once bustling area of the Gifford Pinchot National Forest into a "ghost forest." Now follow the PCT north across the fallow nursery. Heavily forested Bunker Hill rises before you. Elk and deer frequent the meadow you're traversing.

The trail soon enters forest, crossing a wet alder and maple flat and passing a

Wind River valley view

lone bog Douglas-fir. At 0.6 mile from the trailhead, reach a junction (elev. 1220 ft.). The PCT continues right, scooting along the base of Bunker Hill on its way to the Wind River. You want to bear left onto Trail No. 145 and begin your switchbacking charge up Bunker Hill. Despite being a small peak, it's a good little climb, with a pitch that's steep from time to time. But the tread is good, weaving through some beautiful patches of old-growth Douglas-fir.

At 1.8 miles the trail brushes up with a small set of ledges. Carefully work your way toward them for a good view of the Wind River valley and of Dog, Wind, Augspurger, and Big Huckleberry Mountains as well as the top of Mount Adams. Oregon's Mount Defiance dominates the backdrop, and you'll be able to catch a glimpse of the Columbia River at its base. The trail continues for another 0.2 mile to Bunker Hill's 2383-foot forested summit. All that remains of the fire lookout that once graced this peak are the concrete blocks that anchored it.

26 Whistle Punk Trail

RATING/ DIFFICULTY	LOOP	ELEV GAIN/ HIGH POINT	SEASON
**/1	1.5 miles	80 feet/ 1230 feet	Mar–Dec

Crowds: 2; **Map:** Green Trails Wind River No. 397; **Contact:** Gifford Pinchot National Forest, Mount Adams Ranger District; **Notes:** NW Forest Pass or Interagency Pass required. Wheelchair accessible; **GPS:** N 45° 48.605', W 121° 56.615'

 **Saunter back into a time when the forest**

was abuzz with whistle punks, high climbers, loaders, and steam donkeys. Hardscrabble loggers from northern Europe and the Midwest toppled trees 200 feet high, and the rivers boomed with timber during the spring runoff. Learn about the logging practices of yesteryear, and embrace the silence and beauty of a regenerating forest and one spared from the axe.

GETTING THERE

From Stevenson, head east on State Route 14 for 3.2 miles, turning north at the traffic circle onto Wind River Highway. Then drive 8.6 miles and turn left onto Hemlock Road. After 1.2 miles (just beyond the Wind River Work Center), turn right onto Forest Road 43. Proceed for 0.7 mile and turn right onto FR 417. Continue for 0.3 to the trailhead (elev. 1150 ft.). Privy available.

ON THE TRAIL

Whistle Punk Trail No. 59 is littered with logging relics from the 1920s and lined with informative plaques about this bygone era. Start by walking up an old-road-turned-trail, and immediately come to a junction. You'll be returning on the trail straight ahead, so head

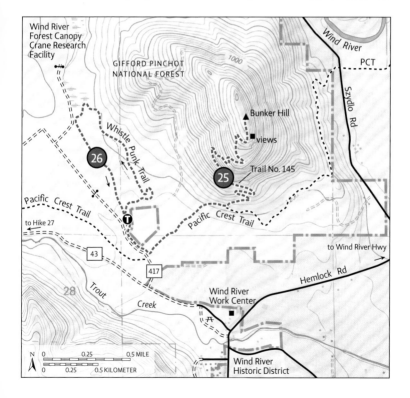

Old logging relics along the Whistle Punk Trail

right through a swamp of Oregon ash, a tree that Northwest forest ecologist Stephen Arno, in his book *Northwest Trees*, describes as "a typical eastern hardwood that got misplaced on the west side of the continent."

After you traverse the wetlands, the trail weaves around a variety of logging artifacts in various degrees of decay before taking to an old logging railroad bed. Following the old railbed, the trail eventually skirts an attractive wetland complete with an observation deck. Across the dogwood-dotted swamp, you may be surprised to see towering firs and cedar—trees hundreds of years old and spared from past harvesting.

Continue hiking, crossing a channel, and enter that ancient forest, part of the Thornton T. Munger Research Natural Area. Munger was a US Forest Service scientist who was responsible for establishing the

nursery and arboretum (Hike 24) at Wind River in the early 20th century and was instrumental in the creation of Portland's Forest Park. The trail returns to the old road that you started on. Turn left and head back to the trailhead to complete your loop.

EXTENDING YOUR TRIP

For a short and very interesting side trip, head right where the loop trail reaches the old road. Hike the road 0.3 mile through spectacular groves of ancient fir, hemlock, and cedar, and come to a No Entry sign at the edge of the Wind River Canopy Crane Research Facility area. You aren't allowed to go near the station, which started off in 1995 as a twenty-eight-story crane allowing scientists to study the canopy of the surrounding ancient forest. Since 2011 it has been retrofitted with ecological monitoring

sensors providing data to the National Ecological Observatory Network. You can catch
a glimpse of it from a viewpoint on nearby
PCT (Hike 27).

27 Sedum Point

RATING/ DIFFICULTY	ROUNDTRIP	ELEV GAIN/ HIGH POINT	SEASON
***/3	9 miles	2130 feet/ 3275 feet	May–Nov

Crowds: 2; **Map:** Green Trails Wind River
No. 397; **Contact:** Gifford Pinchot National
Forest, Mount Adams Ranger District; **Notes:**
NW Forest Pass or Interagency Pass required;
GPS: N 45° 48.684', W 121° 57.383'

*Solitude is possible along
this section of the Pacific
Crest Trail (PCT). Saunter through old-
growth forest groves to a pair of excellent
viewpoints—one north across the Trout Creek
valley to the ancient forests of the Thornton T. Munger Research Natural Area, the
other south down the Wind River valley out
to the Columbia. And sedums? Yep, you'll
see 'em! They're stonecrops, a ledge-clinging,
star-shaped yellow flower that sprouts from
rosettes of fleshy leaves.*

GETTING THERE

From Stevenson, head east on State Route
14 for 3.2 miles, turning north at the traffic

MEXICO TO CANADA

Putting in a long, hard day on the trail can certainly be challenging, but it can be reward-
ing as well. Imagine putting in three, four, or five months on the trail. A small but growing group of hikers from coast to coast do just that each year on any of America's eleven
national scenic (long-distance) trails. The granddaddy of them all, the 2175-mile Appa-
lachian Trail (AT) is the most popular. Completed in 1937, it winds its way from Georgia
to Maine.

Here in the Columbia River Gorge, the Pacific Crest Trail (PCT) works its way 2650 miles
from the Mexican to Canadian borders. Though it was officially completed in 1993, in 1968 the
PCT joined the AT as one of America's first national trails. Administered by the National Park
Service, the National Trails System consists of congressionally designated trails. Inclusion in
the system is based on the trail's cultural, historical, and scenic attributes as well as its draw
for outdoor recreation.

The PCT, like most of the national trails, actually consists of many trails woven together to
form one continuous corridor. While much of the PCT traverses deep wilderness far from population centers and roads, many good day-hiking opportunities exist where the trail crosses or
comes close to travel corridors.

The PCT is well-maintained and is looked after by several citizen groups like the Pacific
Crest Trail Association. In the Columbia River Gorge, take a day hike on this grand trail at
Gillette Lake (Hike 21), Aldrich Butte (Hike 22), Table Mountain (Hike 23), Bunker Hill (Hike
25), Sedum Point (Hike 27), Dry Creek Falls (Hike 84), Benson Plateau (Hike 85), Wahtum Lake
(Hike 96), and Indian Mountain (Hike 98). You can walk across the Bridge of the Gods too,
which is part of the trail, although there is no sidewalk, so use caution.

Penstemons and a view out to Oregon

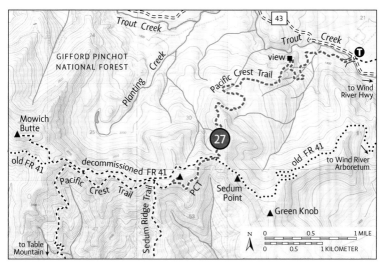

circle onto Wind River Highway. Then drive 8.6 miles and turn left onto Hemlock Road. After 1.2 miles (just beyond the Wind River Work Center), turn right onto Forest Road 43. Proceed for 1.4 miles to the trailhead (elev. 1200 ft.) on your left and parking for two vehicles—additional parking is available on the shoulder just beyond.

ON THE TRAIL

Head south on the PCT, immediately crossing Trout Creek on a sturdy arched bridge. Pass a riverside campsite, and mosey through carpets of mossy greenery in a beautiful grove of old-growth forest. Begin climbing, crossing a few cascading creeks en route. Crest a ridge, and at 1.6 miles come to a ledge (elev. 1750 ft.) with a steep drop-off (use caution) granting excellent viewing north of Trout Creek flowing through a volcanic landscape. Immediately to the right is Bunker Hill (Hike 25), an igneous plug. To the

left is Trout Creek Hill, an ancient shield volcano like Oregon's Larch Mountain (Hike 70).

Scan the Wind River Canopy Crane Research Facility to the left of Bunker Hill for the twenty-eight-story tower that used to host a canopy crane for studying old-growth forests. The tower has since been retrofitted with ecological monitoring sensors providing data to the National Ecological Observatory Network.

The trail now turns southward, gently climbing along a ridge draped in uniform second growth. Occasionally pass a fire-scarred snag, evidence of past fires that resulted in this young forest. After slightly descending into a small depression, the way gains elevation more steadily. Traverse a steep hillside, passing window views of Mount Adams and of the Indian Heaven Wilderness country. Soon afterward, pass through a lovely grove of big old firs, apparently spared from past fires. At 4.1 miles, intersect the decommissioned FR 41 (elev. 2950 ft.). Continue south on the PCT for another 0.3 mile, rounding a knoll. Then leave the trail to the right on a boot-beaten path, ascending steep meadows for 0.1 mile (careful to not damage delicate flowers) to a 3275-foot semi-open summit.

Savor the views! Mounts Adams and Hood! And the Wind River valley to the Gorge—Dog Mountain, Mount Defiance, Tanner Butte, and more. The flower show is good too—and there are even some sedums. But technically you're not on Sedum Point; that's the smaller knoll directly to your east, reached by hiking old FR 41 east for 0.5 mile followed by a short scramble.

EXTENDING YOUR TRIP

For more good views, continue south on the PCT for another 0.4 mile, reaching a junction with the Sedum Ridge Trail. Now, either head back or—if you want more exercise complete with solitude—turn right, and after a couple of hundred feet turn left onto long-closed FR 41. Follow this easy-to-walk old road for 1.2 miles, turning right at a large berm onto another closed road. Then continue for 0.7 mile to the 3513-foot summit of Mowich Butte. The lookout is long gone and vegetation is growing in, obscuring what used to be an excellent view north. But solitude is assured, and there's a good chance of seeing a *mowich* or *chetwoot* ("deer" or "bear" in Chinook Jargon).

Opposite: *Trapper Creek Wilderness protects nearly the entire Trapper Creek drainage (Hike 28).*

trapper creek wilderness, washington

The southernmost federal wilderness in Washington's Cascade Range, Trapper Creek lies about 15 miles north of the Columbia River Gorge. At just shy of 6000 acres, it's not very large, but its importance is grand. Protecting nearly the entire Trapper Creek watershed, this wilderness provides exceptional habitat in an area that has been heavily and intensively logged. Trapper Creek houses superb stands of old-growth forest that are habitat for endangered northern spotted owls and waterways supporting anadromous fish. The heavily forested wilderness contains one lake and several peaks that top 4000 feet and provide excellent viewing. Elk are numerous, as are cougars, bobcats, and black bears. While Trapper Creek ranks among Washington's smaller wilderness areas, it offers exceptional hiking. An excellent network of trails, including many built by the Portland-based Mazamas, traverses the wilderness. Created as part of the 1984 Washington State Wilderness Act, an adjacent 4540-acre roadless area (the Bourbon Tract) of equal ecological importance was left out of the wilderness due to timber pressures at the time. The Bourbon Tract, with its old growth, would make a nice addition to the Trapper Creek Wilderness.

28 Trapper Creek

RATING/ DIFFICULTY	ROUNDTRIP	ELEV GAIN/ HIGH POINT	SEASON
***/3	10 miles	1930 feet/ 2400 feet	Apr–Nov

Crowds: 2; **Maps:** Green Trails Lookout Mountain No. 396, Wind River No. 397; **Contact:** Gifford Pinchot National Forest, Mount Adams Ranger District; **Notes:** NW Forest Pass or Interagency Pass required. Free wilderness permit required, self-issued at trailhead. Wilderness rules apply; **GPS:** N 45° 52.914', W 121° 58.804'

Follow tumbling Trapper Creek through a deep valley into the heart of the wilderness bearing its name. Wend through magnificent groves of towering ancient firs. Stand captivated, admiring cascading side creeks. And embrace the valley's lushness. Steep surrounding ridges capture processions of moisture-laden clouds. Trapper Creek receives in excess of 100 inches of precipitation a year.

GETTING THERE

From Stevenson, head east on State Route 14 for 3.2 miles, turning north at the traffic circle onto Wind River Highway. Then drive 14.4 miles (passing through Carson) to an intersection just beyond the Carson National Fish Hatchery. Continue straight on Mineral Springs Road (Forest Road 3065) for 0.4 mile and turn right onto dirt FR 5401. Proceed 0.4 mile to Trapper Creek trailhead (elev. 1200 ft.). Privy available.

ON THE TRAIL

From the large parking area, enter thick, dark forest and immediately come to a junction. The trail right travels along Dry Creek through the Bourbon Roadless Area (Hike 31) to the Big Hollow Trail (Hike 32). Continue left on the well-maintained Trapper Creek Trail No. 192. At 0.8 mile come to a junction at the wilderness boundary. The trail left heads to a handful of cabins on a US Forest Service road. The trail right travels up Howe Ridge to 4207-foot Observation Peak (Hike 30).

Continue straight and rock hop across a creek. The way then ascends a bench above Trapper Creek before pulling away from the waterway. At 1.6 miles, after a slight descent,

Towering primeval forest

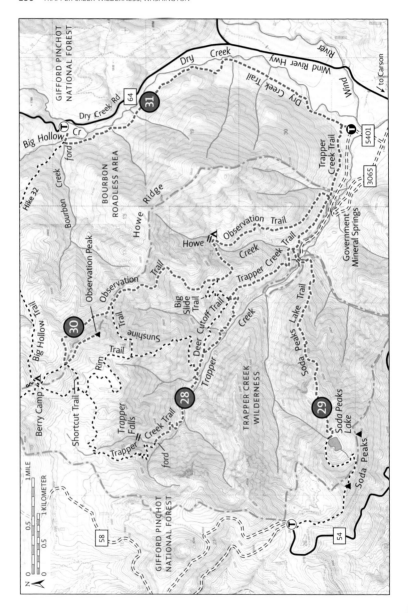

come to Howe Creek (elev. 1450 ft.), which can be difficult to cross in high water. Here the Soda Peaks Lake Trail (Hike 29) veers left. Continue right and start climbing, passing showy Pacific dogwood trees among fire-scarred big firs and cedar snags. Even in this saturated valley, fire plays a major role in forest succession. At 2.6 miles after a slight descent, come to a junction with the Big Slide Trail (elev. 1900 ft.). This side trail, along with others within the valley, was constructed by the Portland-based Mazamas. Many of these trails tend to be primitive and challenging. The Big Slide Trail steeply climbs 700 feet in 0.7 mile to connect with the Howe Ridge Trail, offering a loop option on the return.

Continue left and immediately come to the Deer Cutoff Trail, another Mazamas-built side trail. It offers a short cut up the valley but misses some beautiful old-growth groves. Veer left and drop 300 feet into a spectacular grove of old-growth giants beside Trapper Creek. Good camps can be found here. Continue hiking, meandering through more giant cedars, firs, and hemlocks and passing by a couple of mineral springs too. The tread is now much lighter and the terrain more rugged.

At 3.6 miles reach the second junction with the Deer Cutoff Trail. Now cross a creek and come to the Sunshine Trail (elev. 1800 ft.) junction at 3.8 miles. This primitive path steeply climbs up the southern face of Observation Peak. Continue on the Trapper Creek Trail, now high above the crashing creek. At 4 miles come to Hidden Creek. The bridge here was destroyed in a flood. The rocky creek can now be difficult to cross. Once across, start climbing. Pass two brushy short spurs—one leading right to Hidden Creek Falls and one leading left to Rendezvous Flats on Trapper Creek.

At 5 miles the trail sans bridge (another flooding casualty) crosses Trapper Creek (elev. 2400 ft.). This crossing, too, can be difficult. For most day hikers, this is a good spot to turn around. But if you want to continue, see below.

EXTENDING YOUR TRIP

Beyond the creek crossing, the trail steeply climbs out of the valley, passing a ledge overlook of breathtaking Trapper Falls, which plunges 100 feet. The way then continues, steeply climbing to a broad bench shrouded with towering trees and bountiful huckleberry bushes. At 6.4 miles from the trailhead, the trail once again makes a tricky crossing of Trapper Creek. The way then resumes climbing, passing the Rim Trail and the Shortcut Trail before coming to a 3700-foot saddle. Here at 7.8 miles the trail terminates at Berry Camp and a four-way junction. Head left 1.2 miles for Sister Rocks, or right 0.9 mile for Observation Peak (both Hike 33). Return to the trailhead by either hiking straight on the Big Hollow Trail to Dry Creek (Hikes 32 and 31, respectively) for a 14.8-mile loop, or right on the Observation Peak Trail (Hike 30) for a 14.2-mile loop.

29 Soda Peaks Lake

RATING/ DIFFICULTY	ROUNDTRIP	ELEV GAIN/ HIGH POINT	SEASON
****/5	10 miles	2900 feet/ 3760 feet	June–Nov

Crowds: 3; **Maps:** Green Trails Lookout Mountain No. 396, Wind River No. 397; **Contact:** Gifford Pinchot National Forest, Mount Adams Ranger District; **Notes:** NW Forest Pass or Interagency Pass required. Free wilderness permit required, self-issued at trailhead. Wilderness rules apply; **GPS:** N 45° 52.914', W 121° 58.804'

Early season thaw at Soda Peaks Lake

The only lake within the Trapper Creek Wilderness, Soda Peaks Lake sits in a cirque surrounded by majestic ancient trees. The way is tough—quite steep—but tenacious hikers will be rewarded with tranquility upon reaching this placid subalpine lake. Gargantuan towering trees provide plenty of awe along the way, and a mighty fine viewpoint of the Trapper Creek watershed waits for those who want to push on a little farther.

GETTING THERE

From Stevenson, head east on State Route 14 for 3.2 miles, turning north at the traffic circle onto Wind River Highway. Then drive 14.4 miles (passing through Carson) to an intersection just beyond the Carson National Fish Hatchery. Continue straight on Mineral Springs Road (Forest Road 3065) for 0.4 mile and turn right onto dirt FR 5401. Proceed 0.4 mile to Trapper Creek trailhead (elev. 1200 ft.). Privy available.

ON THE TRAIL

A once shorter option leaving from Government Mineral Springs Guard Station is no longer possible. That trail was severely damaged by flooding and obstructed with large blowdowns. It is possible to reach the lake from the west for a much shorter and easier hike via FR 54, but that approach is long and may include some obstacles. To fully embrace this area's natural beauty and get an all-day satisfying hike, begin on the Trapper Creek Trail.

From the large parking area, immediately enter thick, dark forest. Bear left at a junction with the Dry Creek Trail (Hike 31) and at 0.8 mile come to a junction at the wilderness boundary. Continue straight and rock hop across a creek. The way then ascends a bench above Trapper Creek before at 1.6 miles descending slightly to cross Howe Creek (elev. 1450 ft.), which can be difficult to cross at high water. Once across, head left on Soda Peaks Lake Trail No. 133 and descend. Pass a spur leading left to FR 5401 and at 1.8 miles come to a big bridge spanning Trapper Creek.

Cross the creek and traverse a lush river flat before entering a grove of impressive huge Douglas-firs and western hemlocks. At 2 miles pass the old trail from Government Mineral Springs and begin steeply ascending. Following tight switchbacks, steadily ascend a rib covered in salal, huckleberries, and old-growth greenery—some of the ancient giants seem to defy gravity. Gaps in the forest canopy provide glimpses to a lush junglelike landscape that may very well harbor Sasquatch and legendary plane hijacker D. B. Cooper.

At 3.1 miles the way eases its ascent along a ridge crest. Catch a good view out to Observation Peak and Howe Ridge. Then continue the grueling climb out of the valley. Magnificent hemlocks and noble firs help divert your attention from the strenuous slog. At 4 miles cross a small scree slope that's vibrant in autumn, and then commence to clamber once more, traversing gorgeous primeval forest. At 5 miles reach Soda Peaks Lake (elev. 3760 ft.) cradled in a forested cirque. From near its outlet creek, enjoy a deserved break and embrace the lake's tranquility. Some camps can be found near the lake's eastern shore. Good huckleberry harvesting can be found throughout the basin.

EXTENDING YOUR TRIP
The trail continues, steadily gaining elevation traversing the cirque. About 0.8 mile from the lake, reach a saddle between the two Soda Peaks. Continue for another 0.2 mile, reaching a splendid viewpoint (elev. 4370 ft.) that overlooks the lake, the Trapper Creek valley, and beyond. The trail then leaves the wilderness area to cross scree slopes with good views. It then reenters forest, terminating 1.9 miles from the lake at FR 54 (elev. 3650 ft.), which is an alternative approach to the lake reached by following paved FR 54 from Stabler for about 12 miles.

If time permits after your hike, check out what remains of the Government Mineral Springs area. A hotel and resort were built here in 1910 to accommodate tourists seeking the medicinal waters of the region. A happening place during the prohibition years, the resort burned to the ground in 1934. The Civilian Conservation Corps was responsible for building the guard station in 1937, along with the campground, picnic area, and pump pavilion that still remain. The Iron Mike still stands but sadly no longer flows.

30 Observation Peak via Howe Ridge

RATING/DIFFICULTY	ROUNDTRIP	ELEV GAIN/HIGH POINT	SEASON
****/5	12.8 miles	3100 feet/4207 feet	June–Nov

Crowds: 3; **Maps:** Green Trails Lookout Mountain No. 396, Wind River No. 397; **Contact:** Gifford Pinchot National Forest, Mount Adams Ranger District; **Notes:** NW Forest Pass or Interagency Pass required. Free wilderness permit required, self-issued at trailhead. Wilderness rules apply; **GPS:** N 45° 52.914'; W 121° 58.804'

Mount Hood rises over the Wind River valley

Hike a long and winding, but well-graded, trail through stately old growth to a former lookout site granting sweeping views of Mounts Hood, Adams, Rainier, and St. Helens. Stare down, too, into the uncut forests of the Trapper Creek valley, one of the few remaining unblemished watersheds in the southern reaches of the Gifford Pinchot National Forest.

GETTING THERE

From Stevenson, head east on State Route 14 for 3.2 miles, turning north at the traffic circle onto Wind River Highway. Then drive 14.4 miles (passing through Carson) to an intersection just beyond the Carson National Fish Hatchery. Continue straight on Mineral Springs Road (Forest Road 3065) for 0.4 mile and turn right onto dirt FR 5401. Proceed 0.4 mile to Trapper Creek trailhead (elev. 1200 ft.). Privy available.

ON THE TRAIL

While this route to Observation Peak climbs more than 3000 feet, most of the way is well-graded and well-maintained. Hikers looking for a shorter, much easier way to the 4207-foot former lookout site should take the Observation Trail from FR 58 (Hike 33). Hikers looking to make a long loop hike from either the Trapper Creek Trail (Hike 28) or Big Hollow Trail (Hike 32) should return via this route because of its gentle grade.

From the large parking area, enter thick forest and immediately come to a junction. The trail right travels along Dry Creek through the Bourbon Roadless Area (Hike 31) to the Big Hollow Trail. Head left on the wide and well-graded Trapper Creek Trail, and in 0.8 mile come to a junction (elev. 1300 ft.) after crossing the wilderness boundary.

Now head right onto Observation Trail No. 132 and begin climbing. Steadily yet gently, the well-graded trail winds its way up Howe

Ridge, traversing steep slopes and darting in and out of creek-containing ravines (some difficult to negotiate in high water). At 2.6 miles, come to a nice campsite in a grove of big firs perched above a cascading creek (elev. 2300 ft.). Then pass a massive fir and a small waterfall, and enter a patch of burnt forest from the 2020 Big Hollow Fire. Howe Ridge was spared major burning with patches of mosaic burns. Be alert, however, for hazards in the forms of downed trees, falling limbs, and washout. At 3.2 miles pass the Big Slide Trail (elev. 2550 ft.), one of several primitive trails within the wilderness built by the Portland-based Mazamas. This path drops steeply to lose about 700 feet in 0.7 mile, where it connects with the Trapper Creek Trail. It makes for a good loop option early in the season.

Continue straight, winding up the ridge, crossing side creeks, and traversing patches of burnt forest and green groves of magnificent big trees. At 4.1 miles skirt beneath some cliffs and enjoy an excellent view over the valley to Soda Peaks. Cross a talus slope and continue through a mosaic burn zone reaching the lightly traveled Sunshine Trail (elev. 3500 ft.) at 4.8 miles. Continue straight and gently climb, now traversing northeast-facing slopes. Gaps in the forest canopy provide sneak peeks of Mount Adams and waves of emerald ridges. At 5.8 miles reach a junction in a forested saddle (elev. 3800 ft.). The Observation Trail continues right, passing the Shortcut Trail to Trapper Creek (Hike 28), the Trapper Creek and Big Hollow Trails (Hike 32), and the Sister Rocks spur (Hike 33), before it terminates at FR 58.

You want to continue left, making one last climb to the 4207-foot summit of Observation Peak. At 6.1 miles, pass a spur leading

to good views. At 6.4 miles reach the former lookout site and better views. While not the highest summit in the Trapper Creek Wilderness, Observation Peak provides some of its best views. Stand mouth agape at the showy, snowy, bulky volcanoes surrounding you: Rainier, St. Helens, Adams, Hood, and Jefferson. Stare, too, at all of the little nubbles, buttes, and other volcanic remnants scattered across the landscape. Nothing remains of the lookout, which was decommissioned in the 1960s. But a carpet of wildflowers is rolled out on the summit for most of the summer.

EXTENDING YOUR TRIP
Consider turning this hike into a 14.5-mile loop via the Shortcut and Trapper Creek Trails (Hike 28) or a 14.4-mile loop via the Big Hollow and Dry Creek Trails (Hikes 32 and 31).

31 Dry Creek

RATING/ DIFFICULTY	ROUNDTRIP	ELEV GAIN/ HIGH POINT	SEASON
***/2	7.8 miles	350 feet/ 1500 feet	Year-round

Crowds: 1; **Maps:** Green Trails 396, Wind River No. 397; **Contact:** Gifford Pinchot National Forest, Mount Adams Ranger District; **Notes:** NW Forest Pass or Interagency Pass required. Free wilderness permit required if entering the wilderness, self-issued at trailhead; **GPS:** N 45° 52.914' W 121° 58.804'

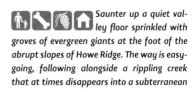 *Saunter up a quiet valley floor sprinkled with groves of evergreen giants at the foot of the abrupt slopes of Howe Ridge. The way is easygoing, following alongside a rippling creek that at times disappears into a subterranean*

channel. While roads lie not far away, the valley exudes a feeling of remoteness and stillness. But these lush woods are anything but still, harboring a cornucopia of critters from flittering wrens to wintering elk.

GETTING THERE

From Stevenson, head east on State Route 14 for 3.2 miles, turning north at the traffic circle onto Wind River Highway. Then drive 14.4 miles (passing through Carson) to an intersection just beyond the Carson National Fish Hatchery. Continue straight on Mineral Springs Road (Forest Road 3065) for 0.4 mile and turn right onto dirt FR 5401. Proceed 0.4 mile to Trapper Creek trailhead (elev. 1200 ft.). Privy available.

ON THE TRAIL

From the large parking area, enter thick, dark forest and immediately come to a junction. The trail left heads into the Trapper Creek Wilderness and is where most people parked at the trailhead are heading. Pay homage to Robert Frost, and head right on Dry Creek Trail No. 194, the trail less taken. This lightly used trail travels along the eastern base of Howe Ridge, traversing lush flats along Dry Creek. The entire way is within the 4540-acre Bourbon Roadless Area, which includes old-growth forest as well as elk and salmon habitat. It would make a good addition to the adjacent Trapper Creek Wilderness.

Follow the trail through a flat of maples. Soon climb a bluff above Dry Creek which

A not-so-dry Dry Creek

may or may not be visibly flowing here. Then follow an old logging railroad bed on a nearly level course through mature second-growth forest. At 1.6 miles come to an inviting gravel bar on the creek and then make a sharp left away from the creek and leave the railroad bed. The way then skirts lush bottomlands and traverses a bluff above the creek.

Continue through a mossy maple and alder flat, and enjoy occasional views to the ridge opposite across the creek. The way then briefly follows an old skid road and enters a grove of massive old Douglas-firs. At 3.5 miles after a couple of bridged side creek crossings, reach a severely scorched stretch of forest from the 2020 Big Hollow Fire. Continue on a bench above Dry Creek, and at 3.8 miles reach Bourbon Creek (elev. 1500 ft.), which can be difficult to cross in high water, requiring a little rock hopping even in the dry months. The trail ends just beyond, at 3.9 miles, at the Big Hollow Trail (Hike 32). Either retrace your steps or continue hiking on the Big Hollow Trail for an ascent up Howe Ridge and Observation Peak.

The 2020 Big Hollow Fire killed large tracts of old-growth forest.

hazards in the form of downed trees and washouts; **GPS:** N 45° 55.569', W 121° 58.794'

Enjoy this quiet and lonely trail through the heart of the 4540-acre Bourbon Roadless Area, a de facto wilderness of primeval forest, recovering burn zones, and clear rushing streams. The way is tough, hastily climbing a steep ridge that divides the Bourbon and Big Hollow Creek watersheds. An alternative approach to Observation Peak, this route helps you appreciate the deeply cut valleys and formidable ridges of this wild corner of the Cascades.

32 Observation Peak via Big Hollow

RATING/ DIFFICULTY	ROUNDTRIP	ELEV GAIN/ HIGH POINT	SEASON
***/4	8.4 miles	2700 feet/ 4207 feet	June–Nov

Crowds: 1; **Maps:** Green Trails Lookout Mountain No. 396, Wind River No. 397; **Contact:** Gifford Pinchot National Forest, Mount Adams Ranger District; **Notes:** Free wilderness permit required if entering the wilderness, self-issued at trailhead. Trail requires two fords, which can be difficult in high water. Trail traverses Big Hollow Fire zone, so expect

GETTING THERE

From Stevenson, head east on State Route 14 for 3.2 miles, turning north at the traffic circle onto Wind River Highway. Then drive 14.4 miles (passing through Carson) to an intersection just beyond the Carson National Fish Hatchery. Bear right at the Government Mineral Springs turnoff and follow Wind River Highway (Forest Road 30) for 2.1 miles. Then turn left onto Dry Creek Road (FR 64) and drive this paved, narrow road for 2.1 miles to the trailhead (elev. 1530 ft.).

ON THE TRAIL

Big Hollow Trail No. 158 takes off into a jungle of greenery, dropping a tad to cross lush bottomlands. At 0.2 mile reach Big Hollow Creek (elev. 1500 ft.) just above its confluence with Bourbon Creek and then farther downstream its confluence with Dry Creek. Yep, in this hollow, the Bourbon runs dry. Big Hollow Creek, however, usually runs pretty strong. Look for a fallen tree across the rushing waterway, otherwise expect to ford it—difficult during high flows. Just beyond, reach a junction with the Dry Creek Trail (Hike 31).

Now continue straight and immediately begin climbing. The way soon enters

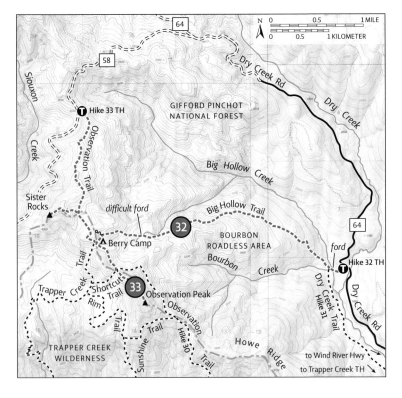

the 2020 Big Hollow Fire zone. Sadly, the old-growth forest here was scorched, replaced with blackened snags. The trail is regularly maintained, but expect a lot of windfall—and avoid hiking during windy periods. On a positive note, now enjoy excellent views out to a series of volcanic buttes and Mount Adams.

The grade doesn't mess around, opting to maximize elevation gain. At 1.8 miles, rejoice a reprieve as you reach a patch of green hemlocks. Then pass through a mosaic burn before soon afterward leaving the burn zone and entering magnificent old-growth forest. The grade now eases. At 2.7 miles come upon a tributary of Big Hollow Creek (elev. 3400 ft.). Prepare to get your feet wet or scout around for a better crossing. Then resume climbing but at a saner grade. Look for old insulators lining the way—this trail once provided the communication line to the lookout that no longer remains on Observation Peak.

At 3.2 miles come to a piped spring that once provided the lookout keepers with water and now provides hikers with a refreshing drink. Just beyond is a short cutoff trail on the left that leads to the Trapper Creek Trail (Hike 28). And just beyond that, at 3.3 miles the Big Hollow Trail terminates at cozy Berry Camp at the junction with the Observation Trail (elev. 3760 ft.) (Hikes 30 and 33).

You've worked hard to get this far, so you might as well continue a little farther to get a visual payoff. Head left and, straddling the Trapper Creek Wilderness boundary, follow the Observation Trail to a junction at 3.7 miles. Then take the summit spur trail 0.5 mile to the 4207-foot summit of Observation Peak. Enjoy the view down into the Bourbon

and Wind River valleys and out to surrounding glacial-clad volcanoes.

33 Sister Rocks and Observation Peak

RATING/ DIFFICULTY	ROUNDTRIP	ELEV GAIN/ HIGH POINT	SEASON
****/3	6.6 miles	1600 feet/ 4268 feet	late June– Oct

Crowds: 2; **Map:** Green Trails Lookout Mountain No. 396; **Contact:** Gifford Pinchot National Forest, Mount Adams Ranger District; **Notes:** Free wilderness permit required, self-issued at trailhead. Trail traverses Big Hollow Fire zone—expect hazards in the form of downed trees; **GPS:** N 45° 56.994', W 122° 02.386'

A backdoor, much easier approach to Observation Peak, this route also grants easy access to the higher and more stunning Sister Rocks. Reaching these two lofty and spectacular viewpoints involves traversing a high ridge across recently burnt forest and a forest of towering old-growth trees. Come in June for wildflowers, September for huckleberries, and all summer and fall for the opportunity to witness bears, elk, and other wild denizens of the Trapper Creek Wilderness.

GETTING THERE

From Stevenson, head east on State Route 14 for 3.2 miles, turning north at the traffic circle onto Wind River Highway. Then drive 14.4 miles (passing through Carson) to an intersection just beyond the Carson National Fish Hatchery. Bear right at the Government Mineral Springs turnoff and follow Wind River Highway (Forest Road 30) for 2.1 miles.

Looking down the Trapper Creek valley to Soda Lake Peaks

Then turn left onto Dry Creek Road (FR 64) and drive this paved, narrow, and brushy road for 6.1 miles (the pavement ends at 4.1 miles). Then turn left onto FR 58 and drive 2.1 miles, bearing left at an unmarked junction at 1.8 miles, and reach the Observation Peak trailhead (elev. 3500 ft.).

ON THE TRAIL

Observation Trail No. 132 immediately enters the 2020 Big Hollow Fire zone. What was once thick, old-growth forest is now a scorched, recovering forest. Watch for downed trees and encroaching brush, and scan the rows of snags for wildlife. Enjoy too-distant views through the trees. As you steadily climb, the forest eventually transitions to old-growth silver fir. This area was set aside in 1967 as a Research Natural Area to study a dominant silver fir forest.

At 1.2 miles, crest a ridge (elev. 4100 ft.) and enter the Trapper Creek Wilderness. An excellent viewpoint to Mount Adams lies left. A boot-beaten but easy-to-follow path to Sister Rocks takes off right. Take it, meandering along a beargrass-lined ridge to reach the juniper-lined ledges of Sister Rocks at 1.7 miles.

Once the site of a fire lookout, this 4268-foot peak offers breathtaking views of Mount St. Helens, the Siouxon Roadless Area, Soda Peaks, Trapper Creek watershed, and Mount Hood. All that remains of the lookout is a lone metal post. The old trail to this summit that came up from the west is also long gone.

After getting your fill of views, retrace your steps back to the main trail and head right to Observation Peak for another excellent vista. The trail winds through magnificent hemlocks and firs, cutting through a carpet of clintonias, bunchberries, and trilliums. As you follow along a ridgeline, the trail loses a few hundred feet, reaching a 3750-foot saddle cradling Berry Camp 0.7 mile from the Sister Rocks trail junction. Here, the Trapper Creek Trail (Hike 28) takes off right, while the Big Hollow Trail ventures left (Hike 32). A small, reliable piped spring can be found just a short distance down the latter trail.

Continue straight for Observation Peak. Notice the Pacific dogwoods en route, their blossoms among the showiest in the Northwest. At 0.4 mile from Berry Camp, the Shortcut Trail branches right to Trapper Creek. Just beyond is another junction. Left winds down long Howe Ridge (Hike 30). Go right, regaining those lost few hundred feet and reaching the 4207-foot summit of Observation Peak in 0.5 mile. Nothing remains of the fire lookout here but the extended views to Mount Rainier, Mount Adams, Mount Hood, and Mount Jefferson that the lucky lookout keeper used to wake up to on a regular basis. Savor the views and a carpet of wildflowers. Then head 2.8 miles back to your vehicle.

34 Falls Creek Falls

RATING/ DIFFICULTY	ROUNDTRIP	ELEV GAIN/ HIGH POINT	SEASON
*****/2	3.4 miles	700 feet/ 2080 feet	Mar–Nov

Crowds: 4; **Map:** Green Trails Wind River No. 397; **Contact:** Gifford Pinchot National Forest, Mount Adams Ranger District; **Notes:** FR 3062 is gated at about 0.4 mile Dec.–Mar. for wildlife protection. During this time, park near gate and walk or bike the road to trailhead; **GPS:** N 45° 54.346', W 121° 56.430'

 *One of the tallest and most stunning waterfalls*

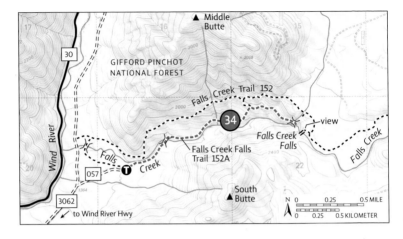

in Washington, the banal name of Falls Creek Falls certainly doesn't even begin to capture the magnitude of this thundering cascade. Hike through old-growth forest along the creek as it crashes through a narrow chasm before reaching the base of the falls. Then stand mesmerized, gazing at the three-tiered 300-plus-foot falls billowing over basalt ledges.

GETTING THERE

From Stevenson, head east on State Route 14 for 3.2 miles, turning north at the traffic circle onto Wind River Highway. Then drive 14.4 miles to an intersection just beyond the Carson National Fish Hatchery. Bear right at the Government Mineral Springs turnoff and follow Wind River Highway (Forest Road 30) for 0.8 mile and turn right onto graveled FR 3062. Drive 2 miles and bear right onto FR Spur 057, continuing 0.4 mile to the trailhead (elev. 1425 ft.) Privy available. Last 0.6 mile can be rough, requiring high clearance.

ON THE TRAIL

Falls Creek Falls Trail No. 152A starts off wide and well-trodden then immediately comes to a junction with the Falls Creek Trail No. 152. Continue right and come upon the tumbling creek, which soon fades from view in a tight chasm. At 0.4 mile cross the creek via a short suspension bridge. Then continue alongside and above the crashing creek (keep dogs and children nearby) in beautiful old-growth forest. Vine maples crowd the understory and add a lot of gold to the dominant green forest come fall.

The trail eventually climbs away from the creek, coming to a junction (elev. 1900 ft.) at 1.2 miles. The trail to the left connects to the Falls Creek Trail. You want to continue right, soon crossing a cascading tributary on a good bridge. The way then crosses a smaller unbridged creek (which will wet your shoes in high water) and skirts beneath some ledges. Falls Creek Falls soon comes into view through the forest, its roaring now

Falls Creek Falls thunders in the spring.

quite audible. After a slight descent, the trail ends at 1.7 miles at a rocky viewpoint near the base of the falls.

The scene is breathtaking. The falls plunge 335 feet through three tiers over steep basalt walls. The upper tier is not visible from this spot, but the lower two are in fine display. The middle tier fans over ledges, while the bottom tier plunges into an amphitheater bowl. The creek flows strong year-round but especially during the wetter months, when you can expect to be misted while admiring the falls.

EXTENDING YOUR TRIP

For a longer and less crowded return, follow the Falls Creek Trail connector for just over 0.1 mile to its junction (elev. 2100 ft.) with the Falls Creek Trail. Then head right on this good but lightly used trail, steadily ascending through open forest and coming to an unmarked junction in 0.6 mile. Head right here for a couple hundred feet to the top of the canyon cradling Falls Creek. Catch a peek of the falls as well as South Butte and Howe Ridge. Then retrace your steps back to the trail and head right another 0.3 mile through old growth, coming to another spur. Take this one right to another viewpoint (elev. 2400 ft.)—this one directly above the top of the falls and looking out to Observation Peak.

Then follow the Falls Creek Trail west back to the trailhead. At 0.9 mile from the upper falls viewpoint, pass the connector junction and continue right, descending through quiet old growth, eventually coming to the creek. At 2.5 miles bear left at a junction and come to a bridge crossing Falls Creek. Then bear left again and head upstream along the creek, returning to the Falls Creek Falls Trail near the trailhead at 3 miles. This alternative makes for a 6.5-mile hike.

Opposite: *Flowers line the base of Horsethief Butte (Hike 58)*

eastern gorge, washington

Plentiful sunshine, prolific wildflowers, fascinating geological formations, and hillsides graced with pine and oak forests are what await you in the eastern reaches of Washington's Columbia River Gorge. Summer can be hot. Fall is lovely. But spring is the best time to visit, despite the abundance of ticks. Some of the best flower shows in the entire Northwest unfurl here in spring and early summer. White Salmon and Bingen offer visitor services, while Columbia Hills Historical and Maryhill State Parks are ideal base camps.

35 Wind Mountain

RATING/ DIFFICULTY	ROUNDTRIP	ELEV GAIN/ HIGH POINT	SEASON
***/3	2.6 miles	1200 feet/ 1907 feet	Mar–Dec

Crowds: 2; **Map:** Green Trails Columbia River Gorge West 428S; **Contact:** Columbia River Gorge National Scenic Area; **Notes:** Summit is an archaeological reserve consisting of culturally and architecturally sensitive areas. Stay on trail and respect all closed areas; **GPS:** N 45° 42.862', W 121° 45.205'

A well-recognized landmark within the Gorge, conical Wind Mountain is a stunning sight from nearby Dog Mountain. A short and steep trail climbs to the summit of this 1907-foot peak. The views out over the Columbia River are good. But more intriguing are the summit's numerous rock pits once used by young Native Americans for vision quests. It's a sacred place that continues to enlighten folks from all backgrounds.

GETTING THERE

From Vancouver, follow State Route 14 east for 50.5 miles, turning left onto Wind Mountain Road. (From Portland, follow I-84 east to exit 44 at Cascade Locks and take the Bridge of the Gods (toll) to SR 14. Turn right and proceed 8.5 miles to Wind Mountain Road.) (From Hood River, take exit 64 off I-84 and cross the Columbia River on a toll bridge

Looking out over Home Valley and the Wind River's confluence with the Columbia River

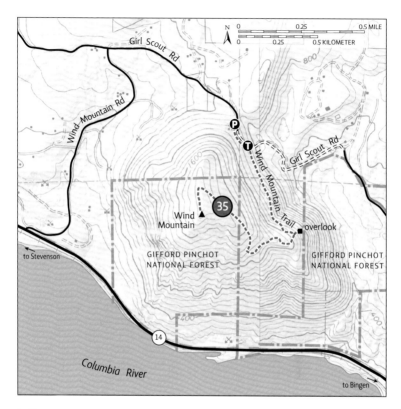

(toll) turning left, or west, onto SR 14. Drive 15.7 miles and turn right on Wind Mountain Road.) Follow Wind Mountain Road, bearing right at 1 mile and reaching Girl Scout Road at 1.4 miles, where you turn right. Drive 0.2 mile to the pavement's end at a clearing; park here (elev. 875 ft.).

ON THE TRAIL

Begin by walking down the dirt road east for 0.1 mile. Here, beside a parking area (elev. 800 ft.) for perhaps two vehicles, locate the unsigned but very obvious trail on your right. The way is short but steep in a couple of sections. While never officially built, the tread is in excellent shape except for one small washed-out area. The trail makes a long traverse across Wind Mountain's steep and thickly forested eastern slope. At 0.5 mile, the way rounds a shoulder (elev. 1200 ft.) and swings west through open forest. A short spur (use caution) leads to an overlook on the left.

Now steeply climbing, the trail crosses a large scree slope before returning to forest just below the summit. A large interpretive sign explains the significance of the numerous rock pits dug into the summit scree slopes. Archaeologists believe the pits were constructed by Native Americans between 200 and 1000 years ago and were used for spirit questing.

Make the final short climb, coming to the 1907-foot summit at 1.3 miles. Do not leave the trail lest you damage this important archaeological and cultural site. Aside from the rock pits, views from the summit are also intriguing. Look west over Home Valley out to Table Mountain and Beacon Rock and northwest up the Wind River valley. There are good views east of Augspurger and Dog Mountains, Wygant Peak, and Mount Defiance. Nick Eaton Ridge forms an imposing wall south across the river. Sit and listen to the wind whistle through the surrounding contorted firs.

36 Dog Mountain

RATING/ DIFFICULTY	LOOP	ELEV GAIN/ HIGH POINT	SEASON
*****/4	6.9 miles	2860 feet/ 2945 feet	Mar–Dec

Crowds: 5; **Map:** Green Trails Columbia River Gorge West 428S; **Contact:** Columbia River Gorge National Scenic Area; **Notes:** NW Forest Pass or Interagency Pass required. Parking area fills fast during flower season. Special limited weekend and holiday day-use permits required from mid-Apr. to mid-June. For details visit: recreation.gov/ticket/facility/273800. Beware of poison oak and rattlesnakes; **GPS:** N 45° 41.956', W 121° 42.464'

One of the most spectacular hikes on the Washington side of the Columbia River Gorge, Dog Mountain offers much to bark about.

Straddling the transition zone between swirling clouds and golden rays of sunshine, Dog affords a beautiful perspective of the multifaceted Gorge. The view straight down to the river and over the cone of Wind Mountain is stunning. And the flowers! From spring throughout the summer, Dog's sun-kissed meadows explode with blossoms. But be forewarned, the way is steep, making it a dog of a hike. And its popularity means you're never far from the pack.

GETTING THERE

From Vancouver, follow State Route 14 east for 54 miles to the trailhead (elev. 150 ft.). Privy available. (From Portland, follow I-84 east to exit 44 at Cascade Locks and take the Bridge of the Gods (toll) to SR 14. Turn right and proceed 12 miles to the trailhead.) (From Hood River, take exit 64 off I-84 and cross the Columbia River on a toll bridge (toll) turning left, onto SR 14. Proceed 12.2 miles to the trailhead.) Columbia Area Transit (CAT) runs a shuttle to Dog Mountain from Hood River, Cascade Locks, and Stevenson. Visit ridecatbus.org/dog-mountain-shuttle for more info.

ON THE TRAIL

Three trails ascend Dog Mountain: the old Dog Mountain Trail, the newer Dog Mountain Trail, and the Augspurger connector. The old trail is the steepest and least interesting. The newer trail is steep but full of views. The connector approach, while considerably longer than the other two, is quiet and well-graded. My suggestion? Up the newer trail for maximum views and down the connector for minimal knee discomfort.

Take Dog Mountain Trail No. 147 and immediately begin climbing. The tread is wide—all the better to keep you from

Dog Mountain's seasonal display of arrowleaf balsamroot

rubbing against the poison oak that grows in profusion here. Passing under scrubby oaks and elegant pines, the way relentlessly climbs. At 0.7 mile reach a junction (elev. 800 ft.). The old trail heads left. Keep right on the newer trail and, now in thick forest, continue ascending steeply. The grade finally begins to ease, and at 1.8 miles you can take a break at a grassy knoll (elev. 1600 ft.), panting over some excellent views.

The way reenters forest and meets up once again with the old trail at 2.2 miles (elev. 2000 ft.). Continue straight, on an insanely steep grade. Break out of the forest and enter the famed flowered upper slopes of the mountain. Sensory overload! From spring through summer, you'll see a sprawling carpet of dazzling flowers: arrowleaf balsamroots, paintbrushes, lupines, desert parsley, cluster lilies, and a myriad of others compete with a gorgeous backdrop of conical Wind Mountain and the buttressed ridges of Oregon's Mount Defiance, Nick Eaton Ridge, and Benson Plateau rising above the river. It's quintessential Columbia Gorge majesty.

At 2.7 miles, reach a junction on an open bluff unofficially known as The Puppy (elev. 2550 ft.), where there was a fire lookout from 1931 until 1967. The right-hand trail makes a gradual ascent to the summit. It's forested and badly overgrown. Skip it and head left, traversing more meadow and skirting over and beneath small cliffs, enjoying nonstop views.

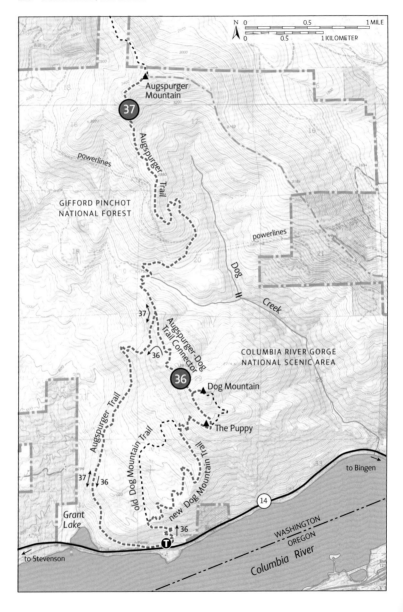

At 3 miles, reach a junction with the Augspurger Trail connector (elev. 2800 ft.), your return route. But first continue right for 0.1 mile, and then turn left on a short spur to reach the 2945-foot Dog Mountain summit. The actual high point is forested and lies just to the east. Don't waste your time crashing brush looking for it. Instead, plop your butt down and soak up the view—from Hood to St. Helens to Silver Star—one of the finest in the Gorge. You earned it.

When ready to descend, retrace your steps to the Augspurger Trail connector. Then turn right and follow this lightly traveled path across windblown meadows, steadily losing elevation. Downward momentum is temporarily halted with a short ascent up a small knoll, and then once again it's downward, back into the forest, to reach the Augspurger Trail (elev. 2250 ft.) after 0.9 mile from the summit.

The way right leads to Augspurger Mountain (Hike 37). The way left heads back to your vehicle. Languidly descend, traversing scree slopes and cool forests of mature trees. Enjoy nice views of Wind Mountain and the Columbia River along the way. The grade is mostly gentle on this former section of the Cascade Crest Trail. At 3.8 miles from the summit, reach the trailhead.

37 Augspurger Mountain

RATING/ DIFFICULTY	ROUNDTRIP	ELEV GAIN/ HIGH POINT	SEASON
***/5	12.8 miles	4650 feet/ 3660 feet	Apr–Nov

Crowds: 2; **Map:** Green Trails Columbia River Gorge West 428S; **Contact:** Columbia River Gorge National Scenic Area; **Notes:** NW Forest Pass or Interagency Pass required. Parking area fills fast during flower season.

Special limited weekend and holiday day-use permits required from mid-Apr to mid-June. For details visit: recreation.gov/ticket/facility/273800. Beware of poison oak and rattlesnakes; **GPS:** N 45° 41.960', W 121° 42.509'

One of the loneliest mountains accessible by trail on the Washington side of the Gorge—Augspurger sits right next to Dog Mountain, one of the most popular peaks in the Gorge. Overlooked by the masses that hike Dog, Augspurger also offers delightful views and beautiful meadows flourishing with flowers. But the distance and elevation required to reach this peak keep the crowds away, assuring you a rare delight in the Gorge—an opportunity for solitude.

GETTING THERE

From Vancouver, follow State Route 14 east for 54 miles to the Dog Mountain trailhead (elev. 150 ft.). Privy available. (From Portland, follow I-84 east to exit 44 at Cascade Locks and take the Bridge of the Gods (toll) to SR 14. Turn right and proceed 12 miles to the trailhead.) (From Hood River, take exit 64 off I-84 and cross the Columbia River on a toll bridge (toll) turning left, onto SR 14. Proceed 12.2 miles to the trailhead.) Columbia Area Transit (CAT) runs a shuttle to the Dog Mountain trailhead from Hood River, Cascade Locks, and Stevenson. Visit ridecatbus.org/dog-mountain-shuttle for more info.

ON THE TRAIL

From Dog Mountain's mall-size parking lot, locate Augspurger Trail No. 4407 to the west and immediately leave the crowds behind. On a gentle grade, the trail wraps around Dog Mountain, traversing several scree slopes providing good views out to Wind Mountain and the Columbia. Once part of

Oregon's Mount Defiance rises above the Columbia River across from Dog Mountain.

the Cascade Crest Trail (precursor to the Pacific Crest Trail), Augspurger fell off most hikers' radar once a new route closer to a bridged crossing of the Columbia was laid around Table Mountain.

At 2.8 miles come to a junction (elev. 2250 ft.) with a trail leading right to Dog Mountain—a trail I have dubbed the Augie Doggie (remember him?) connector. The Augspurger Trail continues left, descending into a thicket of thimbleberries. Reach a saddle (elev. 1800 ft.) and reflect on the climb that awaits your return. Then cross a small creek in a grove of big old hemlocks and firs, and start climbing again. At 3.5 miles reach a dirt service road (elev. 1900 ft.). Turn right and follow it, passing under high-tension wires and coming to the trail again at 4.2 miles. Then through a forest of tall firs and shrubby vine maple carpeted in vanilla leaf, make a long traverse high above Dog Creek. The way switchbacks up a ridge and breaks out onto a flowered basalt ridge. Views!

Flowers! Keep climbing—it gets better. Rising above adjacent powerlines, the trail crests a 2950-foot knoll at 4.9 miles. The Columbia River flows into the west beneath Beacon Rock and Table Mountain. To the south, it's Dog Mountain, Mount Defiance, Nick Eaton Ridge, and Mount Hood. This could be a good place to call it quits, but views to the north await.

Continue along the rolling ridge spine undulating between forest and view-granting meadows. Bear scat is prevalent—be bear aware here. A few brushy sections are encountered, but the tread remains good. After some short steep switchbacks, round a false summit, and at 6.3 miles reach the actual summit (elev. 3660 ft.) cloaked in trees. Disappointed? Don't be—continue on the trail another 0.1 mile, descending 150 feet to flower-dotted meadows with sweeping views west to the Columbia River, the Wind River valley, Trapper Creek Wilderness peaks, and Silver Star. The views to the north are better. Admire Mount St. Helens and Mount Adams rising above the Indian Heaven Wilderness peaks, Grassy Knoll, Big and Little Huckleberry Mountains, and the Big Lava Bed.

EXTENDING YOUR TRIP

The trail continues descending, reaching a rough gravel service road at 2 miles from the viewpoint. If funding becomes available in the future, the Forest Service would like to connect this trail to Grassy Knoll (Hike 38). Consider combining the Augspurger hike with Dog Mountain (Hike 36) by using the connector trail.

38 Grassy Knoll and Big Huckleberry Mountain

RATING/ DIFFICULTY	ROUNDTRIP	ELEV GAIN/ HIGH POINT	SEASON
*****/3	4 miles	1050 feet/ 3648 feet	May–Nov

RATING/ DIFFICULTY	ROUNDTRIP	ELEV GAIN/ HIGH POINT	SEASON
****/4	10.6 miles	2850 feet/ 4209 feet	June–Oct

Crowds: 3/1; **Maps:** Green Trails Wind River No. 397, Willard No. 398; **Contact:** Gifford Pinchot National Forest, Mount Adams Ranger District; **Notes:** FR 6808 is bumpy but passable for cars. Trailhead can also be reached from the east on a slightly better road by following FR 68 from just north of Willard; **GPS:** N 45° 47.858', W 121° 44.470'

 *Longing for views and flowers like Dog Mountain's famous displays but without the crowds and strenuous approach? Then plant yourself down on the Grassy Knoll*

Trail. Shrouded in a kaleidoscope of wildflowers, this former lookout site also offers jaw-slacking views from Hood to Adams. And a craggy knoll on the way grants an eagle's-eye perspective of the massive Big Lava Bed. If you're feeling energetic, continue to Big Huckleberry Mountain, traversing more flowering hillsides.

GETTING THERE

From Stevenson, head east on State Route 14 for 3.2 miles, turning north at the traffic circle onto Wind River Highway. Then proceed 4.1 miles and turn right (just after High Bridge over the Wind River) onto Bear Creek Road. Follow this at-first paved road, which becomes gravel Forest Road 6808 at 3.6 miles, and continue for an additional 7.1 miles to an unsigned junction at Triangle Pass. Then turn left onto FR 68, coming to another junction in 2.1 miles. Bear right and immediately reach the trailhead (elev. 2850 ft.).

ON THE TRAIL

Grassy Knoll Trail No. 146 immediately starts in a small meadow flowering with larkspurs, paintbrushes, desert parsley, and more. The way then enters beautiful old-growth forest and steeply climbs. At 0.7 mile skirt an old gravel pit. At 1.1 miles emerge on a rocky knoll (elev. 3620 ft.) and savor a stunning view over the sprawling Big Lava Bed, with Mount Adams and Little Huckleberry Mountain hovering above. One of the South Cascades' most striking landforms, the massive lava flow originated from a crater some thousands of years ago. Now lodgepole pines and other hardy plants grow within the contorted, jagged, hardened lava, which emits magnetic forces known to thwart compass and GPS systems. Best to appreciate this place from above—but keep children and dogs away from the cliff edges.

Then reenter forest and descend 200 feet to a saddle before steeply climbing to the broad, appropriately named Grassy Knoll (elev. 3648 ft.) at 2 miles. All that remains of the lookout are the support foundation posts.

But a tower isn't necessary to take in the stupendous views. Gaze south to hulking Augspurger Mountain, conical Wind Mountain, icy Mount Hood, and the shimmering Columbia River. Stare west across Sedum Ridge to Silver Star, and turn northeast to capture Mount Adams. And don't forget to cast your glances

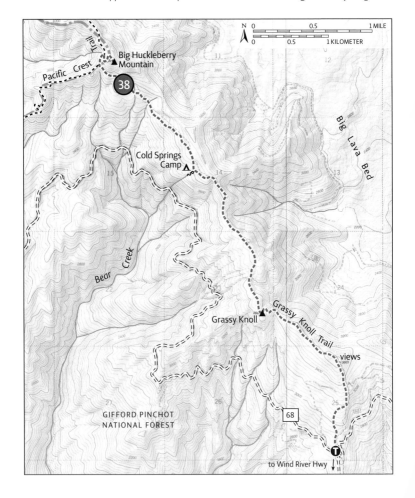

Big Lava Bed spreads in front of Little Huckleberry Mountain and Mount Adams.

downward to a myriad of flowers, including daffodils, planted years ago by a former lookout keeper as a memorial to her husband whom she met at the knoll.

Return content, or keep hiking on a now less trodden trail northward. Soon ascend a broader knoll bursting with even more flowers (elev. 3800 ft.) and then drop to a saddle (elev. 3675 ft.), granting excellent views northwest to the Trapper Creek Wilderness peaks. The trail then steeply climbs an open sun-kissed slope (notice the balsamroot), topping out at about 3875 feet before gently descending across forested slopes to Cold Springs Camp (elev. 3850 ft.) at 3.7 miles.

The way then climbs a little before once again descending. Skirt beneath some ledges (elev. 3650 ft.) and cross two small creeks before climbing steeply to meet the Pacific Crest Trail (elev. 4000 ft.) at 5.1 miles. Turn right and then turn right again onto a short but steep spur to Big Huckleberry Mountain. After 0.2 mile emerge on the 4209-foot summit, which also once sported a fire lookout.

Views here aren't as widespread as from Grassy Knoll, as the forest is obscuring them, but the view south to Hood is good. Enjoy wildflowers and—more than likely—some solitude. And contemplate why Little Huckleberry Mountain across the Big Lava Bed is more than 500 feet higher than Big Huckleberry!

39 Little Huckleberry Mountain

RATING/ DIFFICULTY	ROUNDTRIP	ELEV GAIN/ HIGH POINT	SEASON
***/3	5 miles	1950 feet/ 4781 feet	June–Nov

Crowds: 2; **Map:** Green Trails Willard No. 398; **Contact:** Gifford Pinchot National Forest, Mount Adams Ranger District; **Notes:** Trail also open to mountain bikes; **GPS:** N 45° 54.323', W 121° 42.275'

 Follow this short and occasionally steep trail

through a beautiful ancient forest to a long-ago fire lookout site at the edge of an ancient lava field. Delight in wildflowers and excellent views north to Mount Adams and south to Mount Hood. And marvel at the massive Big Lava Bed spread out to the west and framed by Grassy Knoll and Big Huckleberry Mountain, which is actually shorter than Little Huckleberry Mountain.

GETTING THERE

From Stevenson, head east on State Route 14 for 12 miles, turning left onto Cook-Underwood Road. Continue for 5.1 miles and bear left onto Willard Road. Proceed for 1.5 miles and continue straight 0.7 mile on Oklahoma Road (Forest Road 86). Then turn left onto South Prairie Road (FR 66) and drive 12.1 miles to the trailhead (elev. 3000 ft.).

ON THE TRAIL

Little Huckleberry Trail No. 49 starts off as a wide old road and quickly transitions to a single track. It quickly steepens too, wasting no time gaining elevation. Through open mature forest, steadily ascend. True to this mountain's name, huckleberries flourish in the forest understory. At 1.2 miles the way slightly descends, passing through patches of vine maples that add bright colors in the fall. At 1.6 miles cross a small spring-fed creek and then begin steadily climbing again.

The way bends north to attain the ridge crest, passing through fine old growth. It then emerges in a pocket meadow in a small saddle before, at 2.5 miles, it makes the final climb to the summit graced with junipers and an array of wildflowers. Four concrete support bases are all that remains of Little Huckleberry's fire tower, but the views are to

The author surveys the countryside from the old fire lookout site.

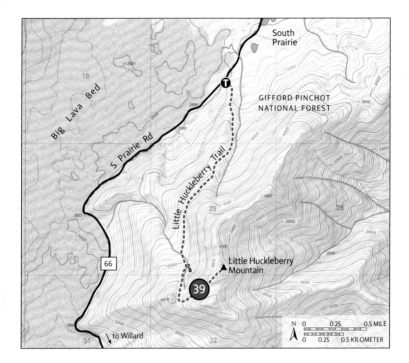

still good northeast across the Monte Cristo Range, Mount Adams, and to the community of Trout Lake. Mount Hood can be seen to the south. And to the west take in an excellent view of the Big Lava Bed with Grassy Knoll and Big Huckleberry (Hike 38) rising behind it. The large flow more than 8 miles long originated from a cinder cone more than 8200 years ago.

Contemplate why Big Huckleberry Mountain is 500 feet lower than Little Huckleberry Mountain. Could it be due to the mountain's girth—or perhaps the size of the huckleberries that grow on these peaks? You'll have to do some random size samplings to see if that's the case. And of course, be sure to eat your results!

40 Buck Creek Falls

RATING/ DIFFICULTY	LOOP	ELEV GAIN/ HIGH POINT	SEASON
**/2	2.9 miles	680 feet/ 1175 feet	Year-round

Crowds: 2; **Maps:** Green Trails Willard No. 398 (not all trails shown), Washington State Department of Natural Resources, Buck Creek map; **Contact:** Washington State DNR, Southeast Region; **Notes:** Discover Pass required. Trail also open to mountain bikes; **GPS:** N 45° 48.226', W 121° 32.191'

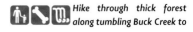 *Hike through thick forest along tumbling Buck Creek to*

Buck Creek Falls crashes into a basalt bowl.

enjoy woodland flowers during the spring as well as peace and quiet through most of the year. Admire small but pretty Buck Creek Falls plunging into a basaltic bowl. And climb a hillside of open forest to admire the Buck Creek valley below.

GETTING THERE

From Stevenson drive east on State Route 14 for 19.4 miles and turn left onto SR 141A. (From exit 64 on I-84 in Hood River take the toll bridge into Washington. Turn left on SR 14 and proceed for 1.6 miles turning right onto SR 141A.) In 2.2 miles bear left onto SR 141 and drive 1.9 miles. Then turn left onto Northwestern Lake Road (which becomes Nestor Peak Road) and drive 0.9 mile. Continue straight on gravel Buck Creek Road (DNR Road B-1000) for 1.4 miles and come to unsigned trailhead (elev. 700 ft.) on the left just before the road crosses Buck Creek.

ON THE TRAIL

Years ago this trailhead and trail were well-signed. While much of the signage is no longer here, the route is pretty defined. Head up the short spur trail and immediately come to a junction with the Buck Creek Trail, which loops 24 miles around the Buck Creek watershed. Head left on the wide trail, which here follows a waterline. Buck Creek provides water for the nearby community of White Salmon.

Gain elevation at a gradual pace with a few short, steep bouts in between. Cross numerous creeks and spring-fed seeps, which can make sections of the trail wet and muddy. Buck Creek provides a nice musical score, drowning out any activity on the nearby paralleling road. At 1 mile a short spur leads right to Buck Creek Falls. Use caution on the wet, uneven basalt ledge as you view the pretty falls.

Then continue north coming to a bridge over Buck Creek, at 1.4 miles, and a developed trailhead (elev. 960 ft.) with picnic tables and privy—an alternative start if you just want to see the falls. Now cross the road, pick up the trail again, and in open forest, start climbing more steadily. At 1.8 miles come to a junction. The Buck Creek Trail heads left toward Monte Cristo (Hike 43). Head right continuing on the loop and now following an old road.

The way soon resumes on trail. Cross a creek in a small ravine and continue to climb. After reaching an elevation of 1175 feet, start descending. Enjoy views through the trees of the valley below and of nearby ridges. Keep

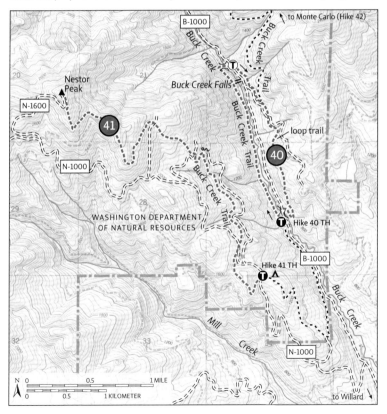

descending and pass some oaks growing among the conifers. At 2.9 miles reach the road at its crossing of Buck Creek. The trailhead is just to the left.

41 Nestor Peak

RATING/ DIFFICULTY	ROUNDTRIP	ELEV GAIN/ HIGH POINT	SEASON
***/3	8 miles	1950 feet/ 3088 feet	May–Nov

Crowds: 3; **Maps:** Green Trails Willard No. 398 (not all trails shown), Washington State Department of Natural Resources, Buck Creek map; **Contact:** Washington State DNR, Southeast Region; **Notes:** Discover Pass required. Trail also open to mountain bikes; **GPS:** N 45° 47.798', W 121° 32.346'

Hike through attractive second-growth forest to an old lookout site in an oft-overlooked state forest. Enjoy good views of Hood River, Mount Hood, Mount Defiance, and Mount Adams. Hike here in the spring and enjoy an array of pretty blossoms in the summit meadows.

GETTING THERE
From Stevenson, drive east on State Route 14 for 19.4 miles and turn left onto SR 141A. (From exit 64 on I-84 in Hood River take the toll bridge into Washington. Turn left on SR 14 and proceed for 1.6 miles turning right onto SR 141A.) In 2.2 miles bear left onto SR 141 and drive 1.9 miles. Then turn left onto Northwestern Lake Road (which becomes Nestor Peak Road) and drive 0.9 mile. Turn left onto gravel Nestor Peak Road (DNR Road N-1000) and drive 2 miles to Buck Creek trailhead 1 (elev. 1400 ft.) at junction with campground spur.

ON THE TRAIL
The way to Nestor Peak is via the Buck Creek Trail. This stretch is by far the busiest of the 24-mile loop trail. The trail is popular with mountain bikers, so stay alert, although most of the way is through open forest with no tight turns. While you can drive farther to access the Buck Creek Trail for a shorter hike to Nestor Peak—why? The whole point is to go hiking!

In mature second-growth forest, head west and start climbing. After a short, steep bout, the way attains a ridge and levels out. It then slightly descends, crossing Road N-1000 (elev. 1520 ft.) at 0.7 mile. Continue losing elevation before passing a spur to a paralleling road, which until recently served as part of the trail. Now on well-built new tread, traverse a hillside. Pass a lot of dips along the way, a feature favored by bikers.

Cross a creek and at 1.6 mile, bear left at a junction at the old trail. Now start climbing steadily and steeply at times as the way attains a ridge. At 2 miles bear right on an old road spur and soon afterward pick up the trail again. Continue ascending. At 2.5 miles cross another road and continue hiking through attractive forest including a cedar grove.

At 2.9 miles pass a small oak grove and wildflower patch. Then steeply climb, catching a preview of the views to come. Ascend a knoll (elev. 2700 ft.) and hike through a pretty patch of open old-growth forest. Then slightly descend and start steeply climbing again. At 3.9 miles the trail reaches a rocky old road. Follow it upward through flowering meadows for 0.1 mile to Nestor's summit. Here you'll find the unattractive remains of the base of the second fire lookout tower, which was removed in 1995.

Mount Adams from the spine of Monte Carlo

The views from the summit, however, are quite sublime, especially of the city of Hood River, Mount Hood, Mount Defiance, and Augspurger Mountain. There's a good view north, too, out to Mount Adams.

42 Monte Carlo

RATING/ DIFFICULTY	LOOP	ELEV GAIN/ HIGH POINT	SEASON
***/4	10.4 miles	2900 feet/ 4045 feet	Mid-May– Nov

Crowds: 1; **Maps:** Green Trails Willard No. 398 (not all trails shown), Washington State Department of Natural Resources, Buck Creek map; **Contact:** Gifford Pinchot National Forest, Mount Adams Ranger District, and Washington State DNR, Southeast Region; **Notes:** Trail open to mountain bikes and horses; **GPS:** N 45° 52.282', W 121° 37.393'

Bearing no resemblance at all to its namesake in Monaco, this Monte Carlo is little visited and little known. This is a tough loop that is long on solitude. Hike through old-growth forest to mountaintop meadows bursting with wildflowers, including many uncommon to the Cascades. And enjoy some fine views, too, of area volcanoes and the Little White Salmon River valley.

GETTING THERE

From Stevenson, head east on State Route 14 for 12 miles, and turn left onto Cook-Underwood Road. (From Hood River take the toll bridge into Washington. Turn left on SR 14 and proceed for 10.2 miles, turning right onto Cook-Underwood Road.) Then continue for 5.1 miles and bear left onto Willard Road. Proceed 1.5 miles to the

Nestor Peak's summit meadows and views out to Mount Hood

old timber town of Willard. Then continue straight on Oklahoma Road, coming to the Oklahoma Campground at 7.6 miles. Continue straight on graveled FR 18 for 0.2 mile to trailhead (elev. 1750 ft.). Park on your left a couple hundred feet before trail located on your right.

ON THE TRAIL

Not the shortest route to Monte Carlo (see Hike 40), this loop makes for a good workout and includes two fine meadows that straight-shot peak baggers will miss. Monte Carlo Trail No. 52 starts off mellow, traversing a forested bottomland. It soon intersects an old logging road and follows it right a short distance. At 0.3 mile leave the old road and steeply climb through a forest that was selectively cut several decades ago. The trail is in good shape, but unfortunately renegade motorcyclists have been illegally using it, damaging the tread in steep spots. Report any scofflaws to the US Forest Service.

At 1 mile reach FR 1840. Go left on the road and pick up the trail again at 1.1 miles on your right. Then resume steeply climbing through old-growth forest. At 1.4 miles head right on an old road and quickly return to the trail, crossing the old road again at 1.7 miles. Next slightly descend before once again climbing. At 2.2 miles start crossing grassy basalt openings that grant views west to Big and Little Huckleberry Mountains. The way then steepens once again, ascending an open hillside bursting with wildflowers in late spring.

The trail then leaves US Forest Service land for Washington State Department of Natural Resources land, reaching a junction (elev. 3375 ft.) in regenerating forest at 2.7 miles. Now turn left on the Buck Creek Trail, coming to the Buck Creek trailhead 2 (an

alternative start via a long dirt road approach) at 3 miles. Continue on the Buck Creek Trail, slowly descending to a bridged crossing (elev. 3200 ft.) of the Middle Fork Buck Creek in a beautiful old-growth forest grove at 3.4 miles.

Then begin climbing a 3650-foot ridge, traversing old cuts and logging roads. The trail then makes a long descent in mature second growth, coming to DNR Road B-1500 in a broad saddle (elev. 3350 ft.) at 4.5 miles. Cross the road and soon cross it again before steeply climbing and reentering the national forest. At 5 miles the trail traverses a large meadow high on the southern slopes of Monte Carlo. Flowers are profuse here in season, and views south to Mount Hood are excellent.

Continue hiking, reentering forest and coming to a junction on the broad summit of 4045-foot Monte Carlo at 5.3 miles. The Buck Creek Trail continues right. You want to head left on the Monte Carlo Trail, following along the narrow nearly level spine of the long peak. The trail traverses lovely swaths of flowering meadows on a basalt escarpment lined with stately trees. At 6.1 miles the way enters forests just above open slopes and ledges. A short spur leads to an excellent viewpoint of Little and Big Huckleberry Mountains, Mount St. Helens, and the Indian Heaven Wilderness peaks.

Continue along the ridge and soon come to one more meadow—this one providing an excellent view of Mount Adams. Then enter open forest and descend at an insanely steep rate, losing 800 feet in 0.6 mile. At 7 miles reach the Monte Cristo Monte Carlo trailhead (elev. 3140 ft.) on FR 1840. This is an alternative approach (See Hike 43) for a much shorter hike.

To continue the loop, head left, cross FR 1840, and pick up the Monte Cristo Trail.

Then make another insanely steep descent, traversing mainly old-growth forest and following spring-fed creeks into the valley. At 8.1 miles reach FR 18 (elev. 2100 ft.). Now turn left and walk this lightly traveled dirt road through the forested Little White Salmon River valley for 2.3 miles back to your start.

43 Monte Cristo

RATING/ DIFFICULTY	ROUNDTRIP	ELEV GAIN/ HIGH POINT	SEASON
****/3	3 miles	1050 feet/ 4171 feet	Mid-May– Nov

Crowds: 1; **Map:** Green Trails Willard No. 398; **Contact:** Gifford Pinchot National Forest, Mount Adams Ranger District; **Notes:** Trail open to mountain bikes and horses; **GPS:** N 45° 53.516', W 121° 34.446'

Arrowleaf balsamroot on Monte Cristo's summit

Hike to an old fire lookout site in the Monte Cristo Range, a little-visited corner of the Cascades that supports a diverse array of plant communities. From the broad, open summit, admire showy wildflowers and patches of stunted Oregon white oaks. Enjoy sweeping views, too, of the Indian Heaven Wilderness peaks, Mount St. Helens, Mount Hood, and Little Huckleberry Mountain.

GETTING THERE

From Stevenson, head east on State Route 14 for 12 miles, turning left onto Cook-Underwood Road. (From Hood River take the toll bridge into Washington. Turn left on SR 14 and proceed for 10.2 miles turning right onto Cook-Underwood Road.) Then continue for 5.1 miles and bear left onto Willard Road. Proceed 1.5 miles to the old timber town of Willard. Then continue straight on Oklahoma Road for 6.9 miles and turn right onto FR 1840. Follow this lightly maintained road (high clearance recommended) for 5.5 miles to trailhead (elev. 3140 ft.) on your right.

ON THE TRAIL

From the grassy trailhead, two trails diverge. The Monte Carlo Trail travels south (Hike 42), steeply climbing 4045-foot Monte Carlo. You want to head north on Monte Cristo Trail No. 53, which starts as an old road skirting an old cut. At 0.6 mile the road ends. Now on real trail, enter old-growth forest and start steeply gaining elevation.

The trail is in decent shape, but illegal motorbike riding has torn into the tread in places. Report any motoring scofflaws to the US Forest Service. At 1.3 miles the trail attains a ridge and begins to traverse more open territory. After a few short switchbacks,

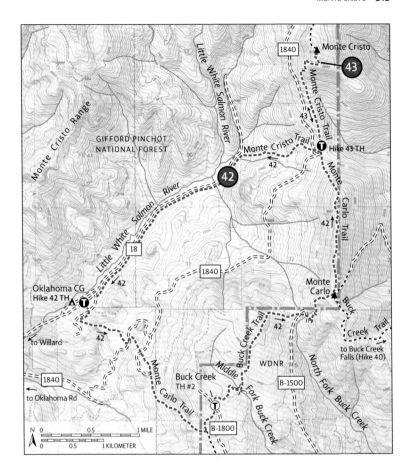

the trail crests Monte Cristo's summit ridge. Now walk across flowering meadows to the 4171-foot former fire lookout site at 1.5 miles.

The views are excellent from this open peak—from Mount Hood south to across the Little White Salmon River valley to Little Huckleberry Mountain west; to Mount St. Helens and the Indian Heaven Wilderness peaks north. Trees block the views east.

From late spring through the summer, the peak's flowers rival its views. The peak and adjacent ridges support a wide variety of plant communities, including Fremont silk-tassel chaparral habitat and open grassland balds such as the summit. Oregon white oaks also grow here, including patches of stunted shrubby ones just below the summit. The region also supports clustered lady's slipper orchids. The forested area just to the east of the summit is a Washington State Department of Natural Resources Natural Area Preserve, established to protect this unique area. Treat the summit area with care as you admire its beauty.

EXTENDING YOUR TRIP
The trail continues north across the open ridge before entering forest in about 0.2 mile. It then climbs to Monte Cristo's 4292-foot high point before descending to a saddle and climbing a knoll. At 1.7 miles from the lookout site, the trail terminates on FR 86 Spur 080.

44 Weldon Wagon Road

RATING/ DIFFICULTY	LOOP	ELEV GAIN/ HIGH POINT	SEASON
***/3	4.6 miles	1230 feet/ 1850 feet	Year-round

Crowds: 2; **Map:** Green Trails Columbia River Gorge East No. 432S; **Contact:** Washington State Department of Natural Resources,

Southeast Region; **Notes:** Crosses private property. Do not stray from trail right-of-way; **GPS:** N 45° 48.170', W 121° 28.171'

Follow an old wagon road high onto a ridge that harbors an exceptional stand of Oregon white oak. Built from 1908 to 1911 to transport White Salmon valley–grown apples to market, the road long ago fell out of use. But it has since been resurrected as a trail—and one of the Gorge's least traveled and most unusual ones at that. Come for the dazzling flower show in spring and the views of Mount Hood year-round. Foraging turkeys and deer will keep you company.

GETTING THERE
From Stevenson, drive State Route 14 east for 19.4 miles, turning left onto SR 141A. (From I-84 exit 64 in Hood River, take the toll bridge into Washington. Turn left on SR 14 and drive 1.6 miles. Then turn right onto SR 141A.) In 2.2 miles bear left onto SR 141,

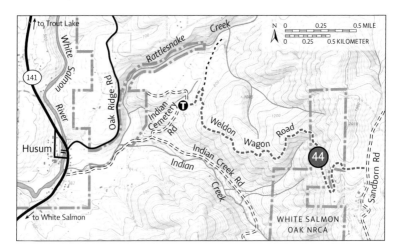

A field of flowering ookow

and after 3.8 miles turn right in Husum onto Indian Creek Road (the turnoff is just before a bridge over Rattlesnake Creek). Follow this good gravel road 0.6 mile, bearing left onto Indian Cemetery Road. Proceed for another 0.4 mile to a gated jeep track on the right. This is the trailhead (elev. 650 ft.). Park at the wide pullout on the left.

ON THE TRAIL

Begin hiking on the old jeep track. At 0.2 mile, the Weldon Wagon Road Trail (signed) takes off to the right. A Klickitat County right-of-way, the trail nevertheless traverses private property at both its eastern and western reaches. Stay on the trail and respect the property owners' privacy and rights.

The way immediately gains elevation, winding through a mixed forest of pine, oak, and Douglas-fir. At 0.4 mile pass a giant ponderosa pine and leave forest for field. The old road continues, meandering across sunny south-facing slopes that radiate with a wide array of blossoms from March to June. Views grow too—especially to the west, of the White Salmon River valley. Royal oaks resembling interpretive dancers and supple gymnasts, with their branches and limbs contorted and juxtaposed, line the way. The scene looks more like it belongs in the Central Valley of California or in the Basque Country of northern Spain.

Continuing higher, the grade steepens, crossing a slope now denuded of trees.

Mount Hood comes into view as well as Nestor Peak and the Monte Cristo Range. At 1.5 miles, high on the ridge (elev. 1570 ft.), a large sign announces your entrance into the Washington DNR White Salmon Oak Natural Resources Conservation Area (NRCA). Encompassing 551 acres, it protects one of the finest representations of this plant community within the state.

At 1.9 miles enter the oak forest (elev. 1700 ft.) the NRCA was created for. This is a good turnaround spot if views were your objective. The trail continues in forest, bending north and then east, skirting private property. Traverse stands of oak, crunching leaves and acorns as you pass. A major food source to deer, the acorns also provide sustenance to woodpeckers and the state's threatened western gray squirrel.

At 2.1 miles, crest the ridge (elev. 1850 ft.) and leave the NRCA, passing a large "boundary bearing" oak. Slightly descend, traveling along the edge of a Christmas tree farm to reach the trail's eastern terminus (elev. 1825 ft.) on Sandborn Road at 2.3 miles. A collection of old farm equipment here should pique your interest.

45 Willard Springs Trail

RATING/ DIFFICULTY	LOOP	ELEV GAIN/ HIGH POINT	SEASON
***/1	3.8 miles	80 feet/ 1860 feet	Mar–Dec

Crowds: 2; **Maps:** USGS Camas Prairie, trail map from refuge's website; **Contact:** Conboy Lake National Wildlife Refuge; **Notes:** Dogs permitted on-leash; **GPS:** N 45° 57.871', W 121° 20.569'

 *Hike along the remains of Conboy*

Lake situated on the Camas Prairie, a high plateau above the White Salmon and Klickitat Rivers at the base of Washington's second-highest summit. Nearly completely drained by late-nineteenth-century settlers, the lake is now more of a marsh but is still rich in wildlife, including nesting greater sandhill cranes. A 7000-acre national wildlife refuge protects remnants of the lake and adjacent forest and prairie lands.

GETTING THERE

From Stevenson, drive State Route 14 east for 19.4 miles, turning left onto SR 141A. (From I-84 exit 64 in Hood River, take the toll bridge into Washington. Turn left, or west, on SR 14 and drive 1.6 miles. Then turn right onto SR 141A.) In 2.2 miles bear left onto SR 141 and continue for 16.2 miles, turning right onto Warner Road (near milepost 21). After 0.8 mile, turn left onto Sunnyside Road and continue for 1.4 miles, turning right onto the Trout Lake Highway. Drive 6.8 miles east, turning right onto Wildlife Refuge Road (signed for the refuge headquarters). Reach the trailhead (elev. 1840 ft.) in 1 mile. Privy and picnic tables available.

ON THE TRAIL

The Willard Springs Trail starts near the ranger station and a few interpretive displays on a small rise overlooking the grassy former lakebed. Follow the path and immediately come to the Whitcomb-Cole Hewn Log House, built in the 1870s and one of the oldest pioneer homes left in the region. The trail then follows an old farm road, crossing a drainage before turning left onto a single track. Now walk north along the small channel on the former lake's western shoreline.

Now a seasonal wetland and especially pronounced in early spring, the old lakebed

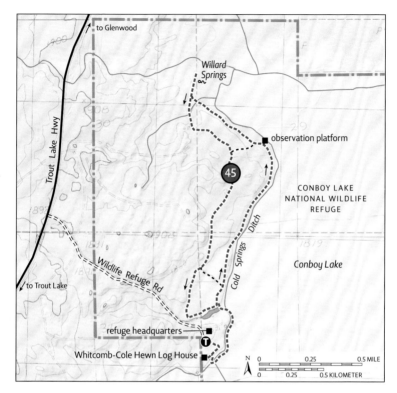

teems with birds. Conboy Lake is the only place in the state where greater sandhill cranes nest. The refuge also harbors the Oregon spotted frog, an amphibian whose numbers have greatly diminished across its West Coast range.

The trail soon crosses the channel and reaches a junction in a small meadow. You'll be returning left so head right, and right again at a shortcut, paralleling the old lakeshore and traveling through a small meadow before traversing pine groves and clusters of aspen. Watch for turkey, deer, elk, coyote, and beaver when not scanning

the grasses and reeds for songbirds and waterfowl. The near-level trail occasionally brushes up alongside the channel, offering excellent viewing out to the lake expanse.

At 1.2 miles, reach an observation platform with a view out to Washington's second-highest summit, 12,276-foot Mount Adams. The trail continues north, passing a giant ponderosa pine before reaching a junction. The trail left is a shortcut to the return leg. Carry on right, through lodgepole pine and grassy wetland prairie. Look for camas—it was once profuse here, sustaining

Mount Adams rises above a high plateau of prairie and pines.

the Klickitat people and leading early settlers to name the area Camas Prairie.

At 1.7 miles, reach a junction. The trail left is your return. But first head right for 0.2 mile to reach Willard Springs, which bubbles from basalt beneath a field. Are there any critters enjoying a drink of fresh spring water?

Now retrace your steps back to the junction and continue right, following the trail on an old road through gorgeous groves of mature ponderosa pine. Stay right at the shortcut junction, and at 3.1 miles, turn left at a junction just before the old-road trail comes to the refuge entrance road and old trailhead. Now hike through a small meadow, returning to a familiar junction at 3.3 miles. Head right and return to the trailhead in 0.5 mile.

46 Coyote Wall

RATING/ DIFFICULTY	ROUNDTRIP	ELEV GAIN/ HIGH POINT	SEASON
****/3	5.4 miles	1500 feet/ 1600 feet	Year-round

Crowds: 5; **Map:** Green Trails Columbia River Gorge East No. 432S; **Contact:** Columbia River Gorge National Scenic Area; **Notes:** Dogs must be on-leash Dec.–June. Heavy mountain bike use. Trails subject to changes and closures; **GPS:** N 45° 42.002', W 121° 24.192'

Hike up the Bingen Anticline, a dramatic uplifted fold of sheer basalt cliffs, stately oak forests, and sprawling meadows that radiate with wildflower brilliance in the spring. The most dramatic feature is the long line of cliffs called the Coyote Wall. Roam along the edge of this lofty wall and howl with delight, admiring thermal-riding raptors, nesting swallows, dazzling blossoms, and a jaw-dropping view of the Gorge spread out before you.

GETTING THERE

From Bingen, drive State Route 14 east for 3.3 miles, turning left (just after milepost 69) onto Courtney Road. (From I-84 exit 64 in Hood River, take the toll bridge into Washington. Turn right onto SR 14 and proceed

4.6 miles to Courtney Road.) From Courtney Road, make an immediate right to the trailhead (elev. 120 ft.). Parking area can fill fast—be sure to park well off roads (and obey no-parking signs) if lot is full.

ON THE TRAIL

At the trailhead notice the "cow catcher," a testament to this area's past use as a ranch before the Forest Service began acquiring it. Large tracts of private property still occupy the area, so respect postings. Also respect Forest Service closures. The trails here were initially user-built without regard to environmental sensitivities. The Forest Service has been closing many of these user trails and, with the help of the Washington Trails Association, upgrading ones that have since become official (numbered and signed).

Start by walking east on a crumbling old paved road (remains of the old Highway 8) along Locke Lake (formed by causeways) and beneath the impressive and formidable face of the Coyote Wall. Notice the big boulders that have come down off of it. Don't loiter! At 0.4 mile come to a junction. Head left here through a gate break and follow Old Ranch Road Trail No. 4426.

Stay on the well-used old jeep track, avoiding eroded shortcuts. After a sharp switchback west, come to a junction with the Little Maui Trail at 0.7 mile. A silly name, like many mountain bike trail names, it offers a nice loop-return option.

Continue straight, traversing open slopes and gradually climbing. Shortly after passing a second switchback, come to a junction with the Little Moab Trail (elev. 360 ft.) at 0.9 mile. The Old Ranch Road Trail continues straight, switchbacking its way up open grassy slopes. You want to go left on a rocky route, soon coming to the edge of the Coyote

Looking down the Coyote Wall to the Columbia River

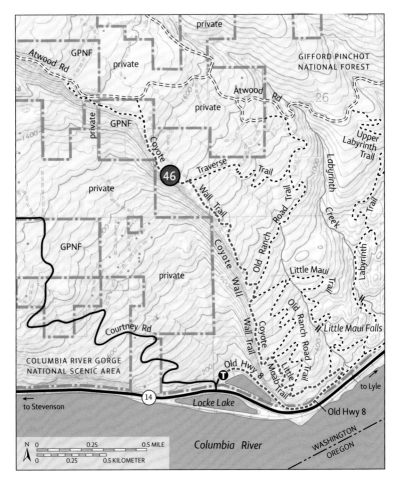

Wall. The way then climbs along the wall edge to grant stunning views. Exercise caution on this route, or stay on the Old Ranch Road Trail if this is too intense.

At 1.2 miles meet up with the Old Ranch Road Trail again. Continue left on the steeper, more intense route. Notice how rocky the terrain is below your feet, with shallow vegetative cover. Thank the Ice Age floods for scouring this terrain down to bedrock. Continue along the cliffy edge, enjoying thrilling views up and down the Coyote Wall. Pass a few tenacious pines along the way.

At 1.6 miles once more come to the Old Ranch Road Trail (elev. 800 ft.). Follow it left a short distance and come to another junction. The Old Ranch Road continues right, heading 0.9 mile to the Atwood Road "trail." Head left on the Coyote Wall Trail, switchbacking across an old jeep track and steadily ascending the broad grassy eastern slope of the Coyote Wall. In early spring profuse patches of arrowleaf balsamroot add golden touches to the emerald hillside. When your eyes aren't fixated on the sheer basalt cliffs angling toward the river, look out over the Columbia Gorge. Mount Hood can be seen to the south.

At 2.3 miles come to a junction with the Traverse Trail (elev. 1375 ft.). Continue straight along the rim of the Coyote Wall coming to an old farm road at forest edge (elev. 1600 ft.) at 2.7 miles. This is a good place to turn around. The Coyote Wall Trail continues another 0.3 mile through oak, pine, and fir forest to the closed-to-vehicles Atwood Road (elev. 1750 ft.). Retrace your steps or consider the options below for a return variation.

EXTENDING YOUR TRIP

To make this hike a loop, on your return, follow the pleasant Traverse Trail through meadows and oak groves 0.8 mile to the Old Ranch Road Trail. Then turn right and follow that trail 2.4 miles back to Old Highway 8. You can also follow the Old Ranch Road back down to Old Highway 8 for 1.8 miles from the upper Little Moab Trail junction. Another option is to follow the Old Ranch Road Trail from the upper Little Moab Trail junction for 0.2 mile to the Little Maui Trail. Then follow this scenic trail, passing a pretty waterfall on the way, 1.2 miles to its terminus on the Old Ranch Road.

47 Catherine Creek: The Labyrinth

RATING/ DIFFICULTY	ROUNDTRIP	ELEV GAIN/ HIGH POINT	SEASON
****/3	4.2 miles	950 feet/ 1000 feet	Year-round

Crowds: 4; **Map:** Green Trails Columbia River Gorge East No. 432S; **Contact:** Columbia River Gorge National Scenic Area; **Notes:** Dogs permitted on-leash. Heavy mountain bike use. Trails subject to changes and closures; **GPS:** N 45° 42.337', W 121° 22.998'

Hike through a spectacular area of sunny skies, alpine flower gardens, and outstanding rock formations. And as this locale's name suggests, you'll wander through a maze of basaltic rock formations. But there's more—gnarly oak groves, delightful waterfalls, and a high open grassy slope granting striking views of the Columbia.

GETTING THERE

From Bingen, drive State Route 14 east for 4.5 miles and turn left (just before milepost 71) onto Old Highway 8. (From I-84 exit 64 in Hood River, take the toll bridge into Washington. Turn right onto SR 14 and drive 5.8 miles to the left turn onto Old Highway 8.) Immediately park at a pullout on the west side of the road, being careful not to park in lanes of traffic (elev. 80 ft.).

ON THE TRAIL

Start by heading west on a crumbling paved stretch of Old Highway 8, this portion long closed to vehicles and littered by rockfall. Stare up at the basalt ledges to look for swallow nests. At 0.2 mile, cross a creek beneath pretty Lower Labyrinth Falls. At 0.5 mile,

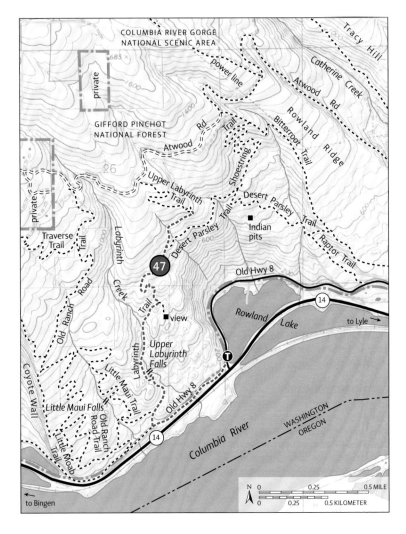

after passing through a road cut, turn right onto Labyrinth Trail No. 4423. Old Highway 8 continues 0.6 mile west to the Coyote Wall trailhead (an alternative start).

Now begin steadily climbing, reaching a junction (elev. 225 ft.) at 0.6 mile. The trail left leads 0.2 mile to the Little Maui Trail (Hike 46). Continue straight, following alongside tumbling Labyrinth Creek. Enter the labyrinth, ascending beneath and around basalt ledges and talus slopes. Come early spring, a myriad of flowers add vibrant colors to the coarse volcanic rock. Lizards and ground squirrels scurry and flit about. And poison oak grows profusely here, so stay on the trail. Be tick aware too.

A miniature version of Wyoming's Devils Tower comes into view. Pass big oaks and a small cave. At 0.9 mile come to Upper Labyrinth Falls in a miniature version of Arizona's Oak Creek Canyon. Now negotiate a steep (and potentially slick) section, and pass more wonderful basalt monuments, columns, and domes.

Cross the creek and continue to climb, coming to a junction (elev. 600 ft.) at 1.3 miles. The short spur right leads to an excellent viewpoint east over the Columbia. Now start climbing up another ledgy area. Ignore an unofficial trail right, pass a barbed-wire fence, and walk beneath a telephone line. The way soon emerges on a high, open grassy slope with stunning views of the river,

Rowland Lake, Columbia Hills, and the Tom McCall Preserve in Oregon.

At 1.9 miles reach a junction (elev. 900 ft.). The Desert Parsley Trail continues right and can be an extension option. The recommended day hike option is to head left on the Upper Labyrinth Trail. Continue climbing, traversing meadows and reaching a broad open area (elev. 1000 ft.) at a switchback at 2.1 miles. Take a break and enjoy sweeping views over Rowland Lake and the Columbia River out to Rowena Gap and the Columbia Hills. Then either head back the way you came or consider one of the options below.

EXTENDING YOUR TRIP

You can continue following the Upper Labyrinth Trail through oak groves and open meadows, reaching the closed-to-vehicles Atwood Road (elev. 1225 ft.) in 0.5 mile. Then head left for 0.5 mile to the Old Ranch Road Trail, and follow this well-graded path 2.7 miles to Old Highway 8. Then turn left and hike 0.7 mile back to your start.

Hikers frolic through meadows high above Rowland Lake.

Another interesting trip is to return via the Desert Parsley Trail, traversing steep slopes and a gully housing a small creek. Upon reentering forest at 0.5 mile, bear right at a junction (elev. 825 ft.) with the unofficial Shoestring Trail. Then switchback down across meadows and return to forest emerging in a valley (elev. 640 ft.) strewn with basalt talus piles. Notice the pits dug among the piles. Similar to the pits on Silver Star (Hike 6) and Wind Mountain (Hike 35), these were once used by young Native men for vision quests.

The trail continues as old road coming to a junction (elev. 520 ft.) at 1.1 miles. The way left climbs to reach the Rowland Trail. Continue right now on the Raptor Trail (which is closed from February 1 to July 15 to protect nesting raptors), skirting the base of basalt cliffs and coming to Old Highway 8 (elev. 240 ft.) at 1.5 miles. Then turn right and walk 1 mile along the narrow road (not recommended on weekends), skirting Rowland Lake (privy available) and returning to your vehicle.

Grass widows

48 Catherine Creek: Universal Access Trail

RATING/ DIFFICULTY	LOOP	ELEV GAIN/ HIGH POINT	SEASON
****/1	1.2 miles	100 feet/ 260 feet	Year-round

Crowds: 3; **Map:** Green Trails Columbia River Gorge East No. 432S; **Contact:** Columbia River Gorge National Scenic Area; **Notes:** Dogs permitted on-leash. ADA accessible; **GPS:** N 45° 42.627', W 121° 21.731'

This is one of the blooming best trails in the Gorge when it comes to displaying the region's floral diversity. Wander down this paved interpretive trail perfect for hikers of all ages and abilities, and delight in a procession of blossoms from February until June. The views, too, are lovely from this loop trail perched on a basaltic bluff above the Columbia.

GETTING THERE

From Bingen, drive State Route 14 east for 4.5 miles and turn left (just before milepost 71) onto Old Highway 8. (From I-84 exit 64 in Hood River, take the toll bridge into Washington. Turn right onto SR 14 and drive 5.8 miles to the left turn onto Old Highway 8.) Continue for 1.4 miles to the trailhead (elev. 260 ft.), located on your right. Park on your left. Privy available from mid-Jan. through mid-June.

ON THE TRAIL

Cross the road and start wandering down Catherine Creek Universal Access Trail No.

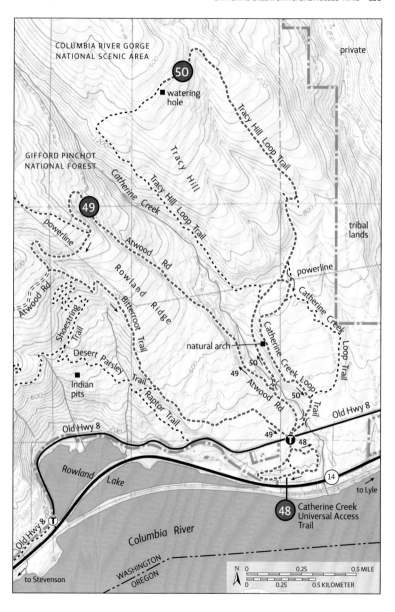

COLUMBIA RIVER GORGE
NATIONAL SCENIC AREA

private

50

watering
hole

Tracy Hill Loop Trail

GIFFORD PINCHOT
NATIONAL FOREST

Catherine Creek

Tracy Hill

Tracy Hill Loop Trail

49

powerline

tribal
lands

Atwood Rd

powerline

Atwood Rd

Rowland Ridge

Catherine Creek

Shoestring Trail

Bitterroot Trail

natural arch

Catherine Creek Loop Trail

Catherine Creek Loop Trail

Desert Parsley Trail

Indian
pits

49

50

Raptor Trail

Atwood Rd

50

Old Hwy 8

49

48

14

Old Hwy 8

Rowland Lake

to Lyle

48 Catherine Creek
Universal Access
Trail

Old Hwy 8

Columbia River

to Stevenson

WASHINGTON
OREGON

N   0   0.25   0.5 MILE
    0   0.25   0.5 KILOMETER

4400, also known as the Catherine Creek Interpretive Trail. It was one of the first trails developed by the Forest Service in the Catherine Creek area after they started acquiring these former ranch lands in the late 1980s. The interpretive panels will shed some insight on the area's cultural and geological history. Interpretive signs will also help tune you in to the area's wide array of blossoms.

While this loop is only 1.2 miles long with an option to make it even shorter, you'll want to linger long. From mid-winter through early summer, the surrounding rocky terrain will be donning showy wildflowers including twinflowers, death camas, grass widows, lupines, bitterroots, Oregon sunshines, penstemons, and a myriad of others.

The way descends slightly, coming to a junction. Head left and pass remnants of the old ranch. The terrain is pretty open with clusters of oaks and pines. Soon the trail reaches an overlook of Catherine Creek cascading in a tight basaltic draw. The trail continues descending then turns west and passes a vernal pool. Stay left at the short-cut junction, pass a few pines and oaks, and then begin climbing. Enjoy excellent views west down the Gorge. The trail then heads east. Veer left at the shortcut junction and again at the initial junction to return to the trailhead.

EXTENDING YOUR TRIP

Four miles east via Old Highway 8 is the Balfour–Klickitat day-use area (NW Forest Pass required) with its lovely 0.7-mile paved wheelchair-accessible loop trail on a bluff above the confluence of the Klickitat and Columbia Rivers. Come during the winter salmon spawning season to witness scores of bald eagles.

49 Catherine Creek: Rowland Ridge

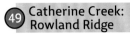

RATING/ DIFFICULTY	ROUNDTRIP	ELEV GAIN/ HIGH POINT	SEASON
****/3	3.5 miles	1100 feet/ 1350 feet	Year-round

Crowds: 3; **Map:** Green Trails Columbia River Gorge East No. 432S; **Contact:** Columbia River Gorge National Scenic Area; **Notes:** Dogs permitted on-leash. Open to mountain bikers. Trails subject to changes and closures; **GPS:** N 45° 42.627', W 121° 21.731'

One of the quieter options in the popular Catherine Creek area, this loop delivers just as fine views and wildflower displays as Coyote Wall and the Labyrinth. Walk up a long-abandoned road through pleasant forest to sprawling meadows high on Rowland Ridge. Then follow a trail along precipitous basalt cliffs, taking in breathtaking views of the Columbia River and its flanking ridges, bluffs, and peaks.

GETTING THERE

From Bingen, drive State Route 14 east for 4.5 miles and turn left (just before milepost 71) onto Old Highway 8. (From I-84 exit 64 in Hood River, take the toll bridge into Washington. Turn right onto SR 14 and drive 5.8 miles to the left turn onto Old Highway 8.) Continue for 1.4 miles to the trailhead (elev. 260 ft.), located on your left. Privy available from mid-January through mid-June.

ON THE TRAIL

Since the late 1980s the Forest Service has been acquiring lands (much old ranch land) at Catherine Creek, but the agency has only

Golden grasses in late fall along the Bitterroot Trail

recently started to implement management plans for this ecologically rich area. This loop follows part of the planned Bitterroot Trail No. 4422, which has not officially been built yet. It follows instead a user-built trail. Expect changes to this route and some much-needed improvements.

From behind a gate, two old roads diverge across the open rocky and grassy country-side. You will be returning on the one to the left. Take the one to the right and immediately come to the new Catherine Creek Loop Trail (Hike 50). Stay on the old road and saunter across a bedrock flat shrouded with flowers and swaying grasses. To protect nesting western meadowlarks, it's imperative to keep your dog leashed. The way soon meets up with Catherine Creek in a small canyon, coming to a junction at 0.3 mile. The way right heads to a natural arch (Hike 50).

You want to continue left on the old Atwood Road.

Now begin steadily climbing on this old county-road-turned-trail. Catch good views through an opening in the forest of the Catherine Creek natural arch across the valley. The trail then enters a thicker forest of oaks and pines bustling with birds and squirrels. Parts of the old road are covered in moss, making for pleasant walking. Pass a growing-over spur leading down to Catherine Creek. Atwood Road steepens, crossing a scree slope and denser forest. At 1.6 miles an old road diverges right while Atwood makes a short hairpin turn left.

The trail then emerges into open meadows on Rowland Ridge. Here at 1.9 miles reach a junction (elev. 1350 ft.) with a service road for a nearby powerline. Head left on the service road, descending open slopes and enjoying bountiful blossoms and wide-open views of the Gorge. At 2.2 miles reach a trail junction. Go right, passing beneath the powerline wires and soon reaching another junction. Now head left on the rocky Bitterroot Trail, using caution as it travels along the edge of a long series of dramatic basalt cliffs. Watch for raptors riding thermals. Enjoy excellent views of the basalt talus piles below—and of Rowland Lake, Mosier Plateau, and Coyote Wall. At 2.8 miles, after crossing a stretch of loose scree, reach a junction (elev. 620 ft.) with a short trail dropping down to connect with the Raptor and Desert Parsley Trails (Hike 47).

Continue straight, leaving the cliffs. After crossing a seasonal creek, reach an old ranch road. Then follow this road trail to return to the trailhead at 3.5 miles.

50 Catherine Creek: Natural Arch and Tracy Hill

RATING/ DIFFICULTY	LOOP	ELEV GAIN/ HIGH POINT	SEASON
***/2	1.9 miles	400 feet/ 630 feet	Year-round

RATING/ DIFFICULTY	ROUNDTRIP	ELEV GAIN/ HIGH POINT	SEASON
****/3	5.1 miles	1300 feet/ 1525 feet	Year-round

Crowds: 4/2; **Map:** Green Trails Columbia River Gorge East No. 432S; **Contact:** Columbia River Gorge National Scenic Area; **Notes:** Dogs permitted on-leash. Open to mountain bikers. Trails subject to changes and closures; **GPS:** N 45° 42.627', W 121° 21.731'

A touch of Utah in the Northwest! Follow an old ranch road to a weathered corral set in a grove of oaks beneath an impressive natural arch. Then wander through pine groves and fields, returning above the arch along ledges that burst with blossoms in the springtime. And if that's not enough, head to the open meadows of Tracy Hill for splendid views.

GETTING THERE
From Bingen, drive State Route 14 east for 4.5 miles and turn left (just before milepost 71) onto Old Highway 8. (From I-84 exit 64 in Hood River, take the toll bridge into Washington. Turn right onto SR 14 and drive 5.8 miles to the left turn onto Old Highway 8.) Continue for 1.4 miles to the trailhead (elev. 260 ft.), located on your left. Privy available from mid-January through mid-June.

ON THE TRAIL
Since the late 1980s the Forest Service has been acquiring lands at Catherine Creek. Much of it was used for ranching, and the agency is now rehabilitating much of the sensitive habitats here. The agency has recently started improving trails here, too, and closing poorly designed and environmentally damaging user trails. Please respect all closures and expect some changes to the trails that are currently open.

From behind a gate, two old roads diverge across the open rocky and grassy countryside. Take the one to the right and immediately come to the new Catherine Creek Loop Trail No. 4419 recently built by the Washington Trails Association. You will be returning on it, so stay left on the old road. The way soon meets up with Catherine Creek in a small canyon, coming to a junction at 0.3 mile. The way left heads to Rowland Ridge (Hike 49). You want to go right.

Cross Catherine Creek on a small bridge and reach an old corral at 0.5 mile (elev. 320

Catherine Creek Natural Arch from an old corral

ft.) in an oak and pine forest at the base of an impressive basalt arch. A rarity in Washington, this intriguing landmark is worth marveling at. But don't go beyond the fence, as this area is culturally and environmentally sensitive. Now continue north on the old road trail, steeply climbing. At 0.7 mile bear right at an old road junction just before a set of powerlines. Continue straight passing the lines and reaching another junction (elev. 600 ft.) at 0.9 mile. Left is the Tracy Hill Loop Trail (see below). The shorter hike option heads right on an old ranch road to come to the Catherine Creek Loop Trail (elev. 630 ft.) at 1 mile. You can go either way (left is longer by 0.2 mile) to return to the trailhead, but right is preferred to travel along the open ridge that backdrops the arch. Pass some great viewpoints near the top of the arch (stay behind fences) and then descend, coming to a junction at 1.6 miles. Now head right,

switchbacking to a bridge spanning Catherine Creek. Cross the waterway and reach the old road trail you started on at 1.8 miles. The trailhead lies 0.1 mile to the left.

For Tracy Hill, head left from the junction at 0.9 mile noted above and emerge from a forested gully to an open ridge graced with patches of ponderosa pine. Ignoring trails to the right, head left up the ridge enjoying growing views. At 2.1 miles (from the trailhead) reach the ridge crest (elev. 1425 ft.) and a paralleling user trail on the right. Head left into an oak forest and emerge on high, open slopes on Tracy Hill. At 2.3 miles come to an old cow watering hole (elev. 1525 ft.) and sprawling views of the Columbia River and Columbia Hills. This is a good spot to turn around. But if you want to make a loop, you can continue on fainter tread, traversing grassy slopes before descending toward Catherine Creek. The way then makes a sharp turn left above the ravine housing the creek. It then descends through meadows and oak groves to reach an old road at the powerlines and terminating at the main trail just north of the natural arch at 3.9 miles. Now turn left and return via the description above for a trip of 5.1 miles.

51 Klickitat Trail: Klickitat River

RATING/ DIFFICULTY	ONE-WAY	ELEV GAIN/ HIGH POINT	SEASON
***/2	10.2 miles	200 feet/ 380 feet	Year-round

Crowds: 3; **Map:** Green Trails Columbia River Gorge East No. 432S; **Contact:** Klickitat Trail Conservancy; **Notes:** Dogs permitted on-leash. Open to mountain bikers and equestrians; **GPS:** N 45° 41.793', W 121° 17.408'

The Klickitat Trail winds 31 miles from the Columbia River through spectacular canyons to the Klickitat River valley—a high plateau between the golden Columbia Hills and piney Simcoe Mountains. This stretch of this spectacular rail trail travels along the wild and scenic Klickitat River. Follow the churning glacier-born river along a basalt chasm, past whitewater rapids, and below a flank of oak-studded hills that burst with brilliant wildflowers in the spring.

GETTING THERE
From Bingen, drive State Route 14 east for 9.4 miles to Lyle and turn left onto SR 142. (From I-84 exit 64 in Hood River, take the toll bridge into Washington. Turn right onto SR 14 and drive 10.7 miles to Lyle, turning left onto SR 142.) After 0.1 mile turn left into Lyle trailhead (elev. 235 ft.). Privy available. For

Pitt trailhead continue north on SR 142 for 10 miles to trailhead on your right (just after the bridge over the Klickitat River). Privy available.

ON THE TRAIL
The Klickitat Trail came to be after a once-active rail line linking Lyle to Goldendale was decommissioned in 1992. However, this spectacular rail trail nearly met its demise due to a contingent of threatening opponents. But thanks to the untiring efforts of the Klickitat Trail Conservancy (KTC) and others, it has become a top area attraction. The trail is managed cooperatively by the KTC, US Forest Service, and Washington State Parks, and it is absolutely imperative that you adhere to all posted regulations—particularly keeping your dog leashed (as the trail traverses active farms) and not leaving the trail right-of-way onto adjacent private property. You can help assuage the concerns of abutting property owners by being a good steward.

This excellent 10.2-mile one-way hike requires a car shuttle to pick you up at the Pitt trailhead (10 miles north on SR 142) afterward. Otherwise, a partial out-and-back will make a great day hike from either direction—or you can always run it out and back! From the Lyle trailhead, begin north on a wide and smooth trail. The 1.6 miles between Lyle and the Fisher Hill Trestle will eventually be paved to allow for wheelchair access. Paralleling SR 142 and passing a few homes, the trail gently climbs out of the Columbia River valley. At 0.8 mile, cross a dirt road leading left, down to a county park on the Klickitat River. At 1.6 miles, leave the Columbia Gorge National Scenic Area and cross the Klickitat River on a high trestle. Stare down into "The Narrows," a deep

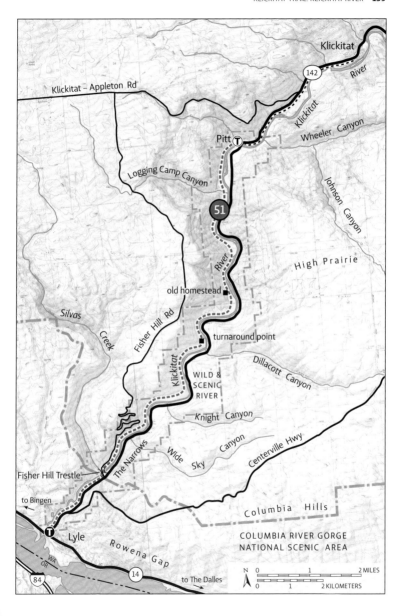

Klickitat

142

River

Klickitat – Appleton Rd

Klickitat

Wheeler Canyon

Pitt T

Logging Camp Canyon

Johnson Canyon

51

River

High Prairie

old homestead

turnaround point

Silvas

Creek

Fisher Hill Rd

Dillacott Canyon

Klickitat

WILD &
SCENIC
RIVER

Knight Canyon

Wide Sky Canyon

Centerville Hwy

The Narrows

Fisher Hill Trestle

to Bingen

Columbia Hills

T Lyle

Rowena Gap

COLUMBIA RIVER GORGE
NATIONAL SCENIC AREA

WA
OR

84

14

to The Dalles

N   0   1   2 MILES

0   1   2 KILOMETERS

A hiker admiring the turbulent Klickitat River after a big rain

basalt chasm. Notice, too, planking suspended above the roiling river. Native Americans dipnet fish from the planking, one of only two areas within the Columbia drainage where this practice continues.

Cross Fisher Hill Road (an alternative trailhead) and continue north, passing tribal land and a fish-gauging station at a small set of falls. With SR 142 now on the opposite side of the river, enjoy miles of roadless, houseless, semi-wild walking. The tread can be rough at times, with rocky sections, but the grade is always gentle. Views are continuous of river rapids and steep oak-covered hills. A federally protected Wild and Scenic River, the Klickitat is coveted by kayakers (watch for them), fishermen and women, and birds. Look for mergansers riding the currents and kingfishers scrutinizing the currents for bounty.

At 5.3 miles, the way is routed around a small washout before passing through a stretch of ponderosa pines away from the river. This is a good turnaround spot if you're hiking out and back. Otherwise, continue and at 7 miles pass a lone homestead connected to the outside world by a cable crossing.

The trail then again brushes up along the river, retreats into forest, and then emerges along the river once again. At 8 miles is a particularly attractive area of basalt ledge along the riverbank. Beyond, the trail bypasses a washout before reaching some homes, a ranch, and small vineyard at 9.3 miles. Be sure to close the several gates you pass through. The trail then follows a right-of-way access for homeowners. At 10 miles come to SR 142 at the community of Pitt, which was once a pit—literally—having been named for a railroad company gravel pit used to help build the railway grade. The Pitt trailhead parking area and privy are just across the road at 10.2 miles.

EXTENDING YOUR TRIP

Continue east on the Klickitat Trail for another 3 miles, passing columnar basalt and an old orchard before paralleling main street in the old mill and railroad town of Klickitat.

Park at the public parking area just east of the historic McCrow Building and Canyon Market in town.

52 Klickitat Trail: Mineral Springs

RATING/ DIFFICULTY	ROUNDTRIP	ELEV GAIN/ HIGH POINT	SEASON
***/1	5.2 miles	100 feet/ 550 feet	Year-round

Crowds: 1; **Map:** Green Trails Columbia River Gorge East No. 432S; **Contact:** Klickitat Trail Conservancy; **Notes:** Dogs permitted on-leash. Open to mountain bikers and equestrians. Watch for ticks, rattlesnakes, and poison oak; **GPS:** N 45° 49.384', W 121° 05.936'

Hike along the tumbling and rippling Klickitat River through fragrant pine groves and wildlife-rich oak forests on this quiet stretch of the 31-mile-long Klickitat Trail. Snoop around the ruins of an old mineral springs bottling operation and admire the remnant structure of an old dry ice factory as you walk this bygone rail line.

GETTING THERE

From Bingen, drive State Route 14 east for 9.4 miles to Lyle and turn left onto SR 142. (From I-84 exit 64 in Hood River, take the toll bridge into Washington. Turn right onto SR 14, drive 10.7 miles to Lyle, and turn left onto SR 142.) Then follow SR 142 (passing through the community of Klickitat) for 16.2 miles. Turn right onto Horseshoe Bend Road and proceed 0.1 mile. Then turn right onto Schilling Road and immediately come to the Wahkiacus trailhead (elev. 550 ft.) on your right. Privy available.

ON THE TRAIL

Due to a missing trestle over the Klickitat River just to the east of the old mill town of Klickitat, this short section of the Klickitat Trail is often bypassed by mountain bikers and ignored by hikers. It's a wonderful stretch of trail nearly all along the scenic river, passing through state wildlife lands and past some intriguing historic structures. It's a great stretch of trail, too, for solitude.

Before starting, check out the kiosk and read about the history of the area. Then begin west, pass through a pine grove, and soon come along the river. The way then passes through dogwoods and alders, coming to a rocky open area. At just shy of a mile, reach the mineral springs and the site of an old dry ice factory that operated here from the Depression until the 1950s. Carbonated water still percolates from one of the wells. Take a sip. Trains used to stop here for passengers to have a swig.

Snoop around the grounds. Aside from the wells, there are foundations as well as the remains of a bridge that once spanned the river. Across the Klickitat River is an attractive Italianate structure which was once part of the dry ice operation. The Washington Department of Fish and Wildlife acquired these lands in the 1950s and left that building standing. Vaux's swifts use its chimney as a roost.

Now continue hiking downriver through oak groves. At 1.2 miles cross a small creek and skirt a rocky outcropping on river's edge. The way then traverses a thickly vegetated area alongside a river channel. It's best to hike here later in the fall when ticks aren't as much of a concern. The trail then comes upon the riverbank again in an area known as Skookum Canyon. After passing by a river bend, the trail comes to a former

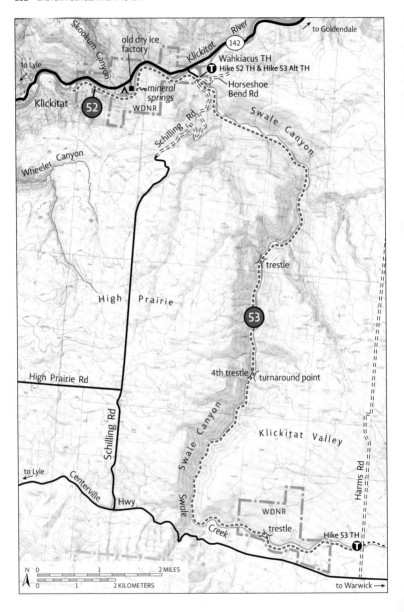

Old mineral springs well

bridge crossing of the river at 2.6 miles. The community of Klickitat lies just beyond. The Klickitat Trail Conservancy is working on securing grants for a replacement bridge. But until the trestle is in place, retrace your steps back to the trailhead.

53 Klickitat Trail: Swale Canyon

RATING/ DIFFICULTY	ROUNDTRIP	ELEV GAIN/ HIGH POINT	SEASON
***/3	11.6 miles	450 feet/ 1550 feet	Mar-July, Oct-Nov

Crowds: 2; **Map:** Green Trails Columbia River Gorge East No. 432S; **Contact:** Klickitat Trail Conservancy; **Notes:** Dogs permitted on-leash. Open to mountain bikers and equestrians. Watch for ticks and rattlesnakes. Trail closed approximately July 1–Oct. 1 because of fire danger; **GPS:** N 45° 43.409', W 121° 01.854'

Hike across a windy open plateau, following alongside a gurgling creek, slowly descending into a deep canyon of pines, dogwoods, oaks, and in spring, a mosaic of wildflowers. Your passage to this wild and remote depression north of the Columbia Hills is via the Klickitat Trail, a 31-mile-long former railroad bed. It's quite a contrast from the western half of the trail, which travels along the Klickitat River (Hike 51) and within sight of roads and homes.

GETTING THERE
From Bingen, drive State Route 14 east for 9.4 miles to a junction with SR 142. (From I-84 exit 64 in Hood River, take the toll bridge into Washington. Turn right onto SR 14, drive 10.7 miles to junction with SR 142.) Then continue east on SR 14 into Lyle for another 0.4 mile, turning left onto Centerville Highway. Follow this good paved road for 14.6 miles, turning left onto gravel Harms

Road. Reach the trailhead in 0.5 mile (elev. 1550 ft.). Privy available.

ON THE TRAIL

The Klickitat Trail almost didn't become a reality because several abutting property owners didn't believe the public had a right to a public right-of-way. But due to the tireless efforts of the Klickitat Trail Conservancy (KTC) and others, the trail prevailed. The 14 miles of trail from Wahkiacus to Warwick are managed cooperatively by the KTC and Washington State Parks. It's absolutely imperative that you adhere to all posted regulations—particularly keeping your dog leashed and not leaving the trail right-of-way onto adjacent private property. Be sure to close all gates you pass through too. Tensions over the trail have simmered, and you can help assuage the concerns of property owners by being a good steward.

If you can arrange a car shuttle at the Wahkiacus trailhead (elev. 550 ft.), then you can make an 11.9-mile one-way trip. (From Lyle, travel 16.2 miles north on SR 142, turning right onto Horseshoe Bend Road, and continuing 0.1 mile south to the trailhead located at the junction with Schilling Road.) But the last 3 miles aren't very appealing, passing several structures (some decrepit) with owners of said structures permitted to drive on this section of trail. Most hikers will prefer the out-and-back option instead, enjoying the best part of the trail—twice!

Starting from the western edge of the Klickitat Valley (actually a plateau between the Columbia Hills and Simcoe Mountains), begin your long, slow descent following Swale Creek into Swale Canyon. In springtime, the wetland pools at the head of the canyon teem with croaking frogs and singing birds. The trail is lined with desert parsley often harboring scads of ticks waiting for a host. Enjoy views up to Stacker Butte and cross the first of many attractively restored trestles, compliments of KTC volunteers. At 1.8 miles pass basalt ledges as you wind down into the canyon. The surroundings are both harsh and beautiful. Shade is at a premium, so slather on the sunscreen. Sage intermixes with willow and dogwood along the creek. At 3.5 miles pass a slick rock

Trestle over Swale Creek near the entrance to Swale Canyon

KLICKITAT RIVER HAUL ROAD

cascade on Swale Creek. At 4 miles traverse a grove of scrappy oaks and tall ponderosa pines. Pass a lovely stretch of creekside before crossing the creek at the fourth trestle at 5.8 miles (elev. 1100 ft.)—a good spot to turn around.

EXTENDING YOUR TRIP

The trail continues across a side creek and, at 7.6 miles, a long trestle. At 7.9 miles pass an old car. At 8.2 miles skirt a rockslide-damaged trestle. Now deep in the canyon, traverse forest and reach the first of the shanties at 9 miles. The way crosses two more trestles before coming to the Wahkiacus trailhead at 11.9 miles.

The 2.2-mile stretch of trail east from Harms Road to Warwick crosses open range and skirts a wildlife-rich marsh providing views of Mount Adams. Unfortunately it's grown over and not yet converted to decent trail tread.

54 Klickitat River Haul Road

RATING/ DIFFICULTY	ROUNDTRIP	ELEV GAIN/ HIGH POINT	SEASON
***/1	7 miles	150 feet/ 650 feet	Year-round

Crowds: 1; **Map:** USGS Wahkiacus; **Contact:** Columbia Land Trust and Washington Department of Fish and Wildlife, Southwest Region; **Notes:** Area subject to closures during high fire danger (consult with Columbia Land Trust). Popular hunting area—don orange during season; **GPS:** N 45° 50.033', W 121° 04.851'

Follow the route of an old company haul road through a beautiful canyon along the untrammeled Klickitat River. Gone are the logging trucks bringing timber to the mill. Thanks to the Columbia Land Trust, this canyon is now once again wild. Walk through groves of stately oaks and pines along the churning river. Watch for wildlife big and small, and savor the serenity and solitude of this special place.

GETTING THERE

From Bingen, drive State Route 14 east for 9.4 miles to Lyle and turn left onto SR 142. (From I-84 exit 64 in Hood River, take the toll bridge into Washington. Turn right onto SR 14, drive 10.7 miles to Lyle, and turn left onto SR 142.) Continue for 17.3 miles and turn left onto the Company Haul Road immediately before the bridge over the Klickitat River. Drive 0.1 mile north and park on the side of road, not blocking the gate (elev. 550 ft.).

ON THE TRAIL

Pass the gate, check out the kiosk, and begin hiking on a paved road (open to bicycles). You're walking on the last stretch of a timber haul road that allowed trucks to whisk logs to a mill in Klickitat via the river corridor. Originally built as a logging rail line and then replaced with pavement in the 1950s, this transportation corridor was built on an important floodplain. In 1994 the Klickitat mill closed, and in 1996 flooding took out a large stretch of the pavement, rendering the road permanently closed. In 2007 the Columbia Land Trust and Yakama Nation Fisheries set out removing 8 miles of roadway and restoring riparian habitat in this dramatic canyon.

Walk north along the wide road along the churning river fed by glaciers high on Mount Adams. Pass through pine, oak, and alder groves. After you pass beneath a set of high-tension wires, SR 142 on the opposite side of the river leaves the canyon. Continue hiking now up a much wilder canyon. At 2

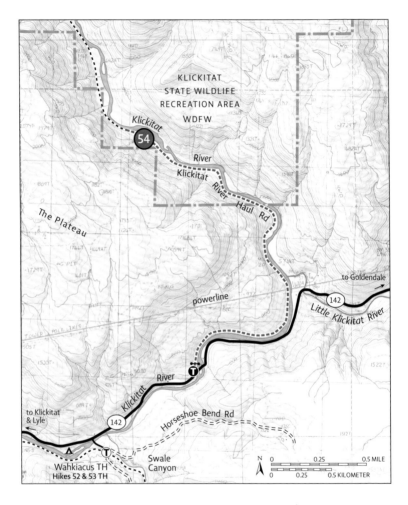

miles the pavement ends near an inviting grassy spot along the river.

Now on trail tread, continue across an outwash area at a river bend. Pass the first of four fence lines and enter the 27,200-acre Klickitat wildlife area, managed by the Washington Department of Fish and Wildlife. The area teems with wildlife and provides important habitat for threatened western gray squirrels and Vaux's swifts. The wildlife area also provides exceptional winter range for black-tailed deer and supports steelhead, spring Chinook, and endangered bull trout.

The trail reaches river level, allowing good viewing for rapid-riding or rock-resting mergansers. Look, too, for bald eagles, kingfishers, and dippers. Continue up the wild canyon, admiring its high, open grassy southern slopes. Soon walk beneath basalt cliffs on a ledge above the roiling river. The trail then pulls away from the river to traverse a pine and fir forest and comes to a gate. Be sure to close the gate upon passing through, as this area is open ranch—and stay on the trail, as private lands abut the trail corridor.

Pass through more oak groves and admire their healthy population of western gray squirrels. At 3.5 miles the trail ends at a marshy backwater along the river. During low river flows, it's possible to get through this area and continue along the former road corridor. The corridor, however, pulls away from the river soon afterward. So for most folks, this is the logical turnaround point.

55 Lyle Cherry Orchard

RATING/ DIFFICULTY	ROUNDTRIP	ELEV GAIN/ HIGH POINT	SEASON
****/3	6.8 miles	1500 feet/ 1220 feet	Year-round

Crowds: 4; **Map:** Green Trails Columbia River Gorge East No. 432S; **Contact:** Friends of the Columbia Gorge; **Notes:** Dogs permitted on leash. Beware of ticks, rattlesnakes, and poison oak. Parking limited, especially on weekends; **GPS:** N 45° 41.185', W 121° 15.950'

If you just want to cherry-pick the best hikes in the Gorge, then by all means, pick this lollipop-loop hike to a century-old cherry orchard. Stemming from the Columbia River,

Desert parsley

this trail winds through a basalt gap to a sprawling grassy bench. It then traverses wide-open slopes ripe with views before topping out at the old orchard sitting plumb above the Gorge. Then follow a new trail back along a ridge to harvest sweet views of Lyle below and the Tom McCall Preserve across the Columbia.

GETTING THERE

From Bingen, drive State Route 14 east for 9.4 miles to Lyle. (From I-84 exit 64 in Hood River, take the toll bridge into Washington. Turn right onto SR 14, drive 10.7 miles to Lyle.) Then continue on SR 14 east for 1.4 more miles to the unmarked trailhead (just after passing through the twin tunnels), located on the left at a wide pullout (elev. 100 ft.).

ON THE TRAIL

Starting in a narrow draw hemmed in by basalt walls, follow the trail upward through a stunted oak forest and soon reach the remnants of the Lyle Convict Road, an unsuccessful precursor to the Columbia River Highway. Veer left on it and come to a trailhead sign where you turn right to continue through the 540-acre Lyle Cherry Orchard Preserve. Owned by Friends of the Columbia Gorge (see sidebar, "Befriending the Gorge" in the western Oregon section), this beautiful property was purchased by the Russell family to protect it from being developed. Nancy Russell (who died in 2008 from Lou Gehrig's disease) founded Friends of the Columbia Gorge and was one of the driving (and most influential) forces behind the establishment of the Columbia River Gorge National Scenic Area in 1986.

Continue upward, crossing basalt scree and then climbing rough terrain teeming with poison oak. At 0.4 mile reach a fantastic overlook of the Columbia complete with intriguing rock formations. Then continue up an open slope where death camas, prairie stars, grass widows, and other showy blossoms begin working their magic on the landscape in the spring. At 0.8 mile, reach a junction (elev. 725 ft.) on a broad, open bench with the Lyle Loop Trail (which you'll be returning on) and an overlook spur.

Continue right on switchbacks before crossing a basalt talus slope. Then steadily ascend, traversing a grassy hillside that grants excellent views of the Rowena Plateau with the tip of Mount Hood in the background. The way then mellows out and reaches an unmarked junction (elev. 1030 ft.) with the Lyle Loop Trail at 1.4 miles. You'll

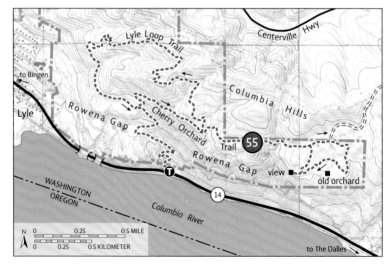

Lyle Cherry Orchard offers a great view of Rowena Gap.

be heading left here on your return, so keep hiking straight to pass an old pasture pool and, shortly afterward, an old fence line. The way then descends 100 feet. Quickly regain the lost elevation and wander through a gorgeous forest of contorted oaks. In spring the forest floor is a stunning gold carpet thanks to a profusion of buttercups.

At 2.1 miles continue straight at a junction. You'll be returning on the right. The trail passes a small vernal pool and comes to an old road (elev. 1100 ft.) at 2.3 miles. The way then loops through an open bluff, the site of an old homestead and cherry orchard. Only one of the cherry trees still survives. Catch good views here east to The Dalles. At 2.8 miles a short spur right leads to a viewpoint west. The way then bends north to close this small loop at 3 miles.

Now head left and at 3.7 miles veer right on the new Lyle Loop Trail that was completed in 2021 by the Washington Trails Association. Gently climb through mature oak forests and grassy openings that grant excellent views west of the Gorge. At 4.3 miles the trail crests a ridge (elev. 1200 ft.) where sweeping views greet you. Look out to the Memaloose Hills and Island, Coyote Wall, Mount Defiance, Dog Mountain, Mount Adams, and more.

The trail then descends, undulating between stunted oak forest and more openings. Views are outstanding. After some switchbacks the trail passes a big ponderosa pine and begins a traverse of steep open slopes above the community of Lyle and below the Lyle marker on the hillside. Wrap around the ridge and come to a familiar broad bench. Flowers are profuse here during the spring. At 5.9 miles veer left where a spur leads right to more viewpoints. At 6 miles return to the main Cherry Orchard Trail. Turn right and return to your start at 6.8 miles.

56 Stacker Butte

RATING/ DIFFICULTY	ROUNDTRIP	ELEV GAIN/ HIGH POINT	SEASON
****/3	5 miles	1150 feet/ 3200 feet	Mar–Nov

Crowds: 2; **Map:** Green Trails Columbia River Gorge East No. 432S; **Contact:** Washington State Department of Natural Resources,

Southeast Region; **Notes:** Dogs prohibited. Discover Pass required; **GPS:** N 45° 41.692', W 121° 05.551'

Hike to a lofty, windswept, flower-carpeted, views-in-every-direction-for-as-far-as-you-can-see high point on the eastern fringe of the Columbia River Gorge. Centerpiece of the 3644-acre Columbia Hills Natural Area Preserve, a land of oak and pine woodlands, grasslands, and rare plants, Stacker Butte stacks up among the area's finest hiking destinations.

GETTING THERE

From Bingen, drive State Route 14 east for 17.4 miles to the junction with US Highway 197. (From The Dalles, follow US 197—exit 87 on I-84—north for 3.3 miles, turning right onto SR 14.) Continue on SR 14 for 0.9 mile, turning left onto gravel Dalles Mountain Road. Proceed 3.4 miles on Dalles Mountain Road (entering Columbia Hills Historical State Park), and turn left just before an old ranch. Pass interpretive displays and continue for 1.4 miles to a small parking area at a gate. Park here, being sure not to block the gate (elev. 2050 ft.). The hike begins on the gated road.

ON THE TRAIL

While this hike consists of walking a service road to a ridge sporting towers of various form and function, in no way does that diminish the journey. The road is rarely driven, and you'll hardly notice the towers. You'll be too busy looking out at nonstop horizon-spanning views. And if you come in April or May, you'll be awestruck by one of the finest floral shows in the entire Pacific Northwest. Arrowleaf balsamroot, lupines, paintbrushes, phlox, larkspurs, desert larkspurs, and others paint this Columbia Hills peak in a radiant array of color.

Before beginning, remember that your four-legged friend is not permitted here, and keep your feet from wandering off the road. Travel is permitted only on the preserve's roadways to help protect one of Washington's last large remnants of Idaho fescue and houndstongue hawkweed grassland communities. The preserve also harbors these three rare plants: obscure buttercup, Douglas' draba, and hot-rock penstemon.

The road climbs steadily across wide-open slopes. Did you pack sunscreen and a wind shell? Views grow increasingly better with each step. From March to May, the flowers are profuse. And while you're busy admiring and identifying flora, don't forget the area's fauna, among them scampering ground squirrels, melodious meadowlarks, and flittering butterflies.

At 1.1 miles (elev. 2650 ft.), a jeep track on the right diverts 0.6 mile to Oak Spring, one of the many springs that dot the Columbia Hills. Feel free to wander this road. The main route continues left, cresting the ridge (elev. 2875 ft.) and reaching a large tower at 1.75 miles. The summit is now in view. Continue climbing another 0.75 mile to reach Stacker Butte's 3200-foot summit, occupied by an oddly arranged and intriguing aviation tower.

Cast it a glance (but stay away from it), and then let your eyes run wild across the horizons: South to The Dalles, endless wheat fields, and Mount Hood pointing to the heavens. West to the heart of the Gorge, with Mount Defiance shadowing surrounding peaks and ridges. East to massive wind turbines across the Columbia Hills. And finally set your sights north to Mount Adams, Mount Rainier, Goat Rocks, the Simcoe Mountains, and directly below to Swale Canyon—a large rift in the Centerville Valley.

EXTENDING YOUR TRIP

Continue walking the service road west along the windy open crest for 0.8 mile to another set of communication towers. You can then walk on the road beyond for another 1.5 miles before coming to private property.

Arrowleaf balsamroot brightens up the Columbia Hills.

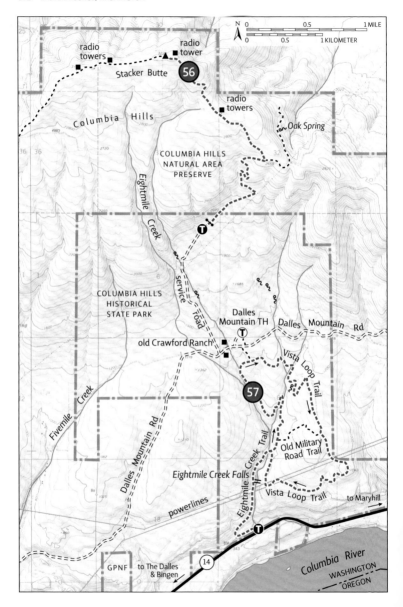

57 Crawford Oaks

RATING/ DIFFICULTY	ROUNDTRIP	ELEV GAIN/ HIGH POINT	SEASON
****/3	6.6 miles	850 feet/ 1200 feet	Mar–Nov

Crowds: 4; **Map:** Green Trails Columbia River Gorge East No. 432S; **Contact:** Columbia Hills Historical State Park; **Notes:** Dogs permitted on leash. Discover Pass required. Trails open to horses and mountain bikes; **GPS:** N 45° 39.426', W 121° 05.249'

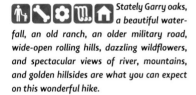 *Stately Garry oaks, a beautiful waterfall, an old ranch, an older military road, wide-open rolling hills, dazzling wildflowers, and spectacular views of river, mountains, and golden hillsides are what you can expect on this wonderful hike.*

GETTING THERE

From Bingen, drive State Route 14 east for 17.4 miles to the junction with US Highway 197. (From The Dalles, follow US 197—exit 87 on I-84—north for 3.3 miles, turning right onto SR 14.) Continue on SR 14 for 3.6 miles, turning left into the trailhead parking (elev. 375 ft.). Privy available.

ON THE TRAIL

Named for the family that homesteaded this tract in 1878, this area has a long human history starting with various tribes. For much of the late 19th and throughout the 20th century the area was a sheep and cattle ranch. In 2003 it became part of the now 3637-acre Columbia Hills Historical State Park.

Start your hike on the gravel entry road, closed to traffic. Immediately start enjoying views of Horsethief Butte (Hike 58), the Columbia River, rolling hillsides, and steep rimrock. Stop at the interpretive signs along the way and at pretty Eightmile Creek Falls tumbling down a basalt wall at 0.4 mile. Then continue following the road-trail through meadows and along oak-lined Eightmile Creek.

At 1 mile rock hop across the creek and reach a junction (elev. 760 ft.). You will be returning from the right on the Vista Loop Trail. So continue straight on the Old Military Road Trail. This trail follows part of the Fort Dalles to Fort Simcoe Military Road, built in 1855–56 to transport supplies between Fort Dalles on the Columbia River and Fort Simcoe north of the Simcoe Mountains in what is now the Yakama Nation.

At 1.3 miles reach a junction. The Old Military Road Trail heads right for 0.4 mile to connect with the Vista Loop Trail, offering a shorter loop option. Head left on the Eightmile Creek Trail and follow a tributary of the cascading creek into a small ravine before rock hopping across it. The trail then traverses a hillside and starts climbing above an oak-harboring ravine cut by Eightmile Creek.

The way then bends east to walk along a fence line of the old Crawford Ranch now visible. Views across the open hillside out to Mounts Hood and Jefferson are excellent. At 2.5 miles come to a junction (elev. 1200 ft.). The trail left leads 0.2 mile to the Dalles Mountain trailhead (alternative start).

Continue straight now on the Vista Loop Trail and traverse former pasture, dipping twice to cross two tributaries. The way then switchbacks and intersects an old ranch road. Bear right and walk along a broad open ridge, enjoying sweeping views of the golden Columbia Hills north to the Columbia River south and Cascades west. At 3.8 miles continue straight at a junction with the Old Military Road Trail.

Grass widows add the first pop of color to the stark landscape in the spring.

Pass under a powerline and descend to traverse a plateau above rimrock outcroppings. Pass a huge glacial erratic and continue to delight in extensive views. And if you're here in the spring, the floral show will blow you away. Grass widows begin blooming in February followed by an array of gorgeous flowers as spring progresses. Listen for meadowlark song against the background highway buzz. The way then bends north, passes back under the powerlines again and follows an old ranch road. At 5.6 miles return to a familiar junction. Head left, returning to the trailhead in 1 more mile.

EXTENDING YOUR TRIP

Hike to the Dalles Mountain trailhead and then walk west 0.25 mile on Dalles Mountain Road to check out the structures, artifacts, and displays at the old Crawford Ranch.

58 Horsethief Butte

RATING/ DIFFICULTY	ROUNDTRIP	ELEV GAIN/ HIGH POINT	SEASON
***/2	1.2 miles	200 feet/ 498 feet	Year-round

Crowds: 3; **Map:** Green Trails Columbia River Gorge East No. 432S; **Contact:** Columbia Hills Historical State Park; **Notes:** Dogs permitted (but not recommended) on leash. Discover Pass required. Watch for rattlesnakes; **GPS:** N 45° 39.012', W 121° 05.964'

A prominent landmark along the Columbia, Horsethief Butte has played host to Native Americans, Lewis and Clark, countless budding climbers, and scads of inquisitive hikers but probably no horse thieves. Created by ancient lava flows and carved by floods of biblical proportions, the butte is an excellent place to contemplate the region's fascinating natural history.

GETTING THERE

From Bingen, drive State Route 14 east for 17.4 miles to the junction with US Highway 197. (From The Dalles, follow US 197—exit 87 on I-84—north for 3.3 miles, turning right onto SR 14.) Continue on SR 14 for 2.8 miles (1.2 miles beyond the Horsethief Lake Campground entrance) to the trailhead (elev. 300 ft.) on your right. Privy available.

ON THE TRAIL

The US Army Corps of Engineers, romanticized by 1950s Western movies, bestowed the name Horsethief on this basaltic monolith. While rustlers probably never used the cavernous butte as a lair, Native peoples frequented it for spiritual rituals. The butte, as well as other parts of the sprawling Columbia Hills Historical State Park, contains numerous pictographs (paintings) and petroglyphs (carvings), among the oldest in the Northwest. Respect all artifacts and area closures within the park.

The hike to the just-shy-of-500-foot butte is short, but you can easily spend hours exploring its many aspects. In spring, the stark walls are decorated with bouquets of flowers. Lizards and snakes (namely bull snakes, a nonvenomous species oft mistaken for a rattler) sun and scurry on the warm ledges. The butte is popular with practicing rock climbers too.

At 0.1 mile come to a junction. The trail left leads into the butte, but it involves some scrambling over loose rock. There's an easier approach, so continue right, skirting along the base of the butte. In spring this sandy, rocky bench comes alive with death camas. At 0.3 mile come to another junction. The trail right continues 0.2 mile along the butte's base to two overlooks above the railroad tracks and Horsethief Lake. Consider checking them out and then return to this spot.

Now take the trail up the butte, climbing 0.1 mile up scree to a gap in the butte and a labyrinth of paths. Feel free to explore. To reach the top of the butte, look for a somewhat trodden way heading southeast up a narrow cleft. You'll need to use your hands, but it's not difficult nor dangerous. Once over this obstacle, follow a path angling northeast to the butte's summit. It's about 0.2 mile from the gap. Enjoy superb views of the Columbia River, Columbia Hills, and Horsethief Lake

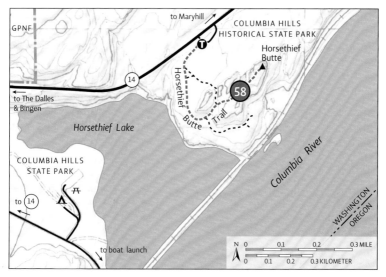

Horsethief Butte is part of a remnant lava flow.

with Mount Hood rising behind it. Return or explore some more.

EXTENDING YOUR TRIP
At Horsethief Lake arrange for a guided hike to the enchanting pictograph *She-Who-Watches*. Visit parks.wa.gov/489/Columbia-Hills for details.

59 Observatory Hill

RATING/ DIFFICULTY	ROUNDTRIP	ELEV GAIN/ HIGH POINT	SEASON
***/2	2.4 miles	350 feet/ 2100 feet	Year-round

Crowds: 2; **Map:** map at trailhead; **Contact:** City of Goldendale Public Works; **Notes:** Dogs permitted on leash. Trails open to mountain bikes; **GPS:** N 45° 50.074', W 120° 49.049'

Wander on a wonderful little trail system on the south slopes of the hill housing the Goldendale Observatory. Three well-built loops wind through oaks, grasses, and—in spring— bountiful blossoming wilflowers. Take in views of Mount Hood, the Columbia Hills, and Columbia Gorge peaks. Plan for a visit to the observatory while hiking and shoot for the stars.

GETTING THERE
From The Dalles follow I-84 east for 19 miles to exit 104 (Biggs Junction). Then drive US Highway 97 north for 13.2 miles and turn left on SR 142 in Goldendale. Proceed for 1 mile and turn right onto N. Columbus Avenue. Continue for 0.6 mile and bear right onto Observatory Drive. After 0.3 mile turn left into trailhead parking (elev. 1900 ft.) near the water tower.

ON THE TRAIL
Bordering the Goldendale Observatory State Park Heritage Site, the volunteer-built Observatory Hill Trails consist of about five miles of looping trails on a 200-acre tract of city-owned property. Signage could use some help, so take a photo of the map at the trailhead.

While you can set out on the 0.7-mile Green, 2-mile Blue, or 2.2-mile Black loops (colors corresponding to their difficulty from easy to strenuous, although there is nothing strenuous here), I suggest the following combo of the three for an introduction to the area. Locate the trailhead to the east of the water tower and follow the trail closest to the access road. Soon cross Observatory Drive and come to a junction at 0.1 mile. You will be returning from the right, so head left.

Now on the Green Loop, enjoy strolling on a wide and well-manicured path. Traverse open oak groves that burst with beautiful blossoms in the spring. The purple blues of the lupines, larkspurs, and bachelor buttons (cornflowers) are particularly striking. At 0.4 mile come to a small ledge granting a view east over US 97 and out to golden hillsides.

The way then bends north. Stay left at a junction. Shortly afterward is another junction. Here head right to connect with the Blue and Black Loops. Now ascend along a ridge crest, climbing higher on Observatory Hill. At 0.7 mile the Blue Loop heads left. Stay right on the Black trail and keep climbing. At 1 mile the trail crosses Observatory Drive at the entrance to the Goldendale Observatory State Park Heritage Site. Walk

right on the road and then a short trail for 0.1 mile to the observatory (elev. 2100 ft.), which contains one of the nation's largest public telescopes.

Then return 0.1 mile to the Black Loop and hike west, traversing a slope of flowers and oaks with window views south of Goldendale. At 1.6 miles come to a junction at a fence line. Here take in a great view of Mount Hood, the Columbia Hills, and the Gorge. Notice the lack of plant diversity on the slopes used for grazing on the other side of the fence.

Now head southeast, taking the trail heading downhill. Shortly afterward come to another junction and stay right on the Black Loop for a steeper descent, passing small ledges and more lovely oak groves. The trail

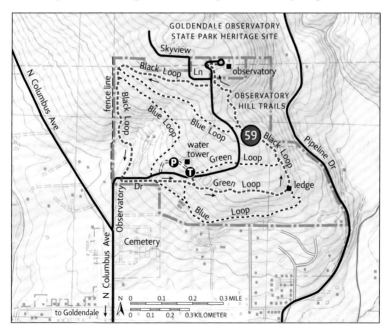

Garry oak

utilizes an old road and then crosses Observatory Drive at 2 miles. Now turn left and veer left at a junction, coming back to the Green Loop at 2.3 miles. Return left 0.1 mile to the trailhead, or go explore more trail segments.

60 Brooks Memorial State Park

RATING/ DIFFICULTY	ROUNDTRIP	ELEV GAIN/ HIGH POINT	SEASON
**/2	3.4 miles	650 feet/ 2800 feet	Apr–Nov

Crowds: 1; **Map:** USGS Satus Pass; **Contact:** Brooks Memorial State Park; **Notes:** Discover Pass required. Dogs permitted on-leash. Beware of ticks; **GPS:** N 45° 56.804', W 120° 40.115'

Located in the forested foothills of the Simcoe Mountains, high above the far eastern reaches of the Columbia River Gorge, Brooks Memorial State Park contains much floral diversity. Take to its quiet trails in spring and summer to admire a wide array of wildflowers. Come in the autumn for a colorful display of deciduous leaves.

GETTING THERE
From The Dalles follow I-84 east for 19 miles to exit 104 (Biggs Junction). Then drive US Highway 97 north for 24.7 miles and turn right into Brooks Memorial State Park. Continue 0.3 mile toward the group camping area to trailhead parking (elev. 2550 ft.). Privy available.

ON THE TRAIL
Named for Judge Nelson B. Brooks, a prominent early settler in nearby Goldendale, Brooks Memorial State Park is a fitting memorial to this civil servant. The park consists of nearly 700 acres complete with a campground and Environmental Learning Center (ELC). It also contains several miles of old roads and trails that are lightly hiked.

Start your hike in a meadow alongside the East Prong Little Klickitat River. The way then bends east, enters forest, and comes to a junction at a park road and the Brooks Nature Trail at 0.2 mile. You will be returning from the left, so head right and parallel the park road, traversing a ponderosa pine forest. At 0.3 mile come to junction with Lady

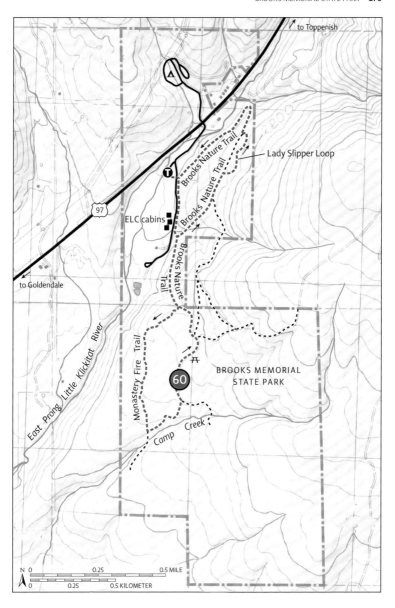

to Toppenish

Brooks Nature Trail

Lady Slipper Loop

Brooks Nature Trail

97

ELC cabins

Brooks Nature Trail

to Goldendale

Brooks Nature Trail

Monastery Fire Trail

60

BROOKS MEMORIAL
STATE PARK

East Prong Little Klickitat River

Camp Creek

N 0   0.25   0.5 MILE

0   0.25   0.5 KILOMETER

Lupines along the Brooks Nature Trail

Slipper Loop. Head straight for a lollipop loop before coming back for this one.

Continue south on the dirt park road, slowly ascending and pulling away from the ELC cabins. At 0.6 mile come to a junction at a gate. Now head right on the Monastery Fire Trail through an open forest of oaks, pines, and Douglas-firs. In spring lupines add purple and a delightful fragrance to the forest.

The way levels out after a couple of little dips and traverses a forest with snags and scarred trees from the 2011 Monastery Complex Fire, named for the adjacent Saint John the Forerunner Greek Orthodox Monastery. The 48-acre monastic order of women operates a popular bakery on the premise, which is a good spot for an after-hike snack.

At 1.2 miles the trail reaches the edge of a large meadow near Camp Creek. Here the tread fades, and travel can be a little tricky. Look for remnants of tread on the bluff above the creek and head left, staying above the creek to reach an old road at 1.4 miles. Now head left following the road across a sprawling meadow that bursts with wildflowers including death camas, meadow larkspurs, cluster lilies, and scores of other showy species. Come to a picnic table at meadow's edge, and enjoy the blossoms and views of distant ridges and peaks.

Then continue on the road, coming to a junction with two other park roads at 1.7 miles. Head left and start descending, passing the Monastery Fire Trail junction and returning to the Brooks Nature Trail at 2.1 miles. Now head right and make a short, steep climb in pleasant fir forest. At 2.4 miles come to the Lady Slipper Loop junction. Head right and look for mountain lady's slippers, one of three endemic lady's slipper orchids in the western United States.

At 2.6 miles leave the Lady Slipper Loop and old road and follow the single track Brooks Nature Trail. After bending back south, the trail travels through a patch of cool old growth along a steep slope above the East Prong Little Klickitat River. At 3.2 miles return to the first junction. Head right 0.2 mile to return to the trailhead.

EXTENDING YOUR TRIP

Explore the other old roads in the park. Note that some travel through private property. Respect all postings and closures.

61 Crow Butte

RATING/ DIFFICULTY	ROUNDTRIP	ELEV GAIN/ HIGH POINT	SEASON
***/2	2.2 miles	380 feet/ 670 feet	Mar 15– Oct 15

Crowds: 1; **Map:** USGS Crow Butte; **Contact:** Crow Butte Park (Port of Benton); **Notes:** $10 day-use fee per car. Dogs permitted on-leash. Watch for rattlesnakes. Park open Mar 15– Oct 15; **GPS:** N 45° 51.066', W°119° 51.198'

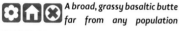 *A broad, grassy basaltic butte far from any population centers, this landmark—culturally significant to local tribes—has much to crow over. Situated on a 1500-acre island in the Columbia River, in the shadow of the Horse Heaven Hills, birdlife here is prolific both in numbers and species. The views are good, too, from the river below to the golden hills, plains, and fields embracing it.*

GETTING THERE

From the junction of US Highway 97 and State Route 14, near Maryhill State Park, drive SR 14 east for 54 miles to Sonava Road at milepost 155 and turn left. (If coming from the east, take exit 131 (Plymouth) off of I-82, drive west on SR 14 for 26 miles, and turn right on Sonava Road.) Then immediately turn right onto W. Crow Butte Road and drive under SR 14, reaching the park day-use area

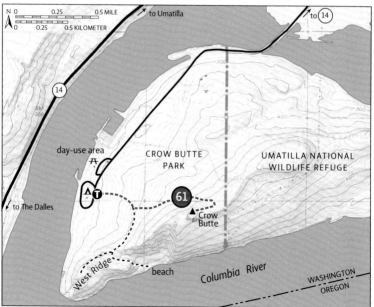

Basalt outcroppings atop Crow Butte

in 2 miles. Park here. The trailhead (elev. 290 ft.) is located in the camping area. Privy and water available.

ON THE TRAIL

Most visitors to the Port of Benton's lovely 275-acre Crow Butte Park (a former Washington State Park, removed with others from the state park system during the Locke administration's 2002 budget woes) never step foot on Crow Butte. They're drawn more to the park's busy campground and marina.

From the day-use area walk 0.2 mile on the road to the campground loop and locate the trail near campsite number 42. Leaving the park's manicured and shaded lawns, the trail enters a grassy, nearly treeless environment fully exposed to the sun and wind. Spring and fall are ideal times to visit, with agreeable temperatures and plenty of migrating birds. The butte is a bird-watcher's paradise, with a dizzying array of species: Bullock's orioles,

loggerhead shrikes, black-headed grosbeaks, Caspian and Forster's terns, American avocets, black-necked stilts, least and western sandpipers, dunlins, Virginia rails, and marsh and rock wrens, among others.

At 0.2 mile from the trailhead come to a junction (elev. 350 ft.). The trail right heads to a secluded beach and West Ridge (see below). For Crow Butte, continue straight on a much lighter-traveled route. Traverse a slope of phlox, prickly pear cactus, and arrowleaf balsamroot. At 0.7 mile, upon reaching the butte's northern ridge, locate light tread heading right across basalt outcroppings. Follow it to the 670-foot summit at 0.9 mile (1.1 miles from day-use area). Although powerlines extend across the butte, the view is quite sublime—from the broad vast flats east to the golden hills north and emerging uplands west. Watch raptors ride the thermals above. You are standing on sacred land to the Umatilla peoples. A land that has seen much change since the Crow family homesteaded here in the 1850s.

Crow Butte Island is anthropogenic, created from flooding by the construction of the John Day Dam. The park and adjacent Umatilla National Wildlife Refuge were created to mitigate some of the dam's environmental impact. The surroundings, however, continue to convert to vineyards, wheat fields, wind turbine farms, and industrial parks.

EXTENDING YOUR TRIP

From the junction hike 0.3 mile south to another junction (elev. 420 ft.). Then hike right for 0.2 mile along West Ridge to a good view of the campground below. Or hike left for 0.3 mile, dropping 175 feet to a small, secluded sandy beach on the Columbia River.

Opposite: Oregon's iconic Multnomah Falls (Hike 69)

western gorge, oregon

Classic scenery and dramatic landscapes are what you'll experience in the Columbia River Gorge, a deep canyon cut by the West's mightiest river through one of its largest and most rugged mountain chains. And on the Oregon side of the river in the Gorge's western half, nothing epitomizes this region more than waterfalls. Perhaps nowhere else in the country is there such a high concentration of cascades, including Multnomah, the state's highest. Here, too, you will find some of the oldest and best loved trails in America, delivering you to old-growth forests, mossy ravines, thundering chasms, breathtaking overlooks, historical sites, and lofty summits.

And this entire splendor is within an hour's drive of more than 2.5 million people!

62 Sandy River Delta

RATING/ DIFFICULTY	ROUNDTRIP	ELEV GAIN/ HIGH POINT	SEASON
**/1	3.5 miles	negligible/ 40 feet	Year-round

Crowds: 5; **Map:** Green Trails Columbia River Gorge West No. 428S; **Contact:** Columbia River Gorge National Scenic Area; **Notes:** Northwest Forest Pass or Interagency Pass required. Dogs permitted off-leash except for on and within 100 feet of the Confluence

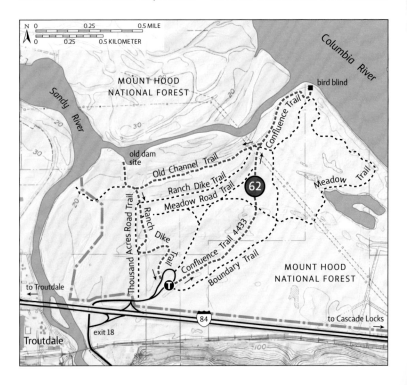

A colonnade of cottonwoods along the Sandy River

Trail, where they need to be leashed. Confluence Trail ADA accessible; **GPS:** N 45° 32.757', W 122° 22.427'

The Sandy River Delta is quite possibly the largest dog park in the Pacific Northwest, where thousands of Portlanders and their four-legged companions come to frolic rain or shine, year-round. But if you're not fond of sharing the trail with scores of off-leash furballs, it's best to wag your tail elsewhere. Otherwise, enjoy exploring nearly 8 miles of level trails along sloughs, across meadows and deciduous forest, and to beaches on the western front of the Columbia River Gorge National Scenic Area.

GETTING THERE

From Portland, follow I-84 east and take exit 18 (Lewis and Clark State Park). After 0.2 mile turn right at a stop sign and proceed under the freeway, continuing 0.4 mile to the trailhead (elev. 20 ft.). Privy available.

ON THE TRAIL

Once a cattle ranch, the 1500-acre Sandy River Delta property was acquired by the US Forest Service in 1991. The flat, lush bottomland was formed by mudflows traveling down the Sandy River from Mount Hood. In this unique part of the Columbia River Gorge National Scenic Area, the Forest Service has been eradicating invasive plants and working on a management plan to help restore this ecosystem to a more natural state. The good news for hikers is that the Delta contains several interconnecting trails, including the 1.3-mile hard-surface, wheelchair-accessible Confluence Trail. This hike follows that trail and a couple others for a good introductory loop.

From the busy parking area, head out northeast on Confluence Trail No. 4433, a multiuse path also open to bikes, horses, and wheelchairs. Your canine companion should be on-leash on this trail. The way skirts a field edge of invasive blackberry backed by rows of oaks and cottonwoods. Views are good across the pasture to Mount Hood and Larch Mountain. Scores of primitive, often muddy, and brushy trails radiate in every direction from this and the other official trails within the delta. Explore at will.

At 0.7 mile, after crossing under a set of transmission wires, reach a junction with the MeadowRoad Trail, and shortly afterward the Boundary Trail, Ranch Dike Trail, and Old Channel Trail. You'll be veering off on the Old Channel Trail on your return. Continue on the Confluence Trail, traversing a restoration area through old dunes and along a channel of the Sandy River. At 1.3 miles reach the bird blind. It depicts the 134 species of plants and animals documented by Lewis and Clark and was designed by Maya Lin, who created the Vietnam Veterans Memorial in Washington, DC.

Scan the surroundings for some of those species, and then retrace your steps 0.5 mile to the Old Channel Trail. Now follow this path west (right) along a shrub-and-cottonwood-lined old river channel, coming to the Thousand Acres Road Trail at 2.4 miles. Before heading back to the trailhead left, follow the old road right. At 2.5 miles bear right and come to the site of the old Sandy River Delta dam at 2.7 miles. The dam was built in 1931 and removed in 2013, reviving a stagnant slough into a healthy river channel.

Now return on the old road. At 3.3 miles leave it left for the Ranch Dike Trail, which leads back to the parking lot in 0.2 mile.

EXTENDING YOUR TRIP

Definitely explore the delta's other trails. For a slightly longer loop around the delta,

follow the Boundary Trail (which can get really muddy in the wet months) to the Old Channel Trail and Thousand Acres Road for a circuit of 3.7 miles.

63 Oxbow Regional Park

RATING/ DIFFICULTY	ROUNDTRIP	ELEV GAIN/ HIGH POINT	SEASON
***/2	4.2 miles	300 feet/ 230 feet	Year-round

Crowds: 3; **Maps:** Green Trails Columbia River Gorge West No. 428S; Oxbow Regional Park; **Contact:** Oxbow Regional Park; **Notes:** Day-use fee $5 per vehicle (pay at entrance, credit cards accepted). Dogs prohibited. Note seasonal park operating hours; **GPS:** N 45° 29.474', W 122° 17.792'

Born of glacial ice on Oregon's highest summit, the Sandy River flows for more than 50 miles on its way to the Columbia. Captain Clark (of Lewis and Clark fame) attempted to wade it back in November of 1805, but as he noted in his journal, to his dismay he "found the bottom a quick sand and impassable." But you don't need to worry about crossing the Sandy when you have miles of lovely trail to hike beside it in this 1200-acre park. A small gorge, big trees, inviting sandbars, and high bluffs are added incentives.

GETTING THERE

From Portland, take exit 17 (Troutdale) off of I-84 and follow the frontage road for 0.6 mile, turning right onto SW 257th Avenue. Continue south on this major arterial for 2.9 miles, turning left onto NE Division Street. (Alternatively, reach this junction from exit 19 on I-205, following NE Division Street east.) Continue east for 2.7 miles, bearing right on SE Oxbow Drive. Then in 2.3 miles turn left onto SE Oxbow Parkway. Proceed 1.6 miles to the park entrance station, and then continue 1.5 miles on the park road, turning left into the large parking area beside the Alder group picnic area (elev. 100 ft.). Privy available.

ON THE TRAIL

With nearly seventy Wild and Scenic River classifications, Oregon leads the nation. The Sandy is one of them, with its upper and lower sections designated Wild and Scenic to forever remain free-flowing. Metro's Oxbow Regional Park protects 1200 acres of prime riverbank, bluff, and riparian forest on the lower Sandy where it exits a small gorge

into a series of oxbows. Mere minutes from metropolitan Portland, the park is popular with anglers, rafters, kayakers, campers, equestrians, and hikers. Laced with 12 miles of trail, Oxbow can easily occupy explorers for days. This loop hike is a nice introduction.

From the Alder group picnic area, head west along a bluff above the river and immediately enter a substantial grove of old-growth forest. Sticking close to the river, ignore several side trails that lead left for shortcuts and right for river access, and come to trail marker "C" at the Happy Creek picnic area (alternative trailhead) at 0.5 mile. Now continue along the river and cross the park road at 0.6 mile, coming to trail junction "B." The trail to the right parallels the road for

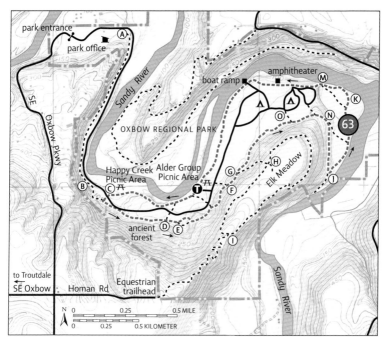

The trail runs along a bluff above the Sandy River.

0.8 mile, passing a plaque commemorating the cleanup after the great flood of 1996.

Head left instead and travel east, paralleling the road and gently climbing, passing through magnificent groves of ancient cedars and firs. Stay right at two junctions where trails lead to post D (alternative trailhead). At 1.2 miles come to marker "E," where the trail diverges. Go either way—the paths soon meet up. At 1.5 miles, after a small climb and dip, intersect a closed-to-traffic dirt road at marker "F." For a shortened loop, head left 0.1 mile back to your vehicle—otherwise, continue right and at 1.6 miles reach marker "G" at a junction (elev. 225 ft.).

Turn left, back onto trail (now open to bikes and horses), gently descending through attractive second-growth forest. Ignore side trails leading left to the campground, and at 2.3 miles come to marker "N" (elev. 125 ft.). Turn right and at 2.5 miles come to a junction at marker "J" (elev. 100 ft.). The trail right follows the river a short way before petering out. Turn left and follow

the river downstream, passing gravel bars and spots along the riverbank that encourage lounging.

Stick to the trail closest to the river, ignoring side trails left that lead to the campground. Come to marker "M" at 3.2 miles. Here a spur leads right to the river. Continue left climbing a bluff (elev. 130 ft.) to the campground. Riverbank erosion here has eaten into the trail, requiring a new route over an old camp road. Walk it and then drop off the bluff, arriving at the boat ramp (elev. 90 ft.) at 3.6 miles. Climb again and then pass through picnic areas perched above the river. Here hike along the bluff edge, enjoying excellent views of the Wild and Scenic Sandy River and reaching your vehicle at 4.2 miles.

EXTENDING YOUR TRIP

Follow that previously crossed closed-to-traffic dirt road 0.2 mile up to Elk Meadow on Alder Ridge (elev. 440 ft.). From there, hike a 1.4-mile nearly level loop, brushing the rim of a gorge above the river. Catch some good but limited views. Also consider hiking the challenging 0.5-mile trail up Alder Ridge to the Equestrian trailhead (elev. 700 ft.).

64 Rooster Rock State Park

RATING/ DIFFICULTY	LOOP	ELEV GAIN/ HIGH POINT	SEASON
**/2	3.2 miles	250 feet/ 210 feet	Year-round

Crowds: 2; **Maps:** Green Trails Columbia River Gorge West No. 428S; Rooster Rock State Park; **Contact:** Rooster Rock State Park; **Notes:** Day-use fee $5 per vehicle (pay at entrance, credit cards accepted). Dogs permitted on-leash; **GPS:** N 45° 32.844', W 122° 13.762'

Known for its miles of gorgeous sandy beaches on the Columbia River, Rooster Rock State Park's quiet trails will delight hikers. Hikers offended by human flesh may want to steer clear of the park's eastern beach—it's one of Oregon's two officially sanctioned clothing-optional beaches, so you'll need to be bare aware while exploring it.

GETTING THERE
From Portland, follow I-84 east and take exit 25 (Rooster Rock State Park). After 0.5 mile pass the park entrance booth and turn right, proceeding 0.4 mile to the farthest-east parking lot. The trail begins to the right of the restroom at the southeast corner of the parking lot (elev. 75 ft.). Privy available.

ON THE TRAIL
Lewis and Clark camped here in 1805, and early settlers named the park's prominent and phallic rock after a different name for a male chicken. It was later changed to

"Rooster" to be less offensive. Several trails take off from the field behind the restroom. The one you want is the Forest Loop Trail, the wide one farthest south next to the Frisbee golf course. Quickly enter forest and stay on the main path, avoiding side trails to Frisbee golf stations for the first 0.25 mile. The trail takes to the spine of a small rolling ridge, traveling through a lush, attractive forest of oak and maple. Mosses drape the hardwoods, while ferns line the way. Winter's lack of cover allows for window views out across the Columbia to Cape Horn.

While the trail makes no significant elevation gain, its constant dipping and climbing along the ridge crest means you'll gain some elevation along the way. Trail runners may find this loop quite enjoyable. At about 0.4 mile you'll pass a small side trail, providing a shortcut. Continue straight on a roller coaster course through hip-high horsetails. At about 0.9 mile, catch glimpses through the trees of Sand Island, with its beautiful dunes.

Mossy, fern-draped maples

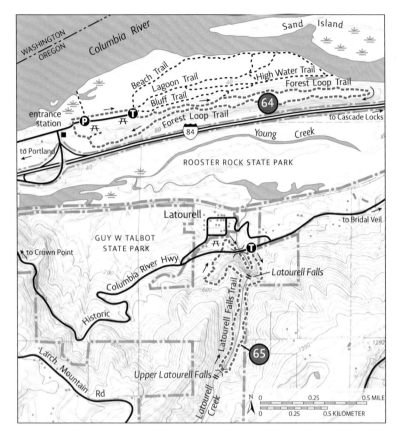

At 1.2 miles the trail loops back at the edge of a grassy slope (elev. 150 ft.). Enjoy the view east of the Columbia River, Angels Rest, Beacon Rock, and Hamilton Mountain. Then continue westward up and down through a forest of attractive contorted hardwoods. At 2.1 miles reach the highest point along the way (elev. 210 ft.). At 2.4 miles return to the Frisbee golf course, with shortcuts back to the trailhead. The main trail continues straight, dropping off the ridge to a meadow by the highway, with good views up to Crown Point. The trail concludes at 2.9 miles at the Group "A" picnic area (elev. 40 ft.). From here follow a paved path to the large parking lot and then walk east 0.3 mile to retrieve your vehicle.

EXTENDING YOUR TRIP

Consider a side trip to Rooster Rock's "Columbia River buffs." The park's beaches are absolutely stunning. Follow the Lagoon

Trail from the left of the restroom down a staircase to the floodplain. Here the Beach Trail leads 0.4 mile left to beaches while the Lagoon Trail continues east 0.6 mile to beaches. The Bluff Trail leads to the High Water Trail terminating in 0.9 mile at a river channel. In summer it's possible to wade across the channel to the spectacular dunes on Sand Island.

65 Latourell Falls

RATING/ DIFFICULTY	LOOP	ELEV GAIN/ HIGH POINT	SEASON
****/2	2.3 miles	650 feet/ 660 feet	Year-round

Crowds: 4; **Map:** Green Trails Columbia River Gorge West No. 428S; **Contact:** Guy W. Talbot State Park; **Notes:** Dogs permitted on-leash; **GPS:** N 45° 32.323', W 122° 13.062'

The closest to Portland of the Columbia River Gorge's major waterfalls, Latourell consists of two spectacular falls. The lower one plunges 224 feet over columnar basalt cliffs and is among the most beautiful waterfalls in the state. The upper waterfall plunges into a horsetail and is not as visited as the lower falls.

GETTING THERE
From Portland, follow I-84 east to exit 28 (Bridal Veil) and proceed 0.4 mile to a junction with the Historic Columbia River Highway. Turn right and continue 2.6 miles to the trailhead (elev. 190 ft.). Privy available.

ON THE TRAIL
Following the lead of other early area homesteaders and civic leaders, in 1929 Guy and Geraldine Talbot donated the land surrounding a pair of gorgeous waterfalls to the Oregon State Parks system. The falls were named for Joseph Latourell, who settled in the area in 1857.

Now follow a paved path 300 feet to a wonderful viewpoint of the breathtaking lower falls. The majority of Latourell's spectators only lumber this far. So carry on, continuing left and leaving the pavement to head upward to gain different perspectives of the lower falls, including a behind-the-scenes look at the plummeting cascade. From a bluff above, enjoy views, too, out to Mounts Pleasant and Zion in Washington.

Lower Latourell Falls

Then walk along Latourell Creek through patches of big firs and moss-draped maples. At 0.4 mile come to an unmarked junction (elev. 370 ft.) with a trail leading right to cross the creek, offering a shortcut to this loop. In winter, however, it may be difficult to cross the swollen waterway.

The loop continues left, working its way into a tight, lush ravine. Cross numerous side creeks (bridged) and attractive cedar groves along the way. At 0.9 mile come to a spray-blasted bridge (elev. 650 ft.) over Latourell Creek just beneath the two-tiered 120-foot horsetail-like upper falls. Savor the mist in warm weather, retreat otherwise. The curious may want to get a closer look of the basalt grotto behind the falls.

The trail continues, now looping back to follow Latourell Creek on its west bank. Traversing steep slopes high above the tumbling waterway, gradually descend and reach the unmarked shortcut trail (elev. 450 ft.) at 1.4 miles. Veer left, climbing to the rim (elev. 550 ft.) of the lower falls basin. A spur steeply drops right to an exposed viewpoint above the falls. Exercise extreme caution—it's a potentially dangerous spot.

After passing a much safer viewpoint, the trail makes a wide swing west before switchbacking east at an oddly shaped and much-admired tree. Gradually losing elevation, the trail reaches the Historic Columbia River Highway. Carefully cross the road here to the park's picnic grounds (elev. 160 ft.) and follow a paved trail beside Latourell Creek underneath a 1914-built bridge, one of the historic highway's remaining concrete arched bridges. Then arrive at the base of the lower falls, one of the most glorious places in the Gorge. Stand mesmerized, staring at streams of silver water plummeting over an amphitheater of columnar basalt.

Then content, cross the creek on a bridge and climb back to the trailhead.

66 Bridal Veil Falls

RATING/ DIFFICULTY	ROUNDTRIP	ELEV GAIN/ HIGH POINT	SEASON
**/1	1 mile	190 feet/ 250 feet	Year-round

Crowds: 3; **Map:** Green Trails Columbia River Gorge West No. 428S; **Contact:** Bridal Veil Falls State Scenic Viewpoint; **Notes:** Dogs permitted on-leash; **GPS:** N 45° 33.209', W 122° 10.967'

A hidden, often overlooked waterfall, Bridal Veil Falls is a wonderful destination for cataract connoisseurs of all ages. The trail is short, making it the ideal add-on to your day after doing one of the many longer nearby hikes. And while the falls is the prime attraction in this small state park, don't skip the bluff-top interpretive loop with its good views and, in late spring, flowering camas.

GETTING THERE
From Portland, follow I-84 east to exit 28 (Bridal Veil) and proceed 0.4 mile to a junction with the Historic Columbia River Highway. Turn right and continue 0.7 mile to Bridal Veil Falls State Scenic Viewpoint and the trailhead (elev. 250 ft.). Privy available.

ON THE TRAIL
Two trails begin near the restrooms. For the falls, head right on a paved path that soon yields to a gravel surface. Making one sweeping switchback, the trail descends into a deep, moist ravine and reaches a bridge over Bridal Veil Creek. The falls is still hidden here but quite audible. Downstream you'll notice

Bridal Veil Falls

the remains of an old industrial operation. In the 1880s a lumber mill was constructed here, sprouting a company town. The mill's wood flume was destroyed by fire in 1937, and milling operations continued on the site until 1960. In 1990, the Trust for Public Land acquired much of the former townsite, demolished the remaining buildings, and transferred the property to the US Forest Service. While I lament the removal of the historical buildings, I welcome the removal of invasive species that have carpeted much of the state park. Volunteers continue to eradicate the vegetative plague.

Cross the bridge and climb a stairway coming to a platform at 0.3 mile to catch

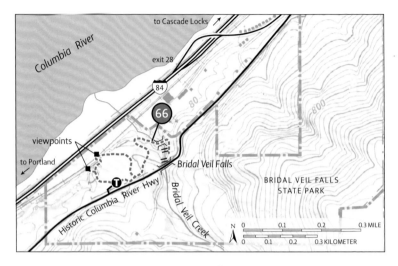

a look at the bridal veil. The gorgeous two-tiered cascade plummets 120 feet down a narrow chasm.

After fawning over its beauty, retrace your steps back to the trailhead and take the mossy paved path that diverts left from the restrooms. Follow this delightful interpretive loop trail for 0.4 mile along the rim of a basalt bluff, taking in good views of Sand Island below and Cape Horn across the river. In springtime enjoy flowering camas, as this bluff supports one of Oregon's largest remaining camas fields in the western half of the Columbia Gorge. Look, too, for other beautiful blossoms, notably checker lily, Oregon iris, and cliff penstemon.

EXTENDING YOUR TRIP

Consider a visit to nearby Shepperds Dell Falls. The short path to this impressive multi-tiered waterfall can be reached by following the Historic Columbia River Highway west for 0.7 mile.

67 Angels Rest

RATING/ DIFFICULTY	ROUNDTRIP	ELEV GAIN/ HIGH POINT	SEASON
*****/3	4.6 miles	1480 feet/ 1600 feet	Year-round

Crowds: 5; **Map:** Green Trails Columbia River Gorge West No. 428S; **Contact:** Columbia River Gorge National Scenic Area; **Notes:** Dogs permitted on-leash. High trailhead break-in area—leave no valuables in your vehicle; **GPS:** N 45° 33.627', W 122° 10.363'

Savor heavenly views from this weathered precipitous outcropping at the western gate of the Columbia River Gorge. But be forewarned—crowding can be hell on this popular trail on weekends and throughout the summer. While Angels Rest may not be too high, it provides some of the best and more unique views in the Gorge of the Columbia directly below.

GETTING THERE

From Portland, follow I-84 east to exit 28 (Bridal Veil) and proceed 0.4 mile to a junction with the Historic Columbia River Highway, where trailhead parking (elev. 125 ft.) is located immediately to your right. (From Hood River, take exit 35 off of I-84 and follow the Historic Columbia River Highway 7.2 miles west.) Overflow parking lies just to the west, on the south side of the highway.

ON THE TRAIL

Carefully cross the old highway and begin hiking the wide and well-beaten Angels Rest Trail No. 415. The way starts in recovering forest from the 2017 Eagle Creek Fire. Much of the forest survived here, although many trees remain scarred from the fire. Gradually gaining elevation, traverse a basalt slope, with views out to Cape Horn, before cresting a bench (elev. 400 ft.) above 150-foot Coopey Falls. Catch glimpses of the cataract and carry on, coming to a bridged crossing of Coopey Creek (elev. 475 ft.) just above a small cascade at 0.6 mile.

Now traversing a slope in a ravine above the crashing creek, steadily climb. At 1.2 miles the forest cover thins as you enter a rather large burn zone from 1991. While the area continues to be recolonized by a wide array of flora, thank the fire for providing some nice views—and flowers! Exercise caution here during windy periods—the snags are prone to losing limbs and being blown over.

Continue climbing, switchbacking over ledge and broken rock, views growing with each step. At 2.2 miles reach an unmarked but obvious junction (elev. 1600 ft.). Head left 0.1 mile to Angels Rest, a small plateau of fractured rock hovering above the Columbia River. The views are simply sublime. Though

you'll see a slight resemblance to the Palisades along the Hudson River, it's no New Jersey you're looking out over. Gaze north across the Columbia to Cape Horn, Silver Star, and Table Mountain, and west over Sand Island out to Crown Point. Keep children close by—it's a hell of a drop from this heavenly spot.

EXTENDING YOUR TRIP

Devils Rest (Hike 68) can also be accessed from this trail. Continue on the main trail another 0.2 mile to a junction. Then head right on the Foxglove Trail, and after passing several junctions, reach Devils Rest (elev. 2450 ft.) in 1.5 miles. Make a long loop by continuing on the Devils Rest Trail to the Wahkeena Trail to the Angels Rest Trail,

Looking out to Archer Mountain

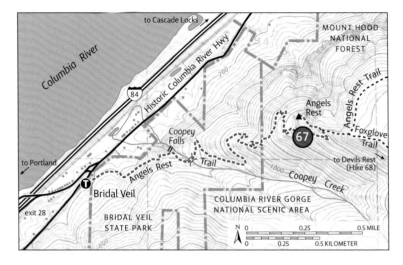

returning to the Foxglove Trail junction in 4.5 miles.

68 Devils Rest

RATING/ DIFFICULTY	LOOP	ELEV GAIN/ HIGH POINT	SEASON
***/3	7.7 miles	2600 feet/ 2450 feet	Year-round

Crowds: 3; **Map:** Green Trails Columbia River Gorge West No. 428S; **Contact:** Columbia River Gorge National Scenic Area; **Notes:** Dogs allowed on-leash. High trailhead break-in area—leave no valuables in your vehicle; **GPS:** N 45° 34.519', W 122° 07.684'

Nearly 1000 feet higher than nearby Angels Rest (Hike 67), Devils Rest may be closer to heaven. But lacking the heavenly views found on Angels Rest, Devils' charm is its stately primeval forest and absence of crowds. The path to the devil's lair is lined with other rewards too, *spectacular waterfalls and a couple of pretty decent views as well.*

GETTING THERE
From Portland, follow I-84 east to exit 28 (Bridal Veil) and proceed 0.4 mile, bearing left (east) onto the Historic Columbia River Highway. Continue for 2.5 miles to the Wahkeena Falls trailhead (elev. 80 ft.). (From Hood River, take exit 35 off of I-84 and follow the Historic Columbia River Highway 4.7 miles west to the trailhead.) Privy and picnic area available.

ON THE TRAIL
This lollipop loop starts on the paved and popular Wahkeena Trail No. 420. In 0.25 mile come to the breathtaking Wahkeena Falls crashing down a basalt chute. Triple-tiered, the 242-foot falls will bring tears (actually mist) to your eyes from its intense spray. Cross the creek beneath the falls on a handsome 1914-built stone bridge. Timber

baron and philanthropist Simon Benson—a Norwegian immigrant born Simon Iversen—donated the land surrounding both Wahkeena and Multnomah Falls to the state.

Continue following the paved path on a switchbacking course, steadily gaining elevation. At 0.5 mile pass the junction with the long-closed Perdition Trail (elev. 325 ft.). A victim of forest fire, subsequent erosion eternally damned Perdition to the land of lost trails. Staying on the paved path, weave up a gap between steep basalt walls.

At 0.8 mile the pavement ends (elev. 625 ft.). Here a short spur leads right to Lemmons Viewpoint, named after a firefighter who lost his life fighting a fire in 1983. The view is good across the river of Beacon Rock and Hamilton Mountain. Continue on good dirt tread, now paralleling Wahkeena Creek. The trail crosses it via bridges twice as it works its way up a tight slot. At 1.2 miles cross a side creek (elev. 920 ft.) beneath 20-foot Fairy Falls, and 0.1 mile beyond come to a junction (elev. 1100 ft.). You'll be returning from the right, so veer left on the Vista Point Trail, rock hopping across a small creek and then gently rounding a ridge with good but limited views. Pass a spur that leads to

BEFRIENDING THE GORGE

The Friends of the Columbia Gorge was organized in 1980, under the leadership of Nancy Russell, to permanently protect the Gorge's natural values. Including such prominent politicians as former Oregon governors Tom McCall and Bob Straub and former Washington governor Dan Evans, the group set out to develop federal legislation to permanently protect the Gorge, create widespread public support for Gorge protection, and challenge inappropriate development proposals in the Gorge.

From 1981 to 1986, the Friends worked tirelessly to build political support for the creation of the Columbia River Gorge National Scenic Area. They worked closely with Senators Hatfield, Packwood, Evans, and Gorton, and Representatives AuCoin, Wyden, Weaver, and Bonker. They were met with much opposition by economic and resource development interests within the Gorge.

However, the Columbia River Gorge National Scenic Area Act was finally passed by both the US Senate and House in October 1986, and the bill was signed by President Reagan on November 17, 1986, just hours before it would have died from a pocket veto. This preservation effort was bipartisan, with powerful Republican support. All four senators sponsoring this bill were Republicans, and Nancy Russell herself was a lifelong Republican.

Since the passage of the legislation, the Forest Service has purchased more than 40,000 acres along the Columbia for resource protection and enhancement. Russell herself personally bought thirty parcels, donating the land to the Friends and protecting it from development. Friends of the Columbia Gorge, which now numbers more than six thousand members (including this author), continues to advocate for and act as a watchdog for this great American landscape. I encourage you to join them.

Nancy Russell passed away in 2008 at the age of seventy-six after a four-year battle with Lou Gehrig's disease. But the great guardian of the Gorge's spirit and inspiration lives on!

Fire-scarred old growth on the Devils Rest Trail

a vista, and at 2 miles, in a grove of big firs, return to the Wahkeena Trail (elev. 1600 ft.).

Now turn left and then immediately right onto the Devils Rest Trail. Any crowds you've contended with so far likely will get left behind here. On good tread, steadily climb steep slopes shaded by big old conifers with blackened trunks from the Eagle Creek Fire. Pass some dead timber and window views of Devils Rest and points north. At 2.9 miles ignore a side trail (elev. 2150 ft.) leading left to the Multnomah Basin Road, continuing right instead, now along the rim of a ridge.

Continue through mostly unburnt primeval forest, crossing a couple of creeks and continuing to climb. Come to a good viewpoint out to Silver Star and company across the Columbia River. Then continue through a gorgeous grove of ancient hemlock and at 3.5 miles come to a short spur leading right to a ledge (elev. 2250 ft.) providing excellent views north to Table Mountain, Hamilton Mountain, Mount Adams, and more.

The main trail climbs a little more, coming to a junction at 3.7 miles, just below the wooded 2450-foot summit of Devils Rest. The trail right is the recently reopened (thanks to volunteers) Primrose Trail. It drops steeply (insanely at times) along a ridge of open forest, granting good views and reaching the Angels Rest Trail in 0.7 mile. It's best hiked uphill.

The better loop option is to head straight on the Foxglove Trail. Steadily lose elevation and reach a junction at 4 miles. The Foxglove Trail continues left passing Lily's Lane Trail before reaching the Angels Rest Trail in 1.2 miles, just 0.2 mile above the Rest. It's a good longer hike option. This loop heads right on the Devils Fork Trail following an old road bed. At 4.1 miles pass the Devils Cutoff Trail, which leads right to the Primrose Trail. At 4.4 miles bear right onto Lily's Lane and reach the Angels Rest Trail at 4.6 miles.

Angels Rest is 1.2 miles to your left here. You want to head right, passing the Primrose Trail at 4.8 miles, just after crossing Mist Creek. Then via switchbacks, steadily descend through an old burn zone with limited views through the trees. After a small spring the trail makes a short gradual ascent. Soon after, in a mossy maple grove, reach the robustly gushing Wahkeena Spring (elev. 1300 ft.) that feeds the showy falls far below.

Just beyond at 6.1 miles come to a junction with the Wahkeena Trail. Veer left, rapidly losing elevation and coming to the familiar Vista Point Trail at 6.4 miles. Then continue left, retracing previously hiked ground for 1.3 miles and returning to your vehicle.

69 Multnomah Falls–Wahkeena Falls Loop

RATING/ DIFFICULTY	LOOP	ELEV GAIN/ HIGH POINT	SEASON
*****/3	5.2 miles	1650 feet/ 1600 feet	Year-round

Crowds: 5; **Map:** Green Trails Columbia River Gorge West No. 428S; **Contact:** Columbia River Gorge National Scenic Area; **Notes:**

A Multnomah Falls Timed Use Permit is required from late May until early September to park at the Multnomah Falls parking area at exit 31. Visit Recreation.gov for details. Parking is extremely limited at Multnomah Falls on Historic Columbia River Highway and will be monitored by concessionaire. Dogs allowed on-leash. High trailhead break-in area—leave no valuables in your vehicle; **GPS:** N 45° 34.656', W 122° 07.034'

Enjoy a spectacular loop to two of the Gorge's most gorgeous waterfalls, plus a handful of not-too-shabby ones. Multnomah is Oregon's tallest and most visited waterfall and the Columbia Gorge's quintessential cataract. And

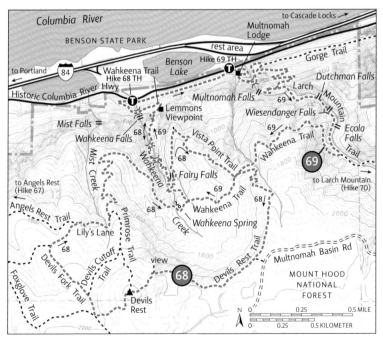

Fairy Falls

Wahkeena—its name derived from a Native American word meaning "most beautiful"—certainly is. This is the ultimate loop for waterfall lovers, and not surprisingly, hordes of hikers barrel up and down these trails. Get an early start, or save it for a rainy day.

GETTING THERE

From Portland, follow I-84 east and take exit 31 (Multnomah Falls). Park and walk through the highway underpass to the trailhead (elev. 50 ft.). Alternatively, also from Portland, follow I-84 east and take exit 28, drive 0.4 mile and bear left (east) onto the Historic Columbia River Highway. Continue for 3 miles to the trailhead, where parking is extremely limited. (From Hood River, take exit 35 off of I-84 and follow the Historic Columbia River Highway 4.2 miles west to the trailhead.) Privy available. Hike can alternatively be started from the Wahkeena Trailhead (see Hike 68 for directions).

ON THE TRAIL

Before proceeding to the falls, you'll pass by the beautiful Multnomah Falls Lodge, a National Historic Landmark built in 1925. The Forest Service maintains a visitors center there, and you can always catch breakfast beforehand or dinner afterward to enhance your hike. Now weaving in and out of selfie-taking tourists, follow the paved-at-first Larch Mountain Trail No. 441 to the base of 620-foot two-tiered Multnomah Falls. Highest in the state and one of the highest in the nation, Multnomah Falls is a breathtaking sight—especially during winter's incessant rains. More than 75 inches of annual precipitation help fan the falls.

At 0.25 mile, cross Multnomah Creek between the two tiers on the elegant and heavily photographed Benson Bridge. It was built in 1915 by entrepreneur and philanthropist Simon Benson, who also bequeathed to the state Multnomah and Wahkeena Falls and hundreds of surrounding acres. Gaze and gape, and then carry on, following a paved path that makes eleven switchbacks.

At the second one, pass a junction with the Gorge Trail (elev. 280 ft.). At switchback number 9, crest a ridge (elev. 785 ft.). Then slightly descend to the pavement's end and a junction (elev. 740 ft.) at 1.1 miles. By all means take the 0.2-mile spur trail right, dropping to the top of the falls (elev. 660 ft.). It's a spiraling and exhilarating view down to the lodge and river and one that may leave you feeling slightly dizzy. Thank heavens for the guardrail!

Return to the main trail and head right, immediately crossing Multnomah Creek on a little bridge. Your route now hugs Multnomah Creek in a cool, moist gorge on blasted ledges and beneath basalt walls. Thankfully the Eagle Creek Fire had little impact here. Pass small Dutchman Falls and soon afterward come to the impressive 50-foot Wiesendanger (also known as Upper Multnomah) Falls, named for a former Forest Service ranger.

The trail then switchbacks above the falls and comes to yet another impressive cascade, 55-foot Ecola Falls (elev. 1050 ft.). Also known as Hidden Falls, Ecola is a rather odd name for this cascade, considering it's the Chinook word for "whale." Keep children and dogs close—the trail here teeters right above the crest of the plummeting water, sans guardrail.

Continue following the creek upward, coming to a junction with the Wahkeena Trail (elev. 1200 ft.) at 1.8 miles. Straight ahead leads to Larch Mountain and Franklin Ridge (Hikes 70 and 72). Turn right instead and climb steadily on good trail, traversing steep slopes cloaked in mostly unburnt forest. Pass some viewpoints out to the river and the Washington side of the Gorge.

Shortly after passing a crashing creek, reach the Devils Rest Trail (elev. 1600 ft.) at 2.7 miles. Continue straight, passing the Vista Point Trail (or take it for a slightly longer return), descending in mature timber to a junction near Wahkeena Spring (elev. 1300 ft.) at 3 miles. Turn right and rapidly descend. At 3.3 miles, turn left at the Vista Point Trail junction (elev. 1000 ft.) to stay on the Wahkeena Trail. Come to 20-foot Fairy Falls soon afterward.

Continue on a steep descent, crossing Wahkeena Creek twice before coming to a lookout and the beginning of paved trail. Lured by yet one more showy waterfall, carry on, reaching the spectacular 242-foot Wahkeena Falls at 4.3 miles. Cross beneath the falls on an impressive old stone bridge and reach the Wahkeena Falls trailhead at 4.6 miles.

Then, locate the connector trail back to the Multnomah Falls trailhead and follow it 0.6 mile back to your vehicle. Have you ever seen so much falling water this side of Brazil and Argentina's Iguazu?

70 Larch Mountain

RATING/ DIFFICULTY	ROUNDTRIP	ELEV GAIN/ HIGH POINT	SEASON
****/4	14.4 miles	4000 feet/ 4055 feet	May–Nov

Crowds: 3; **Map:** Green Trails Columbia River Gorge West No. 428S; **Contact:** Columbia River Gorge National Scenic Area; **Notes:** A Multnomah Falls Timed Use Permit is required from late May until early September to park at the Multnomah Falls parking area at exit 31. Visit Recreation.gov for details. Parking is extremely limited at Multnomah Falls on Historic Columbia River Highway and will be monitored by concessionaire. Dogs allowed on-leash. High trailhead break-in area—leave no valuables in your vehicle; **GPS:** N 45° 34.656'; W 122° 07.034'

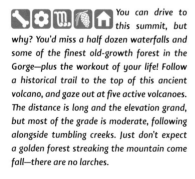 *You can drive to this summit, but why? You'd miss a half dozen waterfalls and some of the finest old-growth forest in the Gorge—plus the workout of your life! Follow a historical trail to the top of this ancient volcano, and gaze out at five active volcanoes. The distance is long and the elevation grand, but most of the grade is moderate, following alongside tumbling creeks. Just don't expect a golden forest streaking the mountain come fall—there are no larches.*

GETTING THERE
From Portland, follow I-84 east and take exit 31 (Multnomah Falls). Park and walk through the highway underpass to the trailhead (elev. 50 ft.). Alternatively, also from Portland, follow I-84 east and take exit 28 (Bridal Veil), drive 0.4 mile and bear left (east) onto the Historic Columbia River Highway. Continue for 3 miles to the trailhead, where parking is extremely limited. (From Hood River, take exit 35 off of I-84 and follow the Historic Columbia River Highway 4.2 miles west to the trailhead.)

ON THE TRAIL
Larch Mountain Trail No. 441 was constructed in 1915 by the Progressive Business Men's Club (which included some of Portland's most prominent citizens), a fledgling US Forest Service, timber baron and philanthropist Simon Benson, and the Trails Club of Oregon (which was officially formed on Larch Mountain). This trail's history is as varied and fascinating as the terrain it traverses.

Start at the Multnomah Falls Lodge, following the paved path past Oregon's most prominent waterfall and maneuvering between hordes of waterfall admirers. At 1.1 miles pass a spur that leads to the upper viewpoint of Multnomah Falls, and leave the majority of the masses behind.

Cross Multnomah Creek, following it upstream past Dutchman, Wiesendanger, and Ecola Falls, coming to the junction with the Wahkeena Trail at 1.8 miles (elev. 1200 ft.). Continue left along Multnomah Creek into a lush and damp rainforest-like valley. Cross the creek on a high bridge and rock hop across several side creeks. At 2.6 miles the trail (elev. 1600 ft.) splits into two routes—high- and low-water routes. The high

Trail along Multnomah Creek

route is slightly longer and involves some climbing. If winter rains have flooded the low route, you'll be heading up!

At 2.9 miles come to the closed Multnomah Basin Road (elev. 1650 ft.). This old dirt road winds east 1 mile to the basin (more a flat) and to the Trails Club of Oregon's Nesika Lodge (currently closed due to fire damage). Continue south on the trail, soon entering the Mark O. Hatfield Wilderness (see sidebar, "Untrammeled Columbia River Gorge"). Some of the finest old growth remaining in the Columbia Gorge can be found on the lower slopes of Larch Mountain and along nearby Bell Creek. These areas' inclusion as wilderness assures its permanent protection. Fill out the day permit and continue.

At 3.2 miles the Franklin Ridge Trail (Hike 71) veers left. Continue right, through groves of ancient hemlock and fir—but no larch. Early

lumbermen erroneously referred to noble fir as larch (which grows on the drier eastern slopes of the Cascades), and a number of Larch Mountains popped up in western Washington and Oregon. Pass a good campsite, and at 3.6 miles enter a large burnt stretch from the Eagle Creek Fire. Cross the East Fork Multnomah Creek using a log bridge, and at 3.9 miles cross the West Fork on a bridge. Multnomah Creek is spring fed, like many of the creeks in the Columbia River Gorge.

Climbing at a moderate grade, the trail veers away from the creek and traverses a large scree slope. Shortly after leaving the scree, reenter green unburnt forest. At 5 miles, leave the wilderness area and come to the Multnomah Creek Way Trail (elev. 2900 ft.). The Larch Mountain Trail continues right, steadily ascending a ridge rife with rhododendrons. At 5.4 miles, intersect an

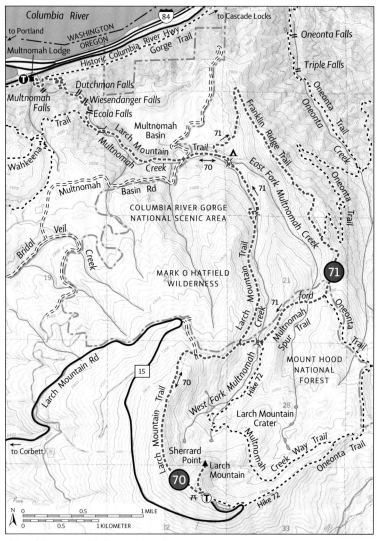

old road (elev. 3300 ft.) that provides hikers and mountain bikers a shortcut from Larch Mountain Road.

Continue ascending through thick woods, reaching picnic tables and (gasp) a road (elev. 3850 ft.) at 6.9 miles. Built in the 1930s as a Depression-era work program project, the paved Larch Mountain Road allows folks to enjoy the views you are about to receive without putting in the work! Try to make this hike in late spring after snowmelt and before the road opens (which varies year to year) to enjoy summit solitude.

Locate the 0.3-mile paved Sherrard Point Trail (named for the forest supervisor at the time of the road's construction) and follow it to the fenced-in rocky and open 4055-foot summit. Wow! From this ancient shield volcano (the caldera is right below you), gaze out at five of the Northwest's most prominent active volcanoes: Hood, Jefferson, Adams, St. Helens, and Rainier. Gaze out over the Gorge too. Somberly assess the extent of the 2017 Eagle Creek Fire (see sidebar, "Burning Down the Forest" in the Silver Star section). And if it's early summer, don't forget to cast your eyes downward to the showy rock gardens adorning the summit.

EXTENDING YOUR TRIP

If you have the energy, consider a loop around the summit crater. See Hike 72 for details.

71 Franklin Ridge

RATING/ DIFFICULTY	ROUNDTRIP	ELEV GAIN/ HIGH POINT	SEASON
***/4	12.3 miles	3300 feet/ 2925 feet	Apr–Nov

Crowds: 1; **Map:** Green Trails Columbia River Gorge West No. 428S; **Contact:** Columbia River Gorge National Scenic Area; **Notes:** A Multnomah Falls Timed Use Permit is required from late May until early September to park at the Multnomah Falls parking area at exit 31. Visit Recreation.gov for details. Parking is extremely limited at Multnomah

Falls on Historic Columbia River Highway and will be monitored by a concessionaire. Dogs allowed on-leash. Trail was heavily impacted by the 2017 Eagle Creek Fire. Expect hazards in the form of downed trees and avoid during high winds. Wilderness rules apply. High trailhead break-in area—leave no valuables in your vehicle; **GPS:** N 45° 34.656', W 122° 07.034'

Separating the Multnomah Creek and Oneonta Creek valleys, two of the Gorge's most popular hiking destinations, stands lonely Franklin Ridge. Once cloaked with stands of old growth, the Eagle Creek Fire was not kind to this ridge—a crying shame. But now views have replaced the thick canopy, and Franklin still offers opportunities for solitude.

GETTING THERE

From Portland, follow I-84 east and take exit 31 (Multnomah Falls). Park and walk through the highway underpass to the Larch Mountain trailhead (elev. 50 ft.). Alternatively, also from Portland, follow I-84 east and take exit 28 (Bridal Veil) drive 0.4 mile and bear left (east) onto the Historic Columbia River Highway. Continue for 3 miles to the trailhead, where parking is extremely limited. (From Hood River, take exit 35 off of I-84 and follow the Historic Columbia River Highway 4.2 miles west to the trailhead.)

ON THE TRAIL

This hike starts at Multnomah Falls, following Larch Mountain Trail No. 441 (Hike 70). Minnie Franklin, whom Franklin Ridge is named for, was instrumental in creating this trail in 1915. After passing Multnomah, Dutchman, Wiesendanger, and Ecola Falls, come to a junction with the Wahkeena Trail at 1.8 miles (elev. 1200 ft.). Continue left on the Larch Mountain Trail, crossing and following alongside cascading Multnomah Creek and reaching the closed-to-traffic Multnomah Basin Road (elev. 1650 ft.) at 2.9 miles. Resume hiking south on the trail, entering the Mark O. Hatfield Wilderness (fill out free permit at box) and coming to the Franklin Ridge Trail No. 427 (elev. 1800 ft.) at 3.2 miles.

Head left on lightly traveled tread, and traverse an open forest of blackened trunks soon transitioning into a completely scorched forest. Brushy tenacious undergrowth is adding greenery to the blackened and silver snags and windfalls. At 4 miles crest the ridge (elev. 2150 ft.) and carry on southward, climbing higher along the once thickly forested ridge. Gaps in the snags now provide good views over the Oneonta Creek valley to the Columbia River, Gorge peaks and ridges, and Mount Adams. The way soon steepens, and after a mile on the ridge, come to a few unburnt green trees. Shortly afterward make a slight descent and traverse magnificent ancient Douglas-firs and hemlocks. At 5.6 miles come to a junction (elev. 2700 ft.) with the Oneonta Trail. Left heads to Triple Falls and the Oneonta Gorge (Hike 73). Proceed right along the ridge and burn zone, dropping 50 feet and then regaining it to reach the Multnomah Spur Trail at 6.2 miles.

Now outside of the wilderness area, veer right on the Multnomah Spur, gently descending through primeval forest. At 6.4 miles come to a potentially difficult ford of the East Fork Multnomah Creek (elev. 2700 ft.). The trail then begins to climb again, bear grass and rhodies lining the way. After reaching a small divide (elev.

Remnant old-growth forest along Franklin Ridge

2925 ft.), descend once again, reaching a junction (elev. 2850 ft.) at 7 miles. The way left leads to Larch Mountain (Hikes 70 and 71). Head right on the Multnomah Creek Way Trail, crossing said creek on a bridge and reaching the Larch Mountain Trail (elev. 2950 ft.) at 7.3 miles. Then head right on the Larch Mountain Trail, eventually passing the Franklin Ridge Trail junction at 9.1 miles. From here it's 3.2 familiar miles back to the trailhead.

EXTENDING YOUR TRIP

Strong hikers can combine Larch Mountain with this hike to make a big loop that follows the Multnomah Creek Way Trail to the summit and returns via the Larch Mountain Trail. See Hikes 70 and 72 for trail descriptions.

72 Larch Mountain Crater

RATING/ DIFFICULTY	LOOP	ELEV GAIN/ HIGH POINT	SEASON
***/3	6.6 miles	1200 feet/ 4055 feet	June–Nov

Crowds: 3; **Map:** Green Trails Columbia River Gorge West No. 428S; **Contact:** Columbia River Gorge National Scenic Area; **Notes:** NW Forest Pass or Interagency Pass required. Dogs permitted on-leash. Road gated at milepost 10 Nov.–May (sometimes longer, depending on snow cover); **GPS:** N 45° 31.781', W 122° 05.301'

If Larch's summit is too much to tackle from Multnomah Falls (Hike 70), but you still want to get a little hiking in on this Columbia Gorge landmark, consider starting from the top of this ancient volcano. Take in the views and then head out on a surprisingly

Pacific rhododendron

quiet loop through some of the finest remaining primeval forest in the region.

GETTING THERE

From Portland, take I-84 east to exit 22 (Corbett) and follow NE Corbett Hill Road south for 1.4 miles to the Historic Columbia River Highway. Turn left, proceeding west for 2 miles. Bear right onto paved Larch Mountain Road (which eventually becomes Forest Road 15) and follow it for 14.2 miles to its end at a summit picnic area (elev. 3850 ft.). Privy available.

ON THE TRAIL

Before beginning the loop, make a beeline on the 0.3-mile paved Sherrard Point Trail to Larch's fenced-in rocky and open 4055-foot summit. From this ancient shield volcano, gaze out at five prominent, still active volcanoes: Hood, Jefferson, Adams, St. Helens, and Rainier. And admire all the less prominent peaks in full view that span the horizon and hug the Columbia River Gorge. Note, too, how dangerously close the Eagle Creek Fire of 2017 came to the old-growth forests of this peak. Then look below at Larch's broad caldera. You'll be making a loop around this heavily forested crater. Don't worry about views—you can always return to Sherrard Point upon completing your loop.

Locate the Larch Mountain Trail No. 441 back at the picnic area and take it. Through forest the way descends—gently at first, then more rapidly. At 1.5 miles come to an old road (elev. 3200 ft.), which leads 0.2 mile west to the Larch Mountain Road, an alternative approach to this loop (2.9 miles west from the summit, with limited parking).

Continue descending, now in attractive old-growth forest. Rhododendrons decorate the understory with plenty of pink and purple blossoms in May and June. At 1.9 miles come to a junction with the Multnomah Creek Way Trail (elev. 2900 ft.). Bear right on it and at 2.1 miles, just after crossing Multnomah Creek on a bridge, come to another junction (elev. 2800 ft.).

The Multnomah Spur Trail leads left 0.8 mile to the Oneonta Trail, offering a slightly longer loop option. Head right, into the crater, skirting a big swamp of pungent skunk cabbage and walking through impressive groves of giant firs and cedars. The way is pretty level for a while, allowing you to concentrate on the surrounding spectacular old-growth forest.

Eventually start climbing, crossing rocky streambeds that may be dry, reaching an old logging railroad bed. No longer in old

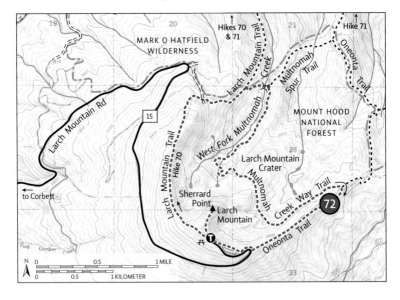

THIS SALAMANDER ROCKS!

While it's more common to see lizards (reptiles) scurrying across rocky areas in the Gorge than amphibians, keep your eyes out for the Larch Mountain salamander. This amphibian, endemic to and threatened in Oregon and Washington, lives in isolated patches of talus habitat, preferring scree, gravelly soils, and other areas of accumulated rock. The Larch Mountain salamander—a small striped salamander that was originally believed to be a sub-species of Van Dyke's salamander—is a unique species and one of the ecological gems of the Columbia River Gorge.

growth (the railroad served its purpose), begin a long gentle traverse in second growth. Cross the headwaters of Oneonta Creek and reach the Oneonta Trail (elev. 3450 ft.) at 4.6 miles.

Now turn right and on good tread hike along a gentle ridge. At 5 miles a short spur leads right to limited views. At 5.6 miles reach the Larch Mountain Road (elev. 3750 ft.). Follow the road to the right for 0.4 mile back to the summit parking lot to complete your loop.

EXTENDING YOUR TRIP

From the Multnomah Creek crossing, follow the Multnomah Spur Trail to the Oneonta Trail for a slightly longer loop (by about 1 mile). There is some nice old-growth forest along the way.

73 Triple Falls

RATING/ DIFFICULTY	ROUNDTRIP	ELEV GAIN/ HIGH POINT	SEASON
***/3	3.6 miles	670 feet/ 600 feet	Year-round

Crowds: 4; **Map:** Green Trails Columbia River Gorge West No. 428S; **Contact:** Columbia River Gorge National Scenic Area; **Notes:** Dogs allowed on-leash. Trail was heavily impacted by 2017 Eagle Creek Fire. Expect

hazards in the form of downed trees and avoid during high winds. Wilderness rules apply. High trailhead break-in area—leave no valuables in your vehicle; **GPS:** N 45° 35.323', W 122° 04.696'

Hike through a deep gorge above and along tumbling Oneonta Creek. Catch some sights and lots of sounds of a series of waterfalls crashing in the gorge's lower reaches. Then after a climb across steep slopes shrouded in trees that succumbed to the 2017 Eagle Creek Fire, stand mesmerized staring at one of the Columbia River Gorge's most unique cataracts, the three-chute Triple Falls.

GETTING THERE

From Portland or Hood River, follow I-84 to exit 35 (Ainsworth State Park) and take the Historic Columbia River Highway west for 2 miles to the Oneonta trailhead (elev. 40 ft.). (Alternatively, from Portland, take exit 28 (Bridal Veil) off of I-84 and follow the Historic Columbia River Highway 5.1 miles east to the trailhead.)

ON THE TRAIL

Starting on Oneonta Trail No. 424 steadily ascend, traversing steep forested slopes. At 0.3 mile bear left at a junction with the

Triple Falls is within the Eagle Creek Fire burn zone.

Gorge Trail (see below). Now switchback east and continue climbing through a forest of blackened trunks. The way skirts cliffs before emerging on a bluff above the deep chasm at the mouth of the Oneonta Gorge. Soon enter scorched forest from the 2017 burn. The way can be brushy at times, and the tread prone to washouts. The Trail Keepers of Oregon (TKO) did (and continue to do) excellent work keeping this trail open.

At 0.9 mile come to a junction (elev. 325 ft.) with the popular Horsetail Falls Trail (Hike 74). Continue straight and enter the Mark O. Hatfield Wilderness (fill out free permit at box). Then continue up the gorge

traversing burnt forest and steep slopes along and above tumbling Oneonta Creek. Catch glimpses of Upper Oneonta Falls before making a switchback across a ledge (keep children close and dogs leashed) that was blasted to accommodate the trail. Soon afterward slightly descend, reaching a fine overlook of triple treat Triple Falls (elev. 600 ft.) at 1.8 miles.

Here Oneonta Creek separates into three channels and plunges 64 feet over a basalt ledge. The falls are spectacular during the wet months. By late summer it's not uncommon for Triple to only be a double. Savor the falls and then head back, or consider longer hiking options below.

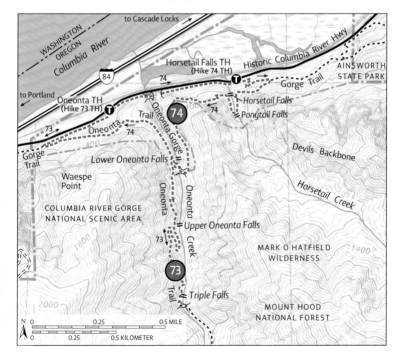

EXTENDING YOUR TRIP

Consider combining the Ponytail Falls Loop (Hike 74) with this one. For a longer and challenging loop continue hiking past Triple Falls. At 1.9 miles cross Oneonta Creek on a sturdy bridge. Then continue heading up the valley, crossing side creeks and entering lush old-growth forest at 2.7 miles.

Cross Oneonta Creek once again on a sturdy bridge, coming to a junction (elev. 1475 ft.) with the Horsetail Creek Trail shortly afterward at 3.2 miles.

Continue right and start climbing out of the valley. Follow long switchbacks through burn patches, old-growth groves, and across a big talus slope. Take in views to the Columbia River and the upper Oneonta Valley. The climb is continuous, but the grade is good. Crest a ridge at the edge of a large burn zone and reach the Franklin Ridge Trail (elev. 2700 ft.) at 5.7 miles.

Then follow the Franklin Ridge Trail (Hike 71) right to the Larch Mountain Trail (Hike 70) to the Gorge Trail. Turn right and follow this stretch of the Gorge Trail for 1.9 miles, traversing mostly green forest and scree slopes granting good views across the river. Return to the Oneonta Trail for a 13-mile loop.

74 Ponytail Falls Loop

RATING/ DIFFICULTY	LOOP	ELEV GAIN/ HIGH POINT	SEASON
****/2	2.7 miles	450 feet/ 380 feet	Year-round

Crowds: 5; **Map:** Green Trails Columbia River Gorge West No. 428S; **Contact:** Columbia River Gorge National Scenic Area; **Notes:** Dogs allowed on-leash. Trail was impacted by 2017 Eagle Creek Fire. Expect hazards in the form of downed trees and avoid during high winds. High trailhead break-in area—leave no valuables in your vehicle; **GPS:** N 45° 35.450', W 122° 04.108'

A Columbia Gorge classic—a tight slot canyon, three spectacular waterfalls, including one you hike behind. Plus, you get a few Columbia River views, a few big old trees, and an old restored tunnel to walk through. Kids will love this hike, but keep 'em close around the many drops-offs.

GETTING THERE

From Portland or Hood River, follow I-84 to exit 35 (Ainsworth State Park) and take the Historic Columbia River Highway west for 1.5 miles to the Horsetail Falls trailhead (elev. 40 ft.). (Alternatively, from Portland, take exit 28 (Bridal Veil) off of I-84 and follow the Historic Columbia River Highway 5.5 miles east to the trailhead.)

ON THE TRAIL

Appropriately named Horsetail Falls plummets 176 feet right next to the trailhead. Stand in awe and click photos away, then head left on well-trodden Horsetail Falls Trail No. 438. After a couple of switchbacks, come to a junction with the Gorge Trail (elev. 200 ft.) after 0.2 mile. Left leads to Ainsworth State Park (an alternative start if you're camping in the park). Continue right, up two more switchbacks, passing the closed Rock of Ages Trail, and at 0.4 mile duck into the cool amphitheater cradling Upper Horsetail Falls (elev. 300 ft.), more widely referred to as Ponytail Falls.

The 80-foot cascade is yet another stunning Columbia Gorge waterfall. Continue hiking, following the trail beneath an overhanging basalt ledge behind the falls. Stare right through the streaming water and feel the pulse of the waterfall! Then continue hiking along steep

Ponytail Falls

basalt walls, traversing a bench where two unmarked side trails lead right to excellent viewpoints over the Columbia out to Washington landmarks. Be extremely careful here, especially watching children, as the edge is abrupt and the drop precipitous.

Now follow the main trail over rocky tread beneath more basalt cliffs and through a stretch of the 2017 Eagle Creek Fire. After climbing to about 380 feet, begin dropping to reach a metal bridge (elev. 275 ft.) that spans the whirling waters of Oneonta Creek. Gaze left, upstream to Upper Oneonta Falls plunging into an emerald punchbowl. Then look downstream toward Lower Oneonta Falls, which is hidden below, within a 20-foot-wide,

200-foot-deep slot canyon. Forty-niner Carleton Emmons Watkins named the falls for his hometown in upstate New York—*Oneonta* is an Iroquois word meaning "place of open rocks." In this case, a name for narrow and mossy rocks would be more apropos.

After staring at the mesmerizing waters, steeply climb and reach a junction (elev. 325 ft.) with the Oneonta Trail at 1.3 miles. For an excellent side trip, consider hiking left 0.9 mile to thrice-delightful Triple Falls (Hike 73). To close the loop, head right instead, skirting cliffs and reentering green old-growth forest. At 1.9 miles come to a junction (elev. 150 ft.) with the Gorge Trail (which leads 1.9 miles west to the Larch Mountain Trail and Multnomah Falls). Continue right, and after 0.3 mile reach the Historic Columbia River Highway.

Now walk to the right along the highway and veer right on a paved trail that crosses Oneonta Creek at the mouth of its gorge (currently closed to the public). An Oregon version of a Utah slot canyon, the basalt Oneonta Gorge is about a half-mile long, 200 feet deep, and only 15 to 20 feet wide. The way then passes through the renovated Oneonta Tunnel, which served motorists from 1914 until 1948, when the highway bypassed it. Horsetail Falls comes back into view shortly afterward, indicating the completion of your loop at 2.7 miles.

75 Bell Creek

RATING/ DIFFICULTY	LOOP	ELEV GAIN/ HIGH POINT	SEASON
****/4	15.8 miles	3400 feet/ 2975 feet	May–Oct

Crowds: 1; **Map:** Green Trails Columbia River Gorge West No. 428S; **Contact:** Columbia River Gorge National Scenic Area; **Notes:**

Dogs allowed on-leash. Wilderness rules apply. Hike requires potentially difficult ford of Oneonta Creek. Trail was impacted by 2017 Eagle Creek Fire and is currently closed. Contact Ranger Station for current status. High trailhead break-in area—leave no valuables in your vehicle; **GPS:** N 45° 35.323', W 122° 04.696'

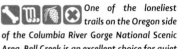 *One of the loneliest trails on the Oregon side of the Columbia River Gorge National Scenic Area, Bell Creek is an excellent choice for quiet contemplation and for admiring a forest several centuries old. Some of the biggest and oldest trees, including massive western red cedars, grace this gentle path. Getting to this trail, however, requires some effort.*

GETTING THERE

From Portland or Hood River, follow I-84 to exit 35 (Ainsworth State Park) and take the Historic Columbia River Highway west for 2.1 miles to the Oneonta trailhead (elev. 40 ft.). (Alternatively, from Portland, take exit 28 (Bridal Veil) off of I-84 and follow the Historic Columbia River Highway 5.5 miles east to the trailhead.)

ON THE TRAIL

Bell Creek Trail No. 459 gently traverses its namesake's watershed along a high forested bench between Larch and Palmer Mountains. The going is pretty mellow, taking you through one of the finest old-growth forests within the national scenic area. What makes this hike difficult is the distance to reach it via other trails and a potentially difficult and dangerous ford of Oneonta Creek.

Starting on the Oneonta Trail, steadily ascend. Bear left at the first junction, with the Gorge Trail at 0.3 mile, and right at the

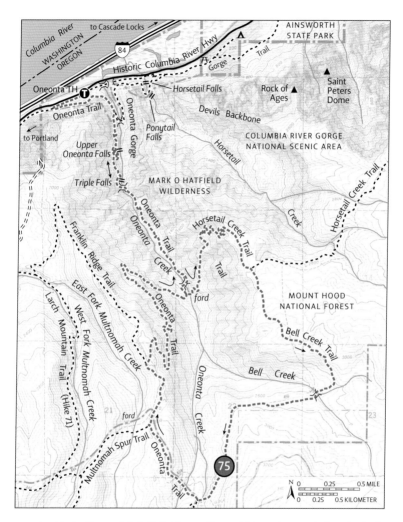

second, with the Horsetail Falls Trail (elev. 325 ft.) at 0.9 mile. Enter the Mark O. Hatfield Wilderness and traverse a large burn zone, following along and above tumbling Oneonta Creek. The trail switchbacks and catwalks (keep children close and dogs leashed), climbing to 700 feet before reaching a fine overlook of triple-treat Triple Falls (elev. 600 ft.) at 1.8 miles. Continue upstream, crossing Oneonta Creek on a big bridge. Then

Lightly-used tread on the Bell Creek Trail

continue alongside tumbling Oneonta Creek and over its cascading tributaries.

Enter gorgeous old growth and cross Oneonta once again on a sturdy bridge, coming to a junction (elev. 1475 ft.) shortly afterward, 3.2 miles from the trailhead. You'll be returning from the right. Head left on the Horsetail Creek Trail, dropping a little to Oneonta Creek. Scout around the rocky creek for a safe place to ford, usually fairly straightforward by midsummer. Once across, steeply climb out of the valley. Reentering a burn zone, the way can be rough. Relentless switchbacks help you

negotiate the steep hillside. Enjoy views out to Franklin Ridge. The grade eases, and finally, at 5.4 miles, come to the Bell Creek Trail (elev. 2875 ft.).

Head right now on a nearly level course on tread that occasionally doubles as a streambed. Skirt the Eagle Creek burn zone, traveling through second-growth forest interrupted with old, fire-scarred snags. At 6.1 miles skirt a cedar swamp. Ascend a broad rise (elev. 2975 ft.), and then begin descending alongside a chattering creek into primeval forest. Savor the beauty of a valley of magnificent coniferous giants—hemlocks, cedars, and Douglas-firs.

After traversing a wet flat, cross pretty Bell Creek (elev. 2725 ft.) on a large log bridge at 7 miles. Then slowly ascend a ridge (elev. 2900 ft.) adorned in old-growth majesty. Cross several creeks and a branch of Oneonta Creek flowing out of a large wetland. At 8.7 miles intersect the Oneonta Trail (elev. 2850 ft.). Left heads to Larch Mountain (Hikes 70 and 71). You'll want to head right, soon crossing Oneonta Creek (here usually a rock hop), before steeply climbing a ridge festooned with rhododendrons (elev. 2950 ft.). Then descend to a huckleberry flat (elev. 2725 ft.), passing the Multnomah Spur Trail (Hike 71) at 9.5 miles.

Now climb 75 feet or so before dropping 50 feet and then once again climbing. At 10.1 miles bear right at the Franklin Ridge Trail junction, cresting said ridge (elev. 2825 ft.) shortly afterward. Then through an open forest and small burn zone, begin a long and gentle descent, passing a few viewpoints of the valley along the way. At 12.6 miles return to the familiar Horsetail Creek Trail junction (elev. 1475 ft.), from where it's 3.2 miles back to your vehicle.

UNTRAMMELED COLUMBIA RIVER GORGE

While much of the Columbia River Gorge region lies within national forest, that doesn't necessarily mean it's fully protected. National forests are managed for "multiple use." While some uses—like hiking—are fairly compatible with land preservation, other uses—such as mining, logging, and off-road vehicle use—are not.

Recognizing that parts of our natural heritage should be altered as little as possible, with bipartisan support, Congress passed the Wilderness Act in 1964 (passage in the House was by an overwhelming 373–1 vote). One of the strongest and most important pieces of environmental legislation in our nation's history, the Wilderness Act afforded some of our most precious wild landscapes a reprieve from exploitation, development, and harmful activities such as motorized recreation. Even bicycles are banned from federal wilderness areas. Wilderness is "an area where the earth and community of life are untrammeled by man," states the legislation. "Where man himself is a visitor who does not remain."

While the Columbia River Gorge had no shortage of qualifying lands for inclusion in the wilderness system back in 1964, no areas were designated. By 1984, however, the Trapper Creek Wilderness and the Columbia Wilderness (later renamed Mark O. Hatfield) were established. And in 2009, the Hatfield Wilderness was greatly expanded when President Obama signed his first piece of wilderness legislation in the form of an Omnibus Public Land Management Act.

Current wilderness acreage in the Columbia Gorge region is as follows:

Trapper Creek Wilderness: 5963 acres

Mark O. Hatfield Wilderness: 65,822 acres

While the expansion of the Hatfield Wilderness was a major environmental achievement, the Trapper Creek Wilderness remains small and should be expanded to include the adjacent 4540-acre Bourbon Roadless Area, with its extensive and impressive old-growth forests.

76 Nesmith Point

RATING/ DIFFICULTY	ROUNDTRIP	ELEV GAIN/ HIGH POINT	SEASON
****/5	10 miles	3800 feet/ 3872 feet	Apr–Nov

Crowds: 3; **Map:** Green Trails Columbia River Gorge West No. 428S; **Contact:** Columbia River Gorge National Scenic Area; **Notes:** Dogs allowed on-leash. Trail was impacted by 2017 Eagle Creek Fire. Expect hazards in the form of downed trees and washouts, and avoid in high wind. High trailhead break-in area—leave no valuables in your vehicle **GPS:** N 45° 36.742', W 122° 00.279'

 *One of the most prominent landmarks on the Oregon side of the Gorge, hulking Nesmith Point looms more than 3800 feet almost directly over the Columbia River. A lung-buster of a climb, Nesmith makes for a great conditioner for mountain climbers and serious trail runners. Once the site of a fire lookout, savor excellent views from the summit and along the way.*

Views from Nesmith Point extend to Mount Adams and Mount Rainier.

GETTING THERE

From Portland, follow I-84 east and take exit 35 (Ainsworth State Park). Turn left toward Dodson, and then immediately turn right onto NE Frontage Road. Continue for 2.1 miles to the John B. Yeon trailhead (elev. 120 ft.). (From Hood River, follow I-84 west and take exit 37, continuing on NE Warrendale Road for 0.5 mile. Turn left and drive under the freeway to a junction with NE Frontage Road. Turn left and continue for 0.4 mile to the John B. Yeon trailhead.)

ON THE TRAIL

A hardy Oregon Trail pioneer, James W. Nesmith made quite a life for himself in his new home as a judge, provisional legislator, congressman, and senator. Like many historic figures, his legacy is complicated. As superintendent of Indian Affairs for Washington and Oregon, his actions were reprehensible. Yet he was only one of two Democratic senators to vote for the 13th Amendment to abolish slavery.

From the trailhead shared with the popular Elowah Falls Trail (Hike 77) pass a leaky wooden water tower and bear right onto Nesmith Point Trail No. 428. Steadily climb through second-growth forest, entering the Mark O. Hatfield Wilderness and coming to a junction (elev. 650 ft.) at 0.9 mile. Here a closed and washed-out section of the Gorge Trail continues west to Ainsworth State Park.

Continue left across a scree slope and then steeply up a draw to a small ridge. The way then enters another draw, before steeply switchbacking to a small basin. The way traverses burnt and recovering forest. After the Eagle Creek Fire, the trail was severely damaged, but tenacious volunteers with the Trailkeepers of Oregon worked hard to restore tread and clear debris, leading to its reopening in the fall of 2022.

Continue up a gully, catching your breath while taking in views out to Mount St. Helens, Table Mountain, Hamilton Mountain, and the Soda Lake Peaks. The uphill grind is relentless, making the distance feel far greater. At about 2.7 miles enter a grove of giant cedars (elev. 2600 ft.). It's then one last push out of the steep basin. Now on a much saner approach, the trail winds through unburnt forest on a broad ridge. At 3.9 miles stop at a spring (elev. 3200 ft.) if you'd like to replenish fluids lost. Then continue climbing,

catching glimpses of heavily burnt Wauneka Point and Tanner Butte. Clumps of rhododendrons add cheerful bouquets along the way come May.

At 4.7 miles come to an old abandoned road (elev. 3750 ft.) that comes up from the Bull Run watershed (closed to public

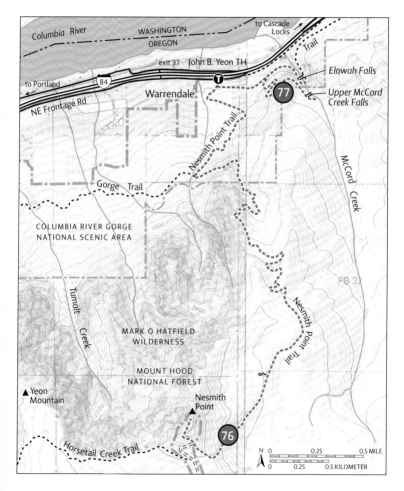

access). Head right, following the old road to Nesmith's 3872-foot summit. While the summit is primarily forested, there are some excellent views to the northwest of Washington's Archer, Silver Star, and Larch Mountains and west to Portland and some Columbia River islands. Past the old tower foundation slabs and the dilapidated privy (a can on its last stand), a path leads a few hundred feet down to a cliff edge (be careful) to an excellent view over the Gorge.

EXTENDING YOUR TRIP

The best views on Nesmith are actually along the Horsetail Creek Trail west of the summit. To reach them, leave the summit and continue down the road 0.3 mile (past the Nesmith Point trail junction). Then turn right, following the trail for 0.7 mile to the viewpoint (elev. 3500 ft.), which shows off Mount St. Helens, Mount Adams, and Nesmith's sheer rocky face.

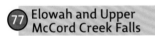

77 Elowah and Upper McCord Creek Falls

RATING/ DIFFICULTY	ROUNDTRIP	ELEV GAIN/ HIGH POINT	SEASON
***/2	2.8 miles	660 feet/ 620 feet	Year-round

Crowds: 4; **Map:** Green Trails Columbia River Gorge West No. 428S; **Contact:** Columbia River Gorge National Scenic Area and Oregon State Parks, John B. Yeon) **Notes:** Dogs allowed on-leash. Bridge across McCord Creek at base of Elowah Falls on Gorge Trail No. 400 is out due to a rock slide. High trailhead break-in area—leave no valuables in your vehicle **GPS:** N 45° 36.742', W 122° 00.261'

Hike to a pair of spectacular waterfalls, one in a deep hidden amphitheater canyon, the other one high above it. Plummeting 213 feet over layered basalt walls, Elowah Falls is one of the Columbia Gorge's greatest water shows. Upper McCord Creek Falls requires a heart-racing approach on a catwalk blasted into sheer ledge—quite a spectacle in its own right.

GETTING THERE

From Portland, follow I-84 east and take exit 35 (Ainsworth State Park). Turn left toward Dodson, and then immediately turn right onto NE Frontage Road. Continue for 2.1 miles to the trailhead (elev. 120 ft.). (From Hood River, follow I-84 west and take exit 37, continuing on NE Warrendale Road for 0.5 mile. Turn left and drive under the freeway to a junction with NE Frontage Road. Turn left and continue for 0.4 mile to the John B. Yeon trailhead.)

Exhilarating stretch of trail en route to Upper McCord Creek Falls

ON THE TRAIL

Before beginning, read the interpretive sign about John B. Yeon, for whom this state park is named. Born Jean Baptiste Yeon in Ontario, Canada, Yeon became a timber magnate and prominent citizen of Portland. He financed what at one time was Oregon's tallest building, and he was a major financial backer of the Columbia River Highway.

Pass a leaky wooden cistern and soon come to a junction with the Gorge Trail. The way right leads to Nesmith Point (Hike 76). You want to veer left and, after steadily climbing 0.4 mile through uniform second-growth forest, reach a second junction (elev. 360 ft.). It's your choice which waterfall you'd like to visit first.

Head right for Upper McCord Creek Falls, switchbacking over mossy scree and passing a couple of rusty old water-diversion pipes. Emerge beneath a steep wall of basalt cliffs. Then traverse it thanks to some past blasting that blazed the trail right into the basalt. Peer straight down upon Elowah Falls, which disappears into a deep, dark ravine. Take in some views, too, along the way, out across the Columbia to Hamilton Mountain. Guardrails help ease any anxiety you may experience along this catwalk above the cataracts. The way then enters burnt and brushy forest to terminate above lovely Upper McCord Creek Falls (elev. 620 ft.) at 1.1 miles. Take time to admire the twin falls and then retrace your steps 0.7 mile back to the second junction.

Now continue right, dropping steeply into the dark and damp amphitheater basin that swallows up Elowah Falls. At 0.3 mile from the junction, stand at the misty base (elev. 200 ft.) of the 213-foot waterfall. Savor the sight of one of the tallest and most stunning waterfalls within the Gorge.

EXTENDING YOUR TRIP

Once the bridge is restored at the base of Elowah Falls, you could continue east on the Gorge Trail passing a picnic area. The trail then continues (with a short stretch on the Historic Columbia River Highway State Trail [HCRHST]) for 3 miles to Tanner Creek, where you can continue farther to Wahclella Falls (Hike 78). Return on the paved and slightly longer HCRHST for a loop. Just don't expect peace and quiet, as the way parallels I-84.

78 Wahclella Falls

RATING/ DIFFICULTY	ROUNDTRIP	ELEV GAIN/ HIGH POINT	SEASON
****/2	2.2 miles	350 feet/ 350 feet	Year-round

Crowds: 5; **Map:** Green Trails Columbia River Gorge West No. 428S; **Contact:** Columbia River Gorge National Scenic Area; **Notes:** NW Forest Pass or Interagency Pass required. Dogs allowed on-leash. Wilderness rules apply. High trailhead break-in area—leave no valuables in your vehicle; **GPS:** N 45° 37.805', W 121° 57.243'

A two-tiered four-star cascade set in a deep slot canyon littered with mossy boulders, Wahclella is one of the prettiest waterfalls in the Gorge. Follow a lollipop loop to the base of the lower falls, soaking up spray while capturing images. Then soak your feet in a nearby pool while watching flittering dippers comb the rapids for appetizing insect larvae.

GETTING THERE

From Portland or Hood River, follow I-84 to exit 40 (Bonneville Dam), turning south and immediately bearing right to the trailhead (elev. 50

Breathtaking Wahclella Falls

ft.). Additional parking can be found at the Tooth Rock trailhead (Hike 79). Privy available.

ON THE TRAIL

Now one of the most popular hikes in the Gorge, up until the 1980s the trail to Wahclella Falls was a rough affair. And the falls have had a wavering history of nomenclature. Originally known as Tanner Creek Falls, then renamed Wahclella by the Mazamas for an old Native American village, then again referred to as Tanner Creek Falls—Wahclella is once again in vogue!

Follow Wahclella Trail No. 436 on an old road alongside Tanner Creek, lined with showy maples and shadowed by the steep walls of Munra Point. At 0.2 mile the road ends at a small dam and intake pipe for the nearby fish hatchery. Now on trail, enter the Mark O. Hatfield Wilderness and immediately come to a bridge directly beneath and within reach of a fanning cascade referred to as Munra Falls.

The canyon tightens as you hike deeper into it. Keep kids and dogs close, as the way climbs high above the river at several points. Steps aid travel along the rocky way. At 0.7 mile the trail splits (elev. 300 ft.). Head left, crossing a gully and climbing higher to about 350 feet before descending to spray-blasted cedars at the base of the falls (elev. 300 ft.). The lower falls drops nearly 80 feet, fanning out of a tight slot across basalt ledge. The upper falls is harder to see as it careens 48 feet down the west side of the narrow chasm above the lower falls.

Cross Tanner Creek on a bridge below the splash pool and travel beneath a mist-soaked overhanging ledge. When sunlight penetrates the canyon floor, nice wading can be found here among mossy boulders. The way then travels beneath stark canyon walls across a floor littered with massive boulders, remnants from a 1973 landslide. Cross Tanner Creek once again, this time on a high bridge (elev. 250 ft.), and then ascend via a few switchbacks to close the loop. Head left and return to the trailhead.

EXTENDING YOUR TRIP

From near the trailhead, follow the Gorge Trail east for 2 quiet miles to the Wauna Viewpoint Trail (Hike 80). Consider, too, a visit to the nearby 1909-built Bonneville Fish Hatchery. Walk its paths and marvel at the sturgeon pool.

79 Tooth Rock

RATING/ DIFFICULTY	ROUNDTRIP	ELEV GAIN/ HIGH POINT	SEASON
**/1	1.8 miles	180 feet/ 270 feet	Year-round

Crowds: 2; **Map:** Green Trails Columbia River Gorge West No. 428S; **Contact:** Columbia River Gorge National Scenic Area; **Notes:** Dogs allowed on-leash. Partially wheelchair accessible. High trailhead break-in area— leave no valuables in your vehicle; **GPS:** N 45° 38.074', W 121° 56.888'

Walk along one of the more interesting and scenic sections of the Historic Columbia River Highway State Trail (HCRHST) to a restored viaduct that wraps around Tooth Rock, a basalt bluff that once impeded travel. Enjoy good views of the river and a short history lesson on transportation through the Gorge on this short and easy hike.

GETTING THERE

From Portland or Hood River, follow I-84 to exit 40 (Bonneville Dam), turning south and immediately bearing left, continuing 0.4 mile to the Tooth Rock parking area (elev. 160 ft.).

ON THE TRAIL

From the trailhead, I-84 spreads out before you, cars and trucks whizzing by at 60-plus miles per hour. But the first vehicles through the Gorge were only allowed to putter. The original Columbia River Highway, a masterpiece of landscape architect and engineer Samuel C. Lancaster, was meant to be driven slowly. Constructed from 1913 until 1922, it was the first planned scenic highway in the country. But by the late 1930s, it was no longer adequate for transportation needs. It was replaced by a new highway, and much of it was later obliterated with the construction of the interstate highway.

In 1996 the Oregon Department of Transportation restored this section of the old highway as the Historic Columbia River Highway State Trail (HCRHST). This paved path is now more than 20 miles long in three sections and, when combined with the old US Highway 30, allows for a safe cycling passage through the Gorge. The trail is also great for walking and running, except for the freeway noise.

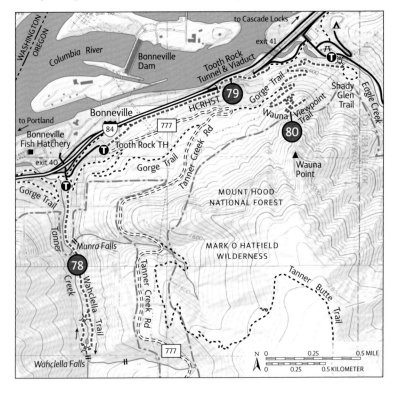

The HCRHST provides good views of the Bonneville Dam and Table Mountain.

Start hiking east, passing an obscure junction at 0.3 mile (elev. 220 ft.). The Eagle Creek Fire burned right up to the trail here, leaving the Pioneer Portage trail to the right buried in blowdown and pioneering invasive plants. Continue on the paved path, soon coming to the viaduct. The freeway tunnels below, through Tooth Rock. Your route wraps around the Tooth, providing good dam (Bonneville dam, that is) views and nice ones, too, of Table Mountain and Eagle Creek's confluence with the Columbia. Admire the arched rubble guardrails. A small pullout, dubbed the Eagle's Nest by Lancaster, was intended for extended viewing but proved a boon to insurance underwriters due to the number of rear-enders.

Continue along the viaduct, crossing over the freeway and coming to a staircase (elev. 190 ft.) at 0.9 mile, which was built in 1996 to reconnect levels of the old highway. Prior to the Eagle Creek Fire you could follow here a portion of an 1850s portage road around Tooth Rock from the south. It can no longer be recommended until it's (hopefully) restored. So, turn around here, or consider the options below.

EXTENDING YOUR TRIP
Continue down the stairs and trail 0.3 mile to the Cascade Salmon Hatchery and continue on the HCRHST for 2.4 miles to Cascade Locks, or for a loop, walk the NE Eagle Creek Loop right for 0.2 mile and then follow the Gorge Trail 2.8 miles (passing the Wauna Viewpoint Trail) back to the HCRHST near the Wahcella Falls trailhead. From here walk the HCRHST 0.3 mile east back to the Tooth Rock trailhead.

80 Wauna Viewpoint

RATING/ DIFFICULTY	ROUNDTRIP	ELEV GAIN/ HIGH POINT	SEASON
***/3	3.6 miles	950 feet/ 1100 feet	Year-round

Crowds: 2; **Map:** Green Trails Columbia River Gorge West No. 428S; **Contact:** Columbia

225

Bonneville Dam

River Gorge National Scenic Area; **Notes:** NW Forest Pass or Interagency Pass required. Dogs allowed on-leash. High trailhead break-in area—leave no valuables in your vehicle; **GPS:** N 45° 38.405', W 121° 55.427'

An oft overlooked location near super popular Eagle Creek, Wauna Point provides exceptional views without the crowds and without having to exert a lot of sweat. From this perch 1000 feet above Eagle Creek, enjoy an eagle's-eye view right down to the creek, Table Mountain, the Bridge of the Gods, and the Bonneville Dam.

GETTING THERE
From Portland, follow I-84 east to exit 41 (Eagle Creek, Fish Hatchery). (From Hood River, leave I-84 West at exit 40, get back on the freeway headed east, and drive 1 mile to exit 41.) Turn right. At 0.1 mile bear right at a parking area and campground entrance and reach another parking area at a picnic area with the trailhead in 0.2 mile (elev. 100 ft.). Privy available.

ON THE TRAIL
Locate Gorge Trail No. 400 taking off from the west side of the parking area at a big bridge spanning Eagle Creek. Take it. In winter watch for spawning salmon. Look for dippers flitting on rocks, diving for larvae, or flying close to the surface of the rippling creek. Once across the bridge, bear right, or take a short side trip on the Shady Glen Trail to the left. This short path meanders along Eagle Creek before looping back to the Gorge Trail in 0.2 mile. The Gorge Trail gently climbs out of the valley, traversing brushy burnt tree groves, a couple of good viewpoints, and a couple of old and weathered stone trail markers.

After an initial steep climb, the grade mellows. At 0.9 mile come to a junction (elev. 600 ft.). The Gorge Trail continues right, crossing mossy scree slopes with good views before reaching the old Tanner Creek Road (Forest Road 777) (elev. 540 ft.) in 0.3 mile, an alternative approach. Head left on Wauna Viewpoint Trail No. 402, traversing some old-growth groves and gently climbing via long switchbacks. The last stretch steepens and crosses a scree slope prone to washing out—so use a little caution. At 1.8 miles reach trail's end (elev. 1100 ft.) at a powerline swath. Don't let the accompanying electrical lines discourage you. The views are excellent.

Stare straight down at the Columbia River. According to the Oregon Historical Society, Wauna is a Klickitat Indian name for a mythological being representing the Columbia River. Look west to Munra Point and Cape Horn; and east to Benson Plateau's Ruckel Ridge, Augspurger Mountain, Grassy Knoll, and Mount Adams. And look north, straight across to Table Mountain and Greenleaf

Peak, and witness the aftermath of the great landslide that blocked the Columbia (see sidebar, "The Gods Must Be Angry" in the western Washington section). The river bends here, around the slumped earth that came crashing off of those peaks. Pretty impressive—it was one earth-shattering event. Back at the viewpoint, that odd concrete monolith is a triangulation installment used to measure any movement of the Bonneville Dam below.

Wauna Point hovers 1000 feet above to the south and is accessible to only the most tenacious and experienced hikers (Hike 81).

81 Dublin Lake

RATING/ DIFFICULTY	ROUNDTRIP	ELEV GAIN/ HIGH POINT	SEASON
**/5	13.2 miles	3990 feet/ 3850 feet	May–Nov

Crowds: 2; **Map:** Green Trails Columbia River Gorge West No. 428S; **Contact:** Columbia River Gorge National Scenic Area; **Notes:** Trail was severely impacted by the 2017 Eagle

Placid Dublin Lake

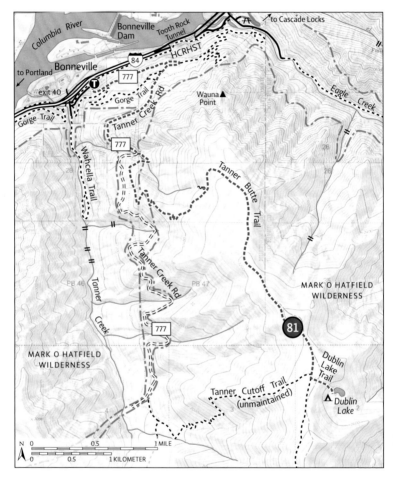

Creek Fire and is currently closed. Check with Ranger Station on its status and once trail is reopened, expect hazards in the form of downed trees, brush, and washouts. Dogs allowed on-leash. High trailhead break-in area—leave no valuables in your vehicle; **GPS:** N 45° 38.061', W 121° 56.894'

A once long, forested hike up a closed road and steep trail to a small lake, this trip—when open again—will be a long, steep hike through a scorched burn zone. The way is long and short on shade—challenging too. The opportunity for solitude is one of this hike's best attributes.

GETTING THERE

From Portland or Hood River, follow I-84 to exit 40 (Bonneville Dam), turning south and immediately bearing left, continuing 0.4 mile to the large Tooth Rock parking area (elev. 160 ft.).

ON THE TRAIL

Walk 0.1 mile on the road you drove in to a gated Forest Road 777 near a water tower. Now walk the road (or consider mountain biking the road section of this hike, allowing for a fast and enjoyable finish to this long trip). Pass a powerline swath and a view down to the river before reaching a junction (elev. 525 ft.) with the Gorge Trail heading east toward the Wauna Viewpoint Trail (Hike 80). Stay on the road and at 1.2 miles come to a junction with the Gorge Trail heading west to Tanner Creek.

Continuing on the road, cross another set of powerlines and steadily climb, traversing scorched forest. At 2.4 miles, in a gulch harboring a couple of small cascades, come to Tanner Butte Trail No. 401 (elev. 1150 ft.) to the left. Take it, immediately entering the Mark O. Hatfield Wilderness. Clamber around those cascades and a few more, possibly getting your feet wet in the process. On a decent grade, the way ascends. Plenty of elevation needs to be subdued!

Once again cross a powerline swath—and enjoy a good view west to Munra Point. Then it's up, up, and away across what was once a verdant forest with pockets of impressive old Douglas-firs. Soon after passing a small creek and spring, come to an unmarked junction (elev. 2750 ft.) at 4.4 miles. Here an unmaintained and mostly obliterated trail heads left, dropping 600 feet in 0.7 mile to Wauna Point, a precipitous viewpoint dangling over Eagle Creek.

For Dublin Lake continue right, now on a gentler grade along a ridge once shrouded with old-growth giants. At 6.2 miles reach a junction (elev. 3800 ft.) with the unmaintained and mostly obliterated Tanner Cutoff Trail. Just beyond at 6.3 miles, turn left on the Dublin Lake Trail (elev. 3850 ft.). Then steeply descend into a hidden forested basin, reaching the little lake (elev. 3550 ft.) at 6.6 miles. Like most of the lakes within the western reaches of the Hatfield Wilderness, Dublin is small and not too impressive. Still, though, it attracts a fair share of backpackers, and the resident newts and ospreys find the lake much to their liking. Rest up for the long haul back.

82 Eagle Creek

RATING/ DIFFICULTY	ROUNDTRIP	ELEV GAIN/ HIGH POINT	SEASON
*****/3	12 miles	1250 feet/ 1200 feet	Mar–Dec

Crowds: 5; **Map:** Green Trails Columbia River Gorge West No. 428S; **Contact:** Columbia River Gorge National Scenic Area; **Notes:** NW Forest Pass or Interagency Pass required. Dogs allowed on-leash. Steep drop-offs—keep children near. Wilderness rules apply. High trailhead break-in area—leave no valuables in your vehicle; **GPS:** N 45° 38.298', W 121° 55.215'

One of the most spectacular trails in America, the route along Eagle Creek travels through a deep chasm on tread that's as much an engineering feat—blasted into ledges and tunneling behind a waterfall—as it is a scenic splendor. Encounter a half dozen waterfalls, old-growth forest, and towering canyon walls. Not surprisingly, Eagle Creek is one of the most popular trails in

Tunnel Falls

the Gorge, so prepare for company. And while dogs are permitted, they're discouraged—the trail is exposed in areas with steep drop-offs. Supervise children closely on this hike.

GETTING THERE

From Portland, follow I-84 east to exit 41 (Eagle Creek, Fish Hatchery). (From Hood River, leave I-84 West at exit 40, get back on the freeway headed east, and drive 1 mile to exit 41.) Turn right. At 0.1 mile bear right at a parking area and campground entrance, continuing for 0.4 mile to the trailhead (elev. 125 ft.). Privy available. If the lot is full, park back at the picnic area near the hatchery.

ON THE TRAIL

Among the oldest trails in the Northwest, Eagle Creek Trail No. 440 was constructed in 1915 in tandem with the Columbia River Highway. The adjacent campground was opened in 1916, becoming the first US Forest Service campground in the country. The recommended hike described here is to Tunnel Falls, but any distance along this trail will suffice.

Start up the trail through the tight canyon. The Eagle Creek Fire (see sidebar, "Burning Down the Forest" in the Silver Star section) surprisingly spared many of the canyon's old-growth trees. But do expect a lot of burnt and dead trees and windfall along the way. Gradually climb along narrow and overhanging ledges nearly 100 feet above the churning creek. Grab onto cable handrails for assurance. The trail crosses many cascading creeks—especially during the wetter months. Catch a glimpse of Eagle

Creek's Metlako Falls, named for the Native word for "the goddess of salmon." The anadromous fish definitely needs a higher power to negotiate this 100-plus-foot plunge, one of the tallest of Eagle Creek's copious cascades. Catch a glimpse, too, of 100-foot Sorenson Creek Falls on Sorenson Creek cascading into Eagle Creek.

After hopping across Sorenson Creek, come to a junction at 1.8 miles. Here a spur leads right 0.2 mile, dropping 150 feet to the base of Lower Punch Bowl Falls. The real treat, however, lies just ahead. At 2 miles come to an overlook of one of the Pacific Northwest's most photographed cascades, 35-foot Punch Bowl Falls plunging into a basaltic amphitheater. If it looks familiar, check your old calendars.

Now continue upstream, crossing Tish Creek on a high bridge and then Fern Creek on an even higher bridge. The surrounding valley walls grow tighter, the scenery more dramatic. Here once again, the trail is blasted into ledges, and there is considerable exposure. Grab onto the cable and keep children and dogs close.

At 3.2 miles stand mesmerized staring at slender 90-foot Loowit Falls tumbling into roiling, thundering Eagle Creek. Then at 3.3 miles clutch your heart—and the railings—and mosey across High Bridge, a solid steel structure spanning a fern-lined, mossy, tight chasm 120 feet above Eagle Creek.

The terrain now becomes a little less intimidating but nevertheless remains spectacular. Oaks and moss cling to basalt walls, and tributary creeks cascade into the canyon. At 3.6 miles come to thundering Skoonichuk Falls (elev. 600 ft.), and shortly afterward pass Tenas Camp, which was damaged by the fire and is no longer usable.

At 4 miles cross Eagle Creek on 4½ Mile Bridge (the trail used to start at the car campground, hence the mileage difference), returning to the east side of the canyon and closer to water level once again. Surviving big trees begin to intersperse with younger growth, recently burnt trees, and old burnt snags—evidence of a large fire that swept through in 1902.

At 4.9 miles cross Wy'East Creek (tricky in high water), pass the old Wy'East Camp (closed for regeneration), and enter the Mark O. Hatfield Wilderness (elev. 900 ft.). At 5.2 miles come to the junction with the Eagle-Benson Trail, a very steep, difficult, and now closed trail heavily damaged by the Eagle Creek Fire. Continue upstream, entering unburnt forest and passing Blue Grouse Camp. The way then gets rockier and at times blasted into ledges before bending left into the amphitheater cradling mind-blowing Tunnel Falls (elev. 1200 ft.) at 6 miles.

Here, Eagle Creek's East Fork plummets 160 feet over sheer basalt walls cloaked with maidenhair ferns into a verdant pool. Impressive, yes, but even more so is the trail that tunnels behind it. The early trail builders blasted a tunnel behind the falls and a catwalk into the surrounding ledge. Wet and potentially treacherous, it's also an exhilarating trek through the tunnel and across the waterfall basin. Take your time and savor this stunning Northwest classic!

EXTENDING YOUR TRIP

If not prone to vertigo, continue 0.2 mile along a heart-racing stretch of steep vertical ledges (clutch that cable) coming to mind-blowing 148-foot Twister Falls (a.k.a. Crossover Falls and several other names). Here the creek plunges into two

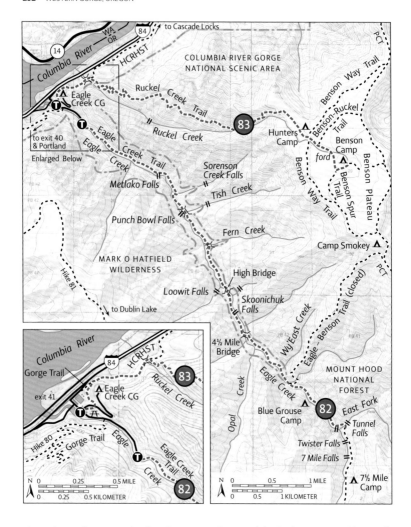

channels crossing over each other. Continue another 0.2 mile to the last of Eagle Creek's major falls, 52-foot Seven Mile Falls (a.k.a. Upper Eagle Creek Falls). The trail continues beyond in old forest, passing 7½ mile

Camp and the Eagle-Tanner Trail (currently closed) at 7.6 miles from the trailhead, before hooking east and winding its way out of the valley to Wahtum Lake (13 miles from the trailhead).

83 Benson Plateau via Ruckel Creek

RATING/ DIFFICULTY	ROUNDTRIP	ELEV GAIN/ HIGH POINT	SEASON
***/5	11.2 miles	3900 feet/ 4000 feet	Late May– Nov

Crowds: 2; **Map:** Green Trails Columbia River Gorge West No. 428S; **Contact:** Columbia River Gorge National Scenic Area; **Notes:** NW Forest Pass or Interagency Pass required. Trail was severely impacted by the 2017 Eagle Creek Fire and is currently closed. Trailkeepers of Oregon is currently working on reopening it. Check with CRGNSA on its status, and once trail is reopened, expect hazards in the form of downed trees, brush, and washouts. Wilderness rules apply. High trailhead break-in area—leave no valuables in your vehicle; **GPS:** N 45° 38.459', W 121° 55.587'

A bulky, imposing, and nearly level peak in the heart of the Columbia River Gorge, the Benson Plateau is the closest thing in western Oregon to a bona fide mesa. While views are

Ruckel Creek flows near its headwaters, before the trail reaches the burn zone.

slim from the thickly forested summit of this flat-topped peak, there are some excellent vistas along the way. Flowers, too, and Native American vision quest pits. A whole lot of elevation gain makes this hike among the Gorge's most challenging.

GETTING THERE

From Portland, follow I-84 east to exit 41 (Eagle Creek, Fish Hatchery). (From Hood River, leave I-84 West at exit 40, get back on the freeway headed east, and drive 1 mile to exit 41.) Turn right and reach the parking area at the campground entrance in 0.1 mile (elev. 100 ft.). Attractive stone privy available.

ON THE TRAIL

From the parking area, follow the road left toward the Eagle Creek Campground. After a few hundred feet, head left on the Gorge Trail. Climb a bluff above the freeway, skirting the campground, and then drop beneath a canopy of big trees to reach a junction with the paved Historic Columbia River Highway State Trail at 0.4 mile. Now head right. At 0.7 mile cross tumbling Ruckel Creek on one of the last remaining old highway bridges. Timber baron and hotel builder Simon Benson was one of the financial backers of the highway. Benson Plateau, however, is named for a local stockman, not the financier.

Now beside the pretty waterway, follow Ruckel Creek Trail No. 405. The trail soon departs its namesake, not nearing it again until approaching Benson's summit. Steeply climbing, cross a powerline swath with a good view to Hamilton Mountain, and enter the Mark O. Hatfield Wilderness. The trail gets steeper, winding through a mosaic burn zone and through a mossy talus slope (elev. 700 ft.). Scan the talus for depressions. Like on several other ridges and peaks

throughout the Gorge, Native peoples dug pits here for vision quests. Respect them by not disturbing them.

The way gets more difficult, traversing scorched forest and steeply climbing a fluted ridge. Pass good viewpoints before emerging at a precipitous clifftop vista (use caution) at about 2.5 miles (elev. 1900 ft.). Enjoy an eagle's-eye perspective of the Bonneville Dam, the Bridge of the Gods, Wauna Lake, and Table and Greenleaf Mountains.

The grade thankfully eases, traveling up grassy slopes bursting with wildflowers and sporting pockets of oaks. Enjoy excellent views down into the Eagle Creek valley. After passing a spring decorated by showy monkey flowers, the trail once again ratchets upward. And as you approach Ruckel Creek, the trail enters cool old growth and begins yet another brutal ascent.

At 4.6 miles a climbing reprieve is finally granted upon cresting the plateau and reaching a junction (elev. 3700 ft.) with the abandoned Rudolph Spur Trail on the left and the unmaintained (and closed) Ruckel Ridge Trail on the right.

To explore Benson Plateau and its unburnt forest and legendary bear grass, continue straight up the Ruckel Creek Trail. Just don't anticipate any views. At 5.1 miles intersect the Benson Way Trail (elev. 3900 ft.) at Hunters Camp. Left heads 1.3 miles north (through a small burn zone) to the Pacific Crest Trail (PCT). Right travels south 1.8 miles to the PCT. Using the PCT, you can make a 5.5-mile loop along the plateau's rim. Otherwise, continue straight, traveling alongside Ruckel Creek, and soon come to the Benson-Ruckel Trail, which heads 0.9 mile northeast to intersect with the PCT, another loop option. The Ruckel Creek Trail continues right, fording Ruckel

Creek before climbing a little to arrive at yet another junction at 5.5 miles. The 0.5-mile Benson Spur Trail leads right here, passing some small wetland pools before reaching the Benson Way Trail, offering yet another loop option.

Continue left 0.1 mile on the Ruckel Creek Trail and come to Benson Camp (elev. 4000 ft.). Perched alongside the creek and some small meadows, it makes a good lunch and turnaround spot.

EXTENDING YOUR TRIP

Continue on the Ruckel Creek Trail for 0.6 mile to the PCT (elev. 4100 ft.). Then craft a loop or follow the PCT south for 1.3 miles to Camp Smokey in a small gap (elev. 3850 ft.). Then continue on the PCT for a short distance beyond to an open knoll for some good views.

84 Dry Creek Falls

RATING/ DIFFICULTY	ROUNDTRIP	ELEV GAIN/ HIGH POINT	SEASON
***/3	4.4 miles	750 feet/ 875 feet	Year-round

Crowds: 3; **Map:** Green Trails Columbia River Gorge West No. 428S; **Contact:** Columbia River Gorge National Scenic Area; **Notes:** NW Forest Pass or Interagency Pass required; **GPS:** N 45° 39.745', W 121° 53.791'

A misnomer, Dry Creek isn't dry at all. Hike a quiet stretch (except when the procession of thru hikers is in session) of the Pacific Crest Trail (PCT) to this pretty 74-foot cascade careening out of a narrow basaltic canyon. Enjoy, too, hiking through green mature forest within the Eagle Creek Fire burn zone.

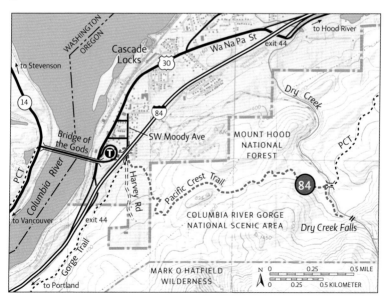

Dry Creek Falls in a columnar basalt basin

GETTING THERE

From Portland, follow I-84 east to exit 44 at Cascade Locks. Proceed for 0.3 mile and then bear right onto the access road for the Bridge of the Gods to Stevenson. (From Hood River, follow I-84 west to exit 44 at Cascade Locks, and proceed for 1.5 miles on Wa Na Pa Street through town, turning left onto the bridge access road.) In 0.2 mile reach the Bridge of the Gods trailhead on your right (before the bridge toll booth; elev. 175 ft.). Privy available.

ON THE TRAIL

From the trailhead in Toll House Park, carefully cross the bridge access road and follow the PCT south. Cross under I-84 and bear right onto SW Moody Avenue. Then immediately walk straight onto Harvey Road and at 0.2 mile come to a parking area (alternative start) on the right for the Gorge Trail. The PCT bids the road adieu and veers left. Follow it.

On smooth tread and climbing gently, the national scenic trail (see sidebar, "Mexico to Canada" in the western Washington section) meanders through an attractive forest of Douglas-firs and vine maples that pretty much survived the Eagle Creek Fire lightly scathed. In autumn the maples streak the understory gold, nicely complementing the emerald canopy. At 1.2 miles come to a powerline swath. Go right on the service road and then immediately left back on trail

The trail continues its moderate ascent, traversing steep forested hillsides and passing beneath a mossy basalt knob, a signature formation in the Columbia Gorge. At about 1.5 miles it makes a slight descent. Cascading water soon replaces the distant lull of traffic and trains. At 2 miles reach a junction with an old woods road at Dry Creek (elev. 725 ft.). Turn right on the old woods road, and after a short and brisk climb, reach Dry Creek Falls (elev. 875 ft.) at 2.2 miles. Plummeting 74 feet into an old catch basin beneath mossy basalt walls, the falls are quite impressive.

But why the dry name? The city of Cascade Locks once diverted water from the creek, causing its creekbed to run dry.

EXTENDING YOUR TRIP

Continue following the PCT to another pretty waterfall, some interesting landforms, and nice views. In 1 mile cross a basalt talus slope that grants good views of Stevenson across the Columbia. At 1.7 miles, after cresting a ridge spur (elev. 975 ft.), reach the two basalt Herman Creek Pinnacles (elev. 835 ft.). Just beyond is a cataract plummeting down a tight chasm. Continue farther still, traversing a long talus slope with excellent views of the Columbia River and Washington peaks and ridges. At 2.2 miles the PCT reaches the Herman Creek Bridge Trail (elev. 1000 ft.), a logical spot to call it quits. If you're interested in what lies beyond, consult Hike 85.

85 Benson Plateau via Pacific Crest Trail

RATING/ DIFFICULTY	ROUNDTRIP	ELEV GAIN/ HIGH POINT	SEASON
****/5	15.6 miles	3980 feet/ 4170 feet	Late May– Nov

Crowds: 2; **Map:** Green Trails Columbia River Gorge West No. 428S; **Contact:** Columbia River Gorge National Scenic Area; **Notes:** NW Forest Pass or Interagency Pass required. Wilderness rules apply; **GPS:** N 45° 40.969', W 121° 50.540'

A geographical oddity in the Gorge, this nearly flat, broad, hulking summit is the remnant of an ancient giant lava flow. The agents of erosion have done a wonderful job over the millennia carving out its steep, fluted ridges and making it appear like a giant citadel. Getting to Benson's expansive flat top requires a bit of storming the castle. Several trails lead to this fortress—all of them steep. The Pacific Crest Trail (PCT) offers the easiest route—but also the longest.

GETTING THERE

From Portland, follow I-84 east to exit 44 for Cascade Locks. Proceed 1.8 miles through town on the Wa Na Pa Street to a stop sign. Go straight, underneath I-84, and then bear left onto Frontage Road for 1.6 miles to the Herman Creek Campground entrance. (From Hood River, leave I-84 West at exit 47 and follow the Frontage Road for 0.7 mile to the campground entrance.) In 0.2 mile bear right, coming to the Herman Creek trailhead (elev. 250 ft.) shortly afterward. Privy available.

ON THE TRAIL

Start hiking on well-traveled Herman Creek Trail No. 406. Shortly after crossing

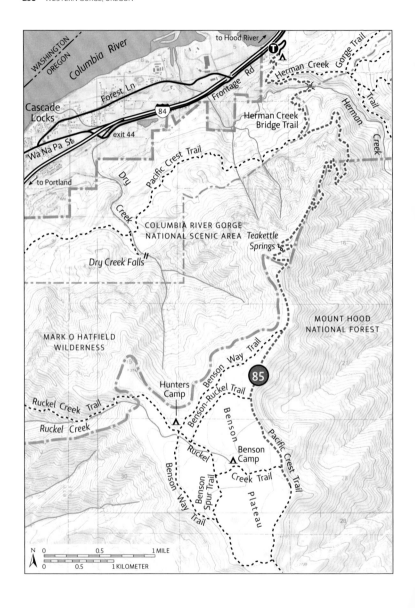

View across Herman Creek to Nick Eaton Ridge

a powerline service road, reach a trail junction (elev. 650 ft.) at 0.6 mile. Bear right onto Herman Creek Bridge Trail No. 406E and traverse a small talus slope with views up to citadel Benson before descending to a sturdy steel bridge spanning cascading Herman Creek (elev. 500 ft.). The forest here succumbed mostly to a surface fire during the Eagle Creek conflagration, leaving the crowns green and intact.

Resume climbing, soon coming to another talus slope with impressive views up the steep basalt parapets of the plateau. At 1.8 miles enter the Mark O. Hatfield Wilderness and come to the PCT (elev. 1000 ft.). Right leads to Dry Creek Falls (Hike 84) and Cascade Locks. Head left. In typical PCT fashion,

the trail climbs at a moderate pace, making long switchbacks to tackle the awaiting 3000 vertical feet.

Cross talus slopes with good views out to the Columbia and Stevenson. At 2.7 miles pass a dry campsite and good viewpoint (elev. 1460 ft.) before beginning a long journey across timbered slopes. Some impressive trees cling to Benson's steep ridges. At about 5 miles crest an open ridge and pause to take in excellent views of the Herman Creek valley, Nick Eaton Ridge, the Columbia River, and more. Enjoy the flowers too, which add colorful touches to the brown rocky slope.

The way continues upward, across patches of burnt forest and slopes of bear grass with their resplendent blossoms in early summer. Enjoy some excellent views, too, along the way. At 5.5 miles, in a grove of big hemlocks, come to Teakettle Springs (elev. 3475 ft.). Now traverse a burn zone. At 6 miles the relentless climb ceases as you crest Benson's long northeastern arm of a ridge (elev. 3775 ft.). Give your quads a break with a slight descent before reaching a junction with the Benson Way Trail (elev. 3790 ft.) at 6.3 miles in a grove of big hemlocks. Catch window views from this forested mesa. Continue left on the PCT for another 0.25 mile of climbing and then enjoy near-flat wandering through colonnades of silver fir and waves of bear grass.

At 7 miles pass the lightly used Benson-Ruckel Trail (elev. 3980 ft.). Continue another 0.7 mile to the Ruckel Creek Trail junction (elev. 4170 ft.)—just beyond, some rimtop views to the east can be had. It's a tough hike to an interesting geological formation. This is a good turnaround point.

EXTENDING YOUR TRIP

If you have more energy, enjoy relatively level wandering on Benson's summit. Hike down the Ruckel Creek Trail 0.7 mile to Benson Camp (elev. 4000 ft.), situated alongside the creek in pocket meadows. Or continue 0.9 mile on the PCT, cresting Benson's 4200-foot high point, and then return to the PCT via the 3.2-mile Benson Way Trail for a trip around the plateau rim. En route pass an excellent viewpoint west over Eagle Creek and traverse a small burn zone. In early season expect wet feet crossing Ruckel Creek.

Opposite: *Glorious vista along the Rowena Plateau (Hike 104)*

eastern gorge, oregon

Expect plentiful sunshine, steep basalt walls, and bluffs that burst with brilliant wildflower blossoms in the spring—in the eastern reaches of Oregon's Columbia River Gorge. Challenge yourself on some of the Gorge's toughest trails and highest peaks, or leisurely meander on nature trails along flower-studded slopes. Hike back into time, exploring historical trails and roads, or venture high above the Gorge into the Mark O. Hatfield Wilderness to alpine lakes and summits providing spectacular views. Explore lovely trails, too, in the communities of Hood River and The Dalles, and be sure to visit the superb Columbia Gorge Discovery Center & Museum in The Dalles. Summer can be hot and winter cold. Fall and spring are best.

86 Herman Creek Ancient Cedars

RATING/ DIFFICULTY	ROUNDTRIP	ELEV GAIN/ HIGH POINT	SEASON
****/4	15 miles	2700 feet/ 2800 feet	Late Apr– Nov

Crowds: 2; **Map:** Green Trails Columbia River Gorge West No. 428S; **Contact:** Columbia River Gorge National Scenic Area; **Notes:** NW Forest Pass or Interagency Pass required. Wilderness rules apply; **GPS:** N 45° 40.969', W 121° 50.540'

Overlooked by many hikers due to its length and lack of views, the Herman Creek Trail is great when you need a break from the neighboring crowded trails. Stretches of this long but moderate hike were burned in 2017, but luckily not its exceptional stand of old-growth red cedars. The trail also wanders through ancient giant noble firs, hemlocks, and Douglas-firs. And there are a couple of

waterfalls along the way too, but Herman Creek remains pretty evasive.

GETTING THERE

From Portland, follow I-84 east to exit 44 for Cascade Locks. Proceed 1.8 miles through town on the Wa Na Pa Street to a stop sign. Go straight, underneath I-84, and then bear left onto Frontage Road for 1.6 miles to the Herman Creek Campground entrance. (From Hood River, leave I-84 West at exit 47 and follow the Frontage Road for 0.7 mile to the campground entrance.) In 0.2 mile bear right, coming to the Herman Creek trailhead (elev. 250 ft.) shortly afterward. Privy available.

ON THE TRAIL

Providing access for several other trails, Herman Creek Trail No. 406 starts off wide and well-trodden. Pass a powerline service road before reaching a junction (elev. 650 ft.) with the Herman Creek Bridge Trail at 0.6 mile. Herman Creek crashes below—about the only evidence for some time that the creek is near. Continue left and soon come to an old road. Bear right and, after a short climb, enjoy fairly level walking to a three-way junction (elev. 1000 ft.) at 1.3 miles. The Gorton Creek Trail to Nick Eaton Ridge (Hike 87) and the Gorge Trail to Wyeth Campground veer left. Continue right, entering the Mark O. Hatfield Wilderness and coming to a junction with the Nick Eaton Trail at 1.4 miles.

Stay right on the Herman Creek Trail, which continues as an old road for a short distance and traverses a recent burn zone. Then slightly descend into a forest of older and bigger trees. Pass a tall slender waterfall and an oak-topped bluff providing valley views before reaching Camp Creek, which may dampen your boots.

Old-growth Douglas-fir

Traverse steep slopes above Herman Creek as you continue deeper up the valley. It's peaceful, and quite a contrast from busy Eagle Creek. Pass another slender waterfall and come to a junction (elev. 1500 ft.) with the extremely steep and lightly maintained Casey Creek Trail at 3.9 miles. An unmarked side spur here drops to the right, losing 400 feet in 0.4 mile to a camp at the confluence of Herman Creek and its East Fork.

Continue on the middle trail, cross Casey Creek, and enter a brushy burn zone. Continue up the valley across more creeks, through old-growth and fire-succession forests, and across a big scree slope before reaching pretty Slide Creek Falls. After two potentially tricky creek crossings—at Mullinix and Whiskey—the way ascends more steadily and enters impressive ancient forest. Giant hemlocks, noble firs, and Douglas-firs line the way. And the East Fork Herman Creek now runs close to the trail.

At 7 miles come to a junction with the Herman Creek Cutoff Trail (elev. 2800 ft.), which leads up Waucoma Ridge. The ancient cedar swamp lies 0.3 mile straight ahead. Campsites dot the magnificent grove—one of the finest old-growth cedar stands in the Gorge. Find a spot to sit and savor this forest, which was old even when our nation was young.

EXTENDING YOUR TRIP

Strong hikers and runners and backpackers can continue 1.9 miles up the Herman Creek Trail, crossing the East Fork and passing more camps to reach the 0.2 mile Mud Lake Trail, although the lake is easier to reach from Wahtum Lake (Hike 96). Alternatively, strong adventurers can make a loop by taking the Herman Creek Cutoff Trail (in good shape) to Nick Eaton Ridge and then returning via either the Nick Eaton Trail or Gorton Creek Trail (expect a lot of fire zone obstacles). This option adds more than 2000 vertical feet and 4.5 miles to the round-trip.

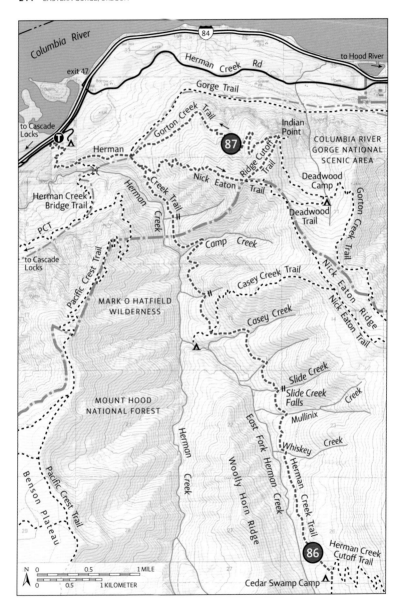

87 Nick Eaton Ridge

RATING/ DIFFICULTY	LOOP	ELEV GAIN/ HIGH POINT	SEASON
****/4	8.3 miles	2900 feet/ 2950 feet	Late Apr– Nov

Crowds: 4; **Map:** Green Trails Columbia River Gorge West No. 428S; **Contact:** Columbia River Gorge National Scenic Area; **Notes:** NW Forest Pass or Interagency Pass required. Wilderness rules apply; **GPS:** N 45° 40.969', W 121° 50.540'

An invigorating loop through beautiful old-growth forest and flower-studded hillsides that largely escaped burning up in the 2017 Eagle Creek Fire. En route enjoy excellent views of the Herman Creek valley and the lofty peaks flanking its watershed. If you're not prone to vertigo, venture down a short steep path to Indian Point, a basalt thumb that precariously hovers 2000 feet above the Columbia River. With a racing heart, enjoy one of the most exhilarating views in the Gorge.

GETTING THERE

From Portland, follow I-84 east to exit 44 for Cascade Locks. Proceed 1.8 miles through town on Wa Na Pa Street to a stop sign. Go straight, underneath I-84, and then bear left onto Frontage Road for 1.6 miles to the Herman Creek Campground entrance. (From Hood River, leave I-84 West at exit 47 and follow Frontage Road for 0.7 mile to the campground entrance.) In 0.2 mile bear right, coming to the trailhead (elev. 250 ft.) shortly afterward. Privy available.

ON THE TRAIL

The starting point for an array of adventures, Herman Creek is a major trail hub in the Gorge. Follow the wide and well-trodden Herman Creek Trail No. 406, passing a powerline service road before reaching a junction (elev. 550 ft.) with the Herman Creek Bridge Trail at 0.6 mile. Continue left, soon following an old road and coming to a three-way junction (elev. 1000 ft.) at 1.3 miles.

The trail to your immediate left is the Gorge Trail, which travels more than 5 miles to Wyeth Campground. The trail just to the right of it is Gorton Creek Trail No. 408, your return route on this lollipop loop. Continue right on the Herman Creek Trail for just over 0.1 mile to another junction. Then head left on Nick Eaton Trail No. 447. Enter the Mark O. Hatfield Wilderness, passing through old-growth forest that mostly survived the 2017 Eagle Creek Fire. The route becomes brutally steep. The tread is generally good, but farther along small, loose rocks act as ball bearings, making slipping easy. It's much easier coming down the gentler and smoother Gorton Creek Trail, hence the counterclockwise direction of this loop.

At 2.6 miles your toil is rewarded as you traverse open grassy slopes. Savor excellent views of the Columbia River, Benson Plateau, and the wild Herman Creek valley with Woolly Horn Ridge (love that name) sitting in the center. In early season pause to marvel at the bountiful blossoms. Then continue climbing into a badly fire-scorched forest. At 3.4 miles come to a junction (elev. 2950 ft.). The Nick Eaton Trail continues right, up its namesake, sprawling ridge, named for ol' Nick who farmed the valley below in the early 1900s.

Here head left (or see below) on good tread in unburnt forest on the Ridge Cutoff Trail, descending to meet the Gorton Creek Trail (elev. 2700 ft.) at 4 miles. But before turning left to close the loop, head right if

The Nick Eaton Trail offers good vistas of the nearby Benson Plateau.

you're not too skittish about heights (best to leave children and dogs behind—with a trusted companion, of course), and immediately come to an unmarked trail heading left. Follow this path through a jumble of vine maples, dropping 200 feet in less than 0.2 mile to emerge at an extremely narrow ledge (use extreme caution) leading to Indian Point, a protruding precipitous basalt thumb hovering more than 2000 feet above the valley. Forget about scaling Indian Point lest you find yourself in Indian Heaven—instead, gasp at its rugged beauty from a safe distance while you take in breathtaking views of the Columbia and points east—Augspurger and Dog Mountains, Wygant Peak, Mitchell Point, Shellrock Mountain . . . and Mount Adams floating above them!

Then return to the Gorton Creek Trail and head right for 2.6 miles on a knee-friendly descent through beautiful, mostly unburnt old-growth forest back to the Herman Creek Trail. From here it's 1.3 familiar miles back to the trailhead.

EXTENDING YOUR TRIP

For a longer loop, from the Ridge Cutoff Trail junction, continue southeast on the Nick Eaton Trail. At 0.1 mile a short spur leads left to a knoll with excellent views north. At 0.5 mile in a burn zone, head left on the Deadwood Trail and descend 0.5 mile in green forest to the Gorton Creek Trail. Then head left, traversing beautiful old growth and coming to the Ridge Cutoff Trail's lower junction in 0.8 mile.

88 North Lake via Wyeth Trail

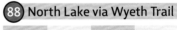

RATING/ DIFFICULTY	ROUNDTRIP	ELEV GAIN/ HIGH POINT	SEASON
***/5	13 miles	4050 feet/ 4000 feet	Late May–Nov

Crowds: 1; **Map:** Green Trails Columbia River Gorge West No. 428S; **Contact:** Columbia

River Gorge National Scenic Area; **Notes:** NW Forest Pass or Interagency Pass required. Trail was heavily impacted by the 2017 Eagle Creek Fire. Expect hazards in the form of downed trees, and avoid during high winds. Wilderness rules apply; **GPS:** N 45° 41.268', W 121° 46.316'

Tucked within a cirque beneath Green Point Mountain and surrounded by old-growth forest, North Lake is a pretty site indeed. While you can reach it by a much shorter and easier route, getting there via the Wyeth Trail up the imposing Gorge Face gives you a great workout and a good assurance of solitude.

GETTING THERE

From Portland or Hood River, follow I-84 to exit 51 (Wyeth). Head south and then immediately turn right on Herman Creek Road. After 0.1 mile turn left into Wyeth Campground, continuing 0.2 mile to the trailhead (elev. 250 ft.). Privy available.

ON THE TRAIL

Begin your journey from Wyeth, Oregon, a tiny outpost named after inventor and explorer Nathaniel Wyeth. Once a train stop, then a Civilian Conservation Corps camp, then a Civilian Public Service Camp for conscientious objectors during World War II—this spot has a fascinating history.

Wyeth Trail No. 411 starts along Gorton Creek on an old road. Bear left at the junction with the Gorge Trail, and immediately climb up and over a knoll and cross a powerline swath. At 0.4 mile rock hop across Harphan Creek, and enter the Mark O. Hatfield Wilderness. Now in beautiful open forest, steadily climb. After about a mile enter the Eagle Creek Fire burn zone. The trail was

heavily impacted by the fire. Volunteers with Trailkeepers of Oregon were able to finally reopen this trail in 2022, but expect a lot of obstacles—blowdowns, brush, and washouts. On a positive note, now enjoy views north over the river and to Mount St. Helens.

The trail ascends a ridge above Harphan Creek, now steeply switchbacking up steep slopes. Cross a brushy talus slope and round an open bluff (elev. 2800 ft.), catching views out to the Wind River valley across the Columbia. Continue higher, passing across another bluff, pretty in summer when it's decked out in blossoms. The way relentlessly gains elevation.

Eventually the grade eases and you leave the burn zone, entering beautiful mature

North Lake

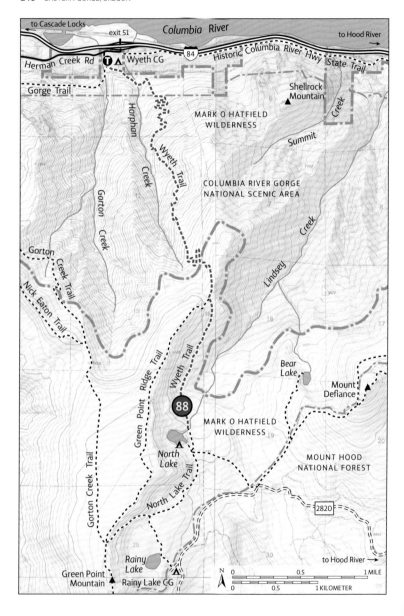

to Cascade Locks

exit 51

Columbia River

to Hood River

Herman Creek Rd

84

Wyeth CG

Historic Columbia River Hwy State Trail

Gorge Trail

Shellrock Mountain

MARK O HATFIELD WILDERNESS

Harphan Creek

Wyeth Trail

Summit

Creek

COLUMBIA RIVER GORGE NATIONAL SCENIC AREA

Gorton Creek

Lindsey Creek

Gorton Creek Trail

Nick Eaton Trail

Green Point Ridge Trail

Wyeth Trail

Bear Lake

Mount Defiance

88

MARK O HATFIELD WILDERNESS

North Lake

Gorton Creek Trail

North Lake Trail

MOUNT HOOD NATIONAL FOREST

2820

to Hood River

Rainy Lake

Green Point Mountain

Rainy Lake CG

N

0   0.5   1 MILE

0   0.5   1 KILOMETER

forest. At 5 miles come to a junction with the Green Point Ridge Trail (elev. 3900 ft.). Stay left on a path lined with huckleberry bushes and tufts of bear grass, traversing gentle terrain beneath Green Point Ridge. Catch occasional glimpses east of towering Mount Defiance. After crossing a talus slope, descend into a beautiful grove of giant firs (elev. 3700 ft.). Then climb again, crossing Lindsey Creek and soon after arriving at a junction (elev. 4000 ft.) at 6.4 miles.

North Lake lies just ahead—follow the path right a few hundred feet to the lake's outlet on what appears to be an old earthen dam. The lake is shallow and surrounded by towering old conifers and steep brushy scree slopes. Not dramatic, but still a nice little spot—and often popular with backpackers coming in from the Wyeth trailhead on Forest Road 2820 a mere 0.8 mile away. Another lake spur (and camps) is reached 0.1 mile ahead where the Wyeth Trail intersects the North Lake Trail.

EXTENDING YOUR TRIP
Follow the North Lake Trail 1.3 miles through gorgeous ancient forest to Green Point Mountain (Hike 99). Then turn right and hike the lonely Green Point Ridge Trail north for 2.7 miles and a gradual descent back to the Wyeth Trail junction. From here head left 5.5 miles back to your start.

89 Mount Defiance

RATING/ DIFFICULTY	LOOP	ELEV GAIN/ HIGH POINT	SEASON
*****/5	13.2 miles	5130 feet/ 4960 feet	Late June– Nov

Crowds: 2; **Map:** Green Trails Columbia River Gorge West No. 428S; **Contact:** Columbia River Gorge National Scenic Area; **Notes:**

Wilderness rules apply; **GPS:** N 45° 41.298', W 121° 41.446'

The granddaddy guardian of the Gorge, Mount Defiance rises nearly one vertical mile above the Columbia River, the highest peak in the Gorge. Many a hiker and trail runner use this mountain's 4800-foot elevation gain to condition for bigger climbs and runs. For a real challenge, follow a spectacular loop to the summit. Savor sweeping views and enjoy one of the Gorge's prettiest subalpine lakes en route.

GETTING THERE
From Portland, follow I-84 east to exit 55 (Starvation Creek Rest Area) and the Starvation Creek trailhead (elev. 150 ft.). Privy available. (From Hood River, follow I-84 west to exit 51 and then double back to exit 55, which is an eastbound exit only.)

ON THE TRAIL
Despite that Defiance's summit is defiled with communication towers, the way up and summit-block scree slopes provide gorgeous views. Defiance can be reached from a much shorter and easier route from the south (see Hike 100), but this route is a classic—and one of the hardest hikes in the Gorge. It's a loop ascending via the insanely steep Starvation Ridge Trail No. 414, which is not advisable to descend unless you hate your knees.

Start by heading west on the paved Historic Columbia River Highway State Trail (HCRHST) alongside busy I-84. At 0.3 mile pass the Starvation Cutoff Trail (currently closed due to a slide). At 0.6 mile head left on Mount Defiance Trail No. 413 and enter a cool ravine. Then cross Warren Creek on a bridge below Hole-in-the-Wall Falls (created in 1938 by highway workers to divert water away from the old highway).

Come to a junction at 0.8 mile. You'll be returning from the right, so head left on the Starvation Ridge Trail, climbing to an airy ledge (elev. 800 ft.). Then drop to cross

Cabin Creek (elev. 560 ft.) and steeply climb. This stretch is rife with poison oak and skirts steep drop-offs—so stay alert. At 1.8 miles pass the upper junction with the cutoff and begin traversing a grassy flowering bluff beneath powerlines. Take in tremendous

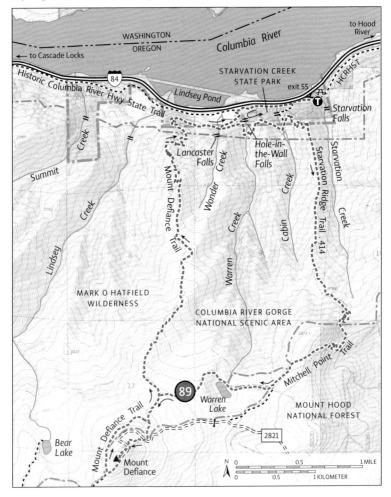

Mount Hood as seen from the talus slopes of Mount Defiance's summit

views of Dog Mountain. Soon crest the narrow bluff (elev. 1200 ft.) by a lone fir and head southward into forest, entering the Mark O. Hatfield Wilderness. Now following a narrow ridge dividing the Cabin and Starvation Creek drainages, vigorously climb. The grade is insanely steep at times. Trekking poles will come in handy.

Cross a talus slope and transition into a forest of hemlock, soon leaving the wilderness area. Then traverse a large talus slope (elev. 3250 ft.) granting a good view north to Mount Adams. Soon afterward, at the edge of an old cut, the hike becomes pleasurable as the Starvation Ridge Trail transitions to the Mitchell Point Trail (which no longer heads to its namesake) on an easy grade along a broad ridge. Enjoy views north to St. Helens along the way.

At 6 miles reach a junction (elev. 3800 ft.). The trail left leads 0.4 mile to the Mount Defiance summit service road (gated at the trailhead). Continue straight back into the wilderness, reaching pretty Warren Lake (elev. 3720 ft.) at 6.4 miles. Set in a bowl surrounded by shiny slabs of scree and lined with vine maples (pretty in autumn), Warren is one of the more picturesque subalpine lakes in the Gorge.

Now clamber over rock toward Defiance's broad rounded summit. Views north to snowy Washington volcanoes and endless verdant ridges are excellent. Swaying bear grass lines the way as you enter scrappy lodgepole pine forest. At 7.1 miles reach the Mount Defiance Trail (elev. 4240 ft.). Turn left here and head up. At 7.3 miles stay left at a junction—you'll be returning from the right. Continue through cool forest, crossing the summit road twice and arriving at the less-than-appealing 4960-foot summit at 7.7 miles.

Congratulate yourself and then leave the towered summit, following trail south across shiny scree speckled with purple penstemon to a junction (elev. 4800 ft.) at 7.9 miles. This is where you'll want to lunch, with excellent views of Mount Hood and the lofty green peaks surrounding Wahtum Lake. The trail left drops 1000 feet over 1.4 miles to FR 2820—it's the easy route up Mount Defiance (Hike 100). Stay right, rounding beneath the summit, traversing several talus slopes. Watch your footing and marvel in unfurling, sprawling views east and south. At 8.6 miles return to the Mount Defiance Trail (elev. 4500 ft.).

Now turn left and begin the long descent. Bear left at 8.8 miles and continue down the Mount Defiance Trail. The grade isn't too bad at first but grows much steeper as you descend. The way skirts the eastern edge of the Eagle Creek Fire zone. Much of the old growth here survived the blaze. Steeply descend, passing a couple of excellent viewpoints. Then a series of steep switchbacks tests your knees for the final descent.

At 12 miles the trail turns east in a powerline swath. It then passes beneath lovely Lancaster Falls (elev. 350 ft.) at 12.3 miles. Soon afterward pass the Starvation Ridge Trail. Then return right on the HCRHST and reach the trailhead at 13.2 miles.

EXTENDING YOUR TRIP

While you're in the area be sure to check out the two-tiered Starvation Falls that drops more than 200 feet. It's a mere 0.1 mile away from the trailhead on a paved path.

90 Wygant Peak

RATING/ DIFFICULTY	ROUNDTRIP	ELEV GAIN/ HIGH POINT	SEASON
***/4	9.2 miles	2280 feet/ 2214 feet	Late Mar–Nov

Crowds: 2; **Map:** Green Trails Columbia River Gorge West No. 428S; **Contact:** Columbia River Gorge National Scenic Area; **Notes:** Construction of the HCRHST in the region expected to be completed by 2024 will change the approach of this trail; **GPS:** N 45° 42.161', W 121° 37.172'

Panorama across the Columbia River to Drano Lake and Nestor Peak

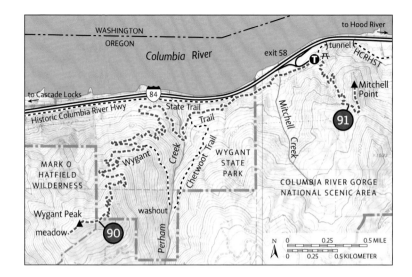

Despite being located right off of busy I-84, the Wygant Trail is one of the quietest hikes in the Gorge when it comes to use. Granted, the summit is forested and reaching it requires some steep climbing. But the trail—thanks to the Trailkeepers of Oregon (TKO)—is in good shape. And there are excellent viewpoints along the way. And wildflowers too—and poison oak, so cover up or save this one for October.

GETTING THERE

From Portland, follow I-84 east to exit 58 (Mitchell Point Overlook). (From Hood River, follow I-84 west to exit 56 at Viento State Park and then double back to exit 58, which is an eastbound exit only.) Drive 0.2 mile to a large parking area (elev. 175 ft.). Privy available.

ON THE TRAIL

Walk back on the road a short distance to the Historic Columbia River Highway State Trail (HCRHST) and follow it west. Pass an old foundation and cross Mitchell Creek. At 0.4 mile leave the HCRHST on the Wygant Trail heading into a little ravine. Beside a small waterfall, steeply switchback out of the gully to a broad forested bench.

At 1.1 miles come to a junction (elev. 300 ft.) with the Chetwoot Trail. Built by volunteers in the 1970s, unfortunately this nice loop into the Perham Creek canyon can no longer be recommended due to a missing bridge and slide damage. Hopefully TKO has this trail on their future work docket. *Chetwoot* means "bear" (hence the trail sign graphic) in Chinook Jargon, a trade language derived from English, French, and Coast Salish. The Wygant Trail was originally built by the Civilian Conservation Corps.

Continue straight, passing a junction at 1.2 miles with a short spur leading along an oak bluff to a fair view of Dog Mountain. Head left, dropping to Perham Creek (elev. 250 ft.), and cross it on a fallen log. Use caution. Then climb out of the ravine through oak forest to a powerline swath, soon afterward coming to an excellent viewpoint (elev. 400 ft.) of Dog Mountain and Cook Hill across the Columbia and Mitchell Point to the east.

The trail continues, switchbacking across the swath and through oak groves, soon reaching another viewpoint (be careful) before intersecting with the upper terminus of the Chetwoot Trail (elev. 1000 ft.) at 2.8 miles. Continue right and switchback through mature forest to a mossy knoll (elev. 1300 ft.) at 3.4 miles. Enjoy excellent viewing here above the river and out to Mount Adams. This is the highlight of this hike.

But a summit (albeit viewless) awaits, so plod on, occasionally steeply upward. At 4.4 miles enter the eastern limits of the Mark O. Hatfield Wilderness and reach Wygant's 2214-foot summit cloaked in Douglas-fir. But a surprise awaits. Continue 0.2 mile farther, dropping about 200 feet to a sprawling meadow, and enjoy excellent views west to Table, Defiance, Greenleaf, Wind, and other peaks.

91 Mitchell Point

RATING/ DIFFICULTY	ROUNDTRIP	ELEV GAIN/ HIGH POINT	SEASON
***/3	2.2 miles	1000 feet/ 1178 feet	Year-round

Crowds: 3; **Map:** Green Trails Columbia River Gorge West No. 428S; **Contact:** Columbia River Gorge National Scenic Area; **Notes:** Final stretch involves some exposure, not safe for children or dogs; **GPS:** N 45° 42.174', W 121° 37.109'

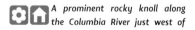 *A prominent rocky knoll along the Columbia River just west of*

Hood River, Mitchell Point was once the site of a beautiful five-window tunnel on the old Columbia River Highway, modeled after Switzerland's Axenstrasse. In 1966 this engineering marvel was destroyed to make way for I-84. Mitchell Point, however, still provides breathtaking views. This hike is short but not easy, and some hikers may find the final few feet a tad too exposed for comfort.

GETTING THERE

From Portland, follow I-84 east to exit 58 (Mitchell Point Overlook). (From Hood River, follow I-84 west to exit 56 at Viento State Park and then double back to exit 58, which is an eastbound exit only.) Drive 0.2 mile to a large parking area (elev. 175 ft.). Privy available.

ON THE TRAIL

Locate the paved path that angles south from the privy to a picnic table, and immediately veer off of it left onto a wide gravel path. Pass an old foundation on your right as you head left into the woods and climb! As the way starts to switchback, ignore a path veering right toward a water intake. The way, once part of a wagon route predating the Historic Columbia River Highway, grows steeper and rockier in places.

At 0.4 mile, ignore a side trail heading left. Soon afterward, switchback up a scree slope. Reenter forest, and then at 0.9 mile come to a saddle in a powerline swath. Turn left and head up the spine of Mitchell Point—first through oaks (and poison oak—be aware) and then onto an open rocky ledge. In spring and early summer, a wide assortment of flowers paints the stark rocky ridge and sheer cliffs.

The ridgeline grows narrower as you approach the 1178-foot summit. Chances are

Cook Hill rises above Drano Lake.

92 Hood River Waterfront Trail

RATING/ DIFFICULTY	ROUNDTRIP	ELEV GAIN/ HIGH POINT	SEASON
***/1	4.6 miles	negligible/ 80 feet	Year-round

Crowds: 5; **Map:** Port of Hood River; **Contact:** Port of Hood River; **Notes:** Trail is ADA accessible; **GPS:** N 45° 42.930', W 121° 30.756'

Follow this lovely urban trail through a string of parks and historic sites along the City of Hood River's Waterfront Park. What was once mostly a drab industrial waterfront is now a vibrant, bustling (especially with wind surfers) recreational center complete with lodging and eating establishments. Allot time along the way for interpretive displays, water play, birdwatching, public art, and perhaps a microbrew or fresh roasted coffee.

GETTING THERE
From I-84 exit 63 in Hood River, head north on N. 2nd Street for 0.3 mile and turn right onto Portway Avenue. Continue for 0.1 mile to the large Hood River Event parking lot (fee). Limited free parking (3-hour limit) can be found along Portway Avenue and N. 2nd Street. Alternative trailheads and parking can be found at the Hook, Port Marina Park, and other area roads.

ON THE TRAIL
A round-trip walk or run on the paved Hood River Waterfront Trail will net you 4.6 miles. You can extend this by adding a few side trips.

Traveling west from the Hood River Event parking area (which you'll want to avoid during events—unless you're attending them), the trail heads through lovely Hood

that the winds will be whipping along it too. The views are both breathtaking and dizzying! Stare down at the highway and across the river to Drano Lake, site of the last log flume in America. Then cast your eyes west to Mount Defiance, Wygant Peak, and Dog Mountain; and east to the town of White Salmon cradled below Hospital Hill. Use caution on the steep descent!

EXTENDING YOUR TRIP
From the trailhead walk east on the newest section (2023) of the HCRHST to a 655-foot tunnel with five arched windows that somewhat replicates the original 1915 tunnel. It's definitely the coolest feature on the HCRHST.

Trail bridge spanning Hood River.

River Waterfront Park, with its kid-friendly beach, picnic area, restrooms, and green lawns. It then skirts a distillery and parallels Portway Avenue out to the Hook, a breakwater popular for kayak launching. The trail ends at the Hook's bend at 0.7 mile.

Traveling east from the Hood River Event parking area, the trail bends south and then skirts the Nichols Natural Area before crossing Nichols Parkway near the Hampton Inn at 0.4 mile. Here you can walk on a road north for 0.2 mile on the Spit, created by Hood River's sediment flow at its confluence with the Columbia River. The area is a popular beach for humans and dogs and kiteboard enthusiasts. You can continue walking on the sandy spit for another 0.25 mile.

From the Hampton Inn, a 0.25-mile connecting side trail heads south ducking beneath I-84 and then bending west to terminate on N. 2nd Street near Hood River's downtown. The Waterfront Trail continues east, spanning Hood River on an attractive bridge and coming to a massive sternwheel at the History Museum of Hood River County. Continue past the museum and cross East Port Marina Drive, coming to a junction. Here the Waterfront Trail splits. Left leads 0.2 mile through manicured lawns in the Port Marina Park to a breakwater. Right, the trail passes some buildings and rounds the marina. It then travels under the Hood River Bridge, continuing along the Columbia River by the Best Western. At 0.8 mile from the trail bridge, the trail terminates at Hood River WaterPlay, where you can rent kayaks or paddleboards.

93 Hood River Penstock Flume Pipeline Trail

RATING/ DIFFICULTY	ROUNDTRIP	ELEV GAIN/ HIGH POINT	SEASON
***/2	2.8 miles	100 feet/ 240 feet	Year-round

Crowds: 3; **Map:** Green Trails Columbia River Gorge East No. 432S; **Contact:** Columbia Land Trust; **Notes:** Trail utilizes a narrow metal grate walkway, which is hard on paws. Trail not recommended for dogs; **GPS:** N 45° 42.244', W 121° 30.321'

Literally a grate trail, hike atop an old penstock pipeline on a narrow metal walkway across and along the churning Hood River. The way travels up a hidden forested canyon just below city neighborhoods and just above the Columbia River. The setting, however, feels much more remote.

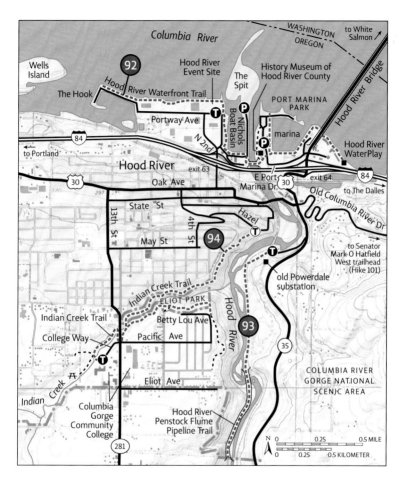

GETTING THERE

From I-84 exit 64 in Hood River, head south on US Highway 30 for 0.4 mile to a four-way stop. Then continue straight on State Route 35 for 0.2 mile and turn on the (easy-to-miss) Powerdale Road. Then continue on this steep and bumpy road (high clearance recommended) for 0.2 mile to the trailhead (elev. 160 ft.).

ON THE TRAIL

Officially named the Hood River Penstock Flume Pipeline Trail (a mouthful indeed), most folks refer to it simply as the Hood River Pipeline Trail. This unique trail follows along and then on the pipeline itself of a now defunct power plant operation. The trail starts near the old Powerdale substation,

A unique catwalk bridge spans Hood River.

now derelict and covered in unsightly graffiti. It began operations in the 1920s and ceased in 2006 upon the destruction of the penstock upriver during a torrential flood. The substation's dam was removed in 2010. The Columbia Land Trust secured this corridor in 2013, allowing for recreational access and habitat restoration and preservation.

Starting on an access road, hike west from the parking lot and cross the still-active (use caution and stay off) Mount Hood Railroad tracks. Then turn left and walk a graveled path along the tracks. The path eventually pulls right from the tracks to follow remnants of the old penstock close to the crashing river. At 0.7 mile pass a small sandy beach. Then hike on an exposed part of the penstock.

At 0.8 mile the fun begins. Come to a rocky bluff above the crashing river. Then begin walking via a metal grated catwalk with handrails on the penstock on a bridge crossing the river. It's pretty exhilarating—and a tight passageway that'll involve some

maneuvering upon meeting others along the way. At 1 mile a gap in the railing with a ladder descending the elevated penstock allows access to the river. The grated trail now heads along the river in a thickly forested canyon of cottonwoods, firs, and maples. The way gains a little elevation and passes another access point to the river before coming to its end at 1.4 miles. This is where a devastating flood washed out a huge section of the penstock in 2006.

94 Indian Creek Trail (East)

RATING/ DIFFICULTY	ROUNDTRIP	ELEV GAIN/ HIGH POINT	SEASON
**/2	4.2 miles	400 feet/ 490 feet	Year-round

Crowds: 3; **Map:** Green Trails Columbia River Gorge East No. 432S; **Contact:** Hood River Valley Parks and Recreation; **Notes:** Trail open to bicycles. Trail borders private property—stay on trail; **GPS:** N 45° 41.689', W 121° 31.563'

 Follow a small creek and an old wooden flume through a forested canyon right in the small city of Hood River. Pass big trees, listen to raucous scrub jays, and enjoy good views of Hood River tumbling below. Come in spring for an array of showy woodland wildflowers. And visit anytime for a break from the bustling waterfront.

GETTING THERE

From I-84 exit 62 in Hood River, travel east on Cascade Avenue (US Highway 30) for 1.2 miles and turn right onto 13th Street (State Route 281). Continue south for 1 mile and turn right onto College Way. Proceed 0.1 mile to trailhead (elev. 490 ft.) at western end of Columbia Gorge Community College parking lot.

ON THE TRAIL

This trail consists of three separate sections, but Hood River Valley Parks and Recreation staff hope to someday secure an easement to bring the whole network together. This hike features the two adjoining eastern stretches. Any segment of them makes for a good short hike or run.

Starting at the community college parking lot, follow the trail to a bridge over Indian Creek and a junction at 0.1 mile. The trail straight leads 0.1 mile to the Devon Court trailhead in a quiet residential neighborhood. The trail left is the Indian Creek Trail, but it only continues for 0.1 mile to a picnic table, beyond which is the private property currently creating the gap in the trail. So head right on the Indian Creek Trail, following the cascading creek and an old wooden flume (penstock) which once supplied water to a fruit cannery near the city center.

The trail here can be wet and muddy at times. Soon the trail bends right, crosses Indian Creek, and comes to busy 12th Street at 0.3 mile. Walk to the crosswalk at the intersection to the south and pick up the trail again next to Dutch Bros. Coffee. Now on good tread come to a junction at 0.4 mile. Head right on an extension of the trail through Eliot Park crossing a side creek on a bridge and then climbing to a spur trail leading right to 8th Street at 0.6 mile. Continue straight along the edge of a high bluff. Indian Creek disappears into a deep ravine. Amble through a grove of big oaks and enjoy window views through the forest to the Columbia River. At 0.9 mile the trail ends on Betty Lou Avenue. Turn around and retrace your steps 0.5 mile back to the main line of the Indian Creek Trail.

The trail traverses high above Indian Creek.

Next turn right, cross the creek, and hike along it. Skirt a power substation and residences, and pass the Union Street and 7th Street trailheads. In attractive forest the trail begins to descend while Indian Creek cascades below in a deep ravine. Traverse steep open slopes providing good views to roaring Hood River and the old Powerdale substation (Hike 93) below. Enjoy excellent views, too, up the river valley.

Continue steadily descending, passing groves of oaks and coming to the Hazel Avenue trailhead (elev. 260 ft.), an alternative starting point (limited street parking) at 1.1 miles from the junction. Then turn around and hike 1.5 miles back to your start.

EXTENDING YOUR TRIP

Check out the western segment of the Indian Creek Trail (access at Arrowhead Avenue) for an additional 2.8-mile round-trip hike or run through a more pastoral and rural stretch along the creek.

95 Punchbowl Falls County Park

RATING/ DIFFICULTY	ROUNDTRIP	ELEV GAIN/ HIGH POINT	SEASON
****/2	2.2 miles	250 feet/ 920 feet	Year-round

Crowds: 3; **Map:** Oregon Hikers; **Contact:** Hood River County Parks & Buildings; **Notes:** Dogs permitted on leash. Trail open from dawn to dusk. Steep drop-offs—keep kids and dogs close; **GPS:** N 45° 36.021', W 121° 38.091'

Less known than Eagle Creek's Punch Bowl Falls, these falls of same name (but different spelling) deliver a lot of captivating natural beauty without the crowds. Hike along the rim of a narrow canyon

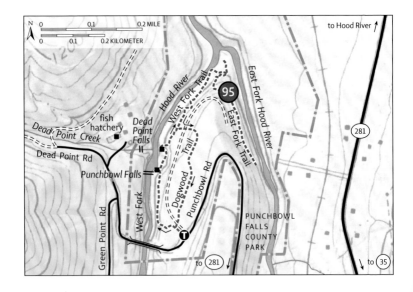

The confluence of the East and West Forks of Hood River

of columnar basalt where the West Fork Hood River crashes below, and witness two falls—one deep in the canyon and one tumbling down the canyon's stark, steep walls.

GETTING THERE

From I-84 exit 62 in Hood River, travel east on Cascade Avenue (US Highway 30) for 1.2 miles and turn right onto 13th Street (State Route 281). Continue south on Dee Highway (SR 281) for 11.4 miles and turn right in Dee (signed for Dee-Lost Lake). After 0.2 mile turn right on Punchbowl Road and continue 1.1 miles to trailhead (elev. 915 ft.).

ON THE TRAIL

Hood River County's newest park, this little gem on the confluence of the East and West Forks Hood River came to fruition thanks to the Western Rivers Conservancy. They purchased the 102-acre property and turned it over to the county in 2016. Trailkeepers of Oregon came onboard shortly afterward to construct some trails.

Start your hike on an old road, soon coming to a junction. You'll be returning from the right on the Dogwood Trail. Head left on the West Fork Trail, soon emerging along the edge of the deep basaltic canyon housing the West Fork Hood River. Use extreme caution walking along the rim while admiring oak groves and canyon walls of columnar basalt. Catch views south of the Punchbowl Road bridge spanning the river gorge and Mount Hood hovering in the distance. In spring an array of wildflowers blossom along the canyon edge.

At 0.3 mile come to an overlook of Punchbowl Falls. The falls are small, but the amphitheater punchbowl they tumble into is impressive, flanked by steep canyon walls. A fish hatchery and a precarious set of stairs leading to a fish ladder lie across the canyon. Keep hiking, coming to a spur at 0.4 mile leading to an overlook of Dead Point Creek cascading 75 feet over two tiers into the canyon. Then retrace your steps back along the spur and continue left, coming to a junction at 0.5 mile with the Dogwood Trail. Head left on the West Fork Trail, following along an old road and the tumbling West Fork. Descend in big timber along the edge of steep slopes, passing a good viewpoint of Hood River's East and West Fork confluence before reaching a junction at 0.8 mile.

Here the East Fork Trail heads right. Head left first, reaching at 0.9 mile a gravel bar at the river's confluence (elev. 775 ft.). The two forks roar here as they emerge from their canyons. Now retrace your steps 0.1 mile and hike 0.3 mile along the East Fork Trail.

The way climbs and then steeply descends via rock steps, passing beneath a 1929-built waterline bridge to a beautiful lush spot along the East Fork.

Make your way back to the West Fork Trail junction and hike 0.3 mile left to the Dogwood Trail junction. Then head left on this peaceful path through open forest, returning to the access road near the trailhead in 0.3 mile. Your vehicle is just a short distance to the left.

96 Wahtum Lake and Chinidere Mountain

RATING/ DIFFICULTY	LOOP	ELEV GAIN/ HIGH POINT	SEASON
*****/3	4 miles	1075 feet/ 4673 feet	June–Oct

Crowds: 4; **Map:** Green Trails Columbia River Gorge West No. 428S; **Contact:** Mount Hood

Wahtum Lake from Chinidere Mountain, with Indian Peak in the background

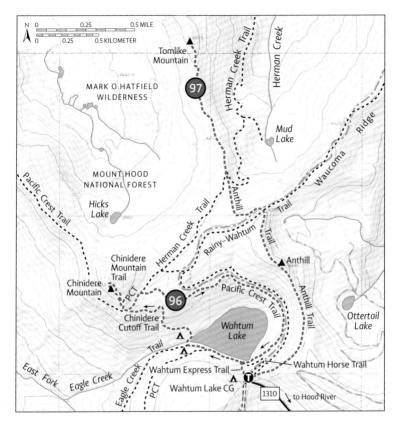

National Forest, Hood River Ranger District; **Notes:** NW Forest Pass or Interagency Pass required. Wilderness rules apply; **GPS:** N 45° 34.635', W 121° 47.566'

Enjoy some of the finest views and one of the largest lakes within the 65,822-acre Mark O. Hatfield Wilderness. Walk among old-growth giants flanking rippling Wahtum Lake before climbing to the windblown open summit of Chinidere Mountain, where five volcanoes and practically every prominent peak lining the Gorge vie for your attention.

GETTING THERE

From I-84 exit 62 in Hood River, travel east on Cascade Avenue (US Highway 30) for 1.2 miles and turn right onto 13th Street (State Route 281). Continue south on Dee Highway (SR 281) for 11.4 miles and turn right in Dee (signed for Dee-Lost Lake) and cross the Hood River. Immediately afterward bear left onto Lost Lake Road and follow for 4.9 miles.

Then bear right onto paved but narrow and brushy (use caution) Forest Road 13. After 4.3 miles bear right onto paved FR 1310 and continue 5.9 miles to the trailhead at Wahtum Lake Campground (elev. 3950 ft.). Privy available.

ON THE TRAIL

From the small campground take Wahtum Express Trail No. 406J and immediately enter the wilderness area, steeply descending in old growth to the lake via more than 250 steps. If your knees are fretting, opt for the adjacent slightly longer Wahtum Horse Trail No. 406H instead. The two approaches reach the Pacific Crest Trail (PCT, elev. 3750 ft.) at 0.2 mile and 0.4 mile, respectively. You'll be returning from the right, so head left along Wahtum's old-growth-graced shores, passing a good swim spot. At 0.5 mile reach a junction with the Eagle Creek Trail near an inviting and well-used backcountry camping area.

Turn right and at 0.6 mile reach a junction. Left heads 13 glorious miles down the Eagle Creek valley. You want to veer right on the Chinidere Cutoff Trail, crossing the lake's outlet on a log jam and catching a good view of the lake. The word *wahtum* is Native American in origin, meaning "lake," and therefore Wahtum Lake is a bit redundant—but it's never tiresome to visit.

Pass more campsites and then steeply climb through old silver firs and showy bear grass, following alongside an old waterline. Shortly after crossing a creek, reach the PCT (elev. 4200 ft.) at 1.4 miles. Turn left and almost immediately afterward head right on the Chinidere Mountain Trail.

Steeply climb, passing a ledge halfway that grants views south and west before skirting scree and reaching the juniper-clutching,

flowers-swaying, covered-in-shale, wind-blown, and wide-open 4673-foot summit at 1.8 miles. From where a fire lookout cabin once stood, savor the stunning sweeping views. Five volcanoes—count 'em: Jefferson, Hood, Adams, St. Helens, and Rainier! Marvel at Indian Mountain to the south, Tanner Butte in the west, Mount Defiance in the east, and rocky Tomlike Mountain and mesa-like Benson Plateau to the north. Named after a Wasco Indian chief, this former lookout site ranks chief among Columbia Gorge viewpoints.

Once you've had your share of alpine rhapsody, retrace your steps to the PCT. Turn left and follow it back, bearing left at the Chinidere Cutoff Trail junction and right at the Herman Creek Trail junction, and gently rounding the lake basin to descend back to the Wahtum Express in 1.8 miles. Then take the gentler Wahtum Horse Trail back to your vehicle for a satisfying 4-mile hike.

EXTENDING YOUR TRIP

Hike too short? Follow the Herman Creek Trail 1 mile to the Anthill Trail and combine this hike with Tomlike Mountain (Hike 97).

97 Tomlike Mountain and the Anthill

RATING/ DIFFICULTY	ROUNDTRIP	ELEV GAIN/ HIGH POINT	SEASON
*****/3	5.8 miles	1300 feet/ 4555 feet	June–Oct

Crowds: 2; **Map:** Green Trails Columbia River Gorge West No. 428S; **Contact:** Mount Hood National Forest, Hood River Ranger District; **Notes:** NW Forest Pass or Interagency Pass required. Wilderness rules apply; **GPS:** N 45° 34.654', W 121° 47.551'

Mount Hood stands out on the horizon from Tomlike Mountain.

⚙ 🌲 *A spectacular rocky and wind-swept peak, Tomlike Mountain's much-to-like, flower-adorned, view-bursting summit has only an Anthill in the way. The Anthill is actually a moundlike ridge rising above the shimmering waters of Wahtum Lake. It's decked with swaying bear grass—not crawling insects. This hike starts high and stays high, but there are a few ups and downs along the way.*

GETTING THERE

From I-84 exit 62 in Hood River, travel east on Cascade Avenue (US Highway 30) for 1.2 miles and turn right onto 13th Street (State Route 281). Continue south on Dee Highway (SR 281) for 11.4 miles and turn right in Dee (signed for Dee-Lost Lake) and cross the Hood River. Immediately afterward bear left onto Lost Lake Road and follow for 4.9 miles. Then bear right onto paved but narrow and brushy (use caution) Forest Road 13. After 4.3 miles bear right onto paved FR 1310 and continue 5.9 miles to the trailhead at Wahtum Lake Campground (elev. 3950 ft.). Privy available.

ON THE TRAIL

Locate the often overlooked Anthill Trail No. 406B taking off from behind the privy. Through old growth, gradually ascend the spine of a ridge dividing the Eagle Creek and Hood River watersheds. En route take in excellent views of Wahtum Lake, Chinidere Mountain, Mount Hood, and even Mount Jefferson.

At 1 mile crest the Anthill's high point (elev. 4475 ft.), and gradually descend through huckleberry patches to reach an old road—now the Rainy-Wahtum Trail—at 1.4 miles. Continue straight, entering the Mark O. Hatfield Wilderness and coming to the Herman Creek Trail (elev. 4150 ft.) at 1.9 miles.

Turn right, and after a few strides locate an unmarked trail heading left, just before the main trail bends right and descends. Now follow the trail to Tomlike's summit. Never officially built, this path involves some brushy and rocky sections, but it's a pretty straightforward route along the ridge crest.

After climbing a small knoll granting views of Mud Lake below, drop into a small saddle (elev. 4140 ft.). Then continue along ledges lined with stunted pines. Hikers who hail from the Northeast may feel they're hiking in New Hampshire's rocky White Mountains. At 2.5 miles veer to the left and, using caution, follow cairns up and over a rocky knoll. At 2.7 miles emerge from a lodgepole pine grove, with the summit block now in full view. Carefully work your way up shale and scree, reaching the 4555-foot summit at 2.9 miles.

Hold on to your hat, for if the strong winds don't knock it off, the horizon-spanning views will! From Washington's Larch Mountain to Oregon's Larch Mountain, Silver Star, Rainier, St. Helens, Adams, Dog, Tanner Butte, the fluted flattop Benson Plateau, and glistening Mount Hood rising above them all. Admire wildflowers and bear grass too, swaying in the strong breezes.

Tomlike was Chief Chinidere's son, and naming this beautiful mountain and the adjacent peak just to the south after these two members of the Wasco Tribe is a fitting honor. And you'll probably be honoring the beauty of the Columbia River Gorge country from atop this peak.

EXTENDING YOUR TRIP

Despite the less-than-enticing name, little Mud Lake twinkling below is actually quite lovely once the mosquitoes dissipate. From the Herman Creek Trail junction, follow it north 0.8 mile and then take a spur trail right

0.2 mile to the lake (elev. 3600 ft.). Dippers, newts, and osprey will keep you company.

98 Indian Mountain

RATING/ DIFFICULTY	ROUNDTRIP	ELEV GAIN/ HIGH POINT	SEASON
*****/3	9 miles	1440 feet/ 4892 feet	June–Oct

Crowds: 2; **Map:** Green Trails Columbia River Gorge West No. 428S; **Contact:** Mount Hood National Forest, Hood River Ranger District; **Notes:** NW Forest Pass or Interagency Pass required. Wilderness rules apply; **GPS:** N 45° 34.635', W 121° 47.566'

 *Hike to an old fire lookout site and some of the finest views in the Gorge. From Indian Mountain's windswept rocky and juniper-hugging north ridge, enjoy unsurpassed views of the Eagle Creek watershed and its lofty Columbia Gorge guardian peaks. And from Indian's open summit, stare right into the glistening ice adorning Oregon's majestic Mount Hood.*

GETTING THERE

From I-84 exit 62 in Hood River, travel east on Cascade Avenue (US Highway 30) for 1.2 miles and turn right onto 13th Street (State Route 281). Continue south on Dee Highway (SR 281) for 11.4 miles and turn right in Dee (signed for Dee-Lost Lake) and cross the Hood River. Immediately afterward bear left onto Lost Lake Road and follow for 4.9 miles. Then bear right onto paved but narrow and

Indian Mountain provides a close-up view of Mount Hood.

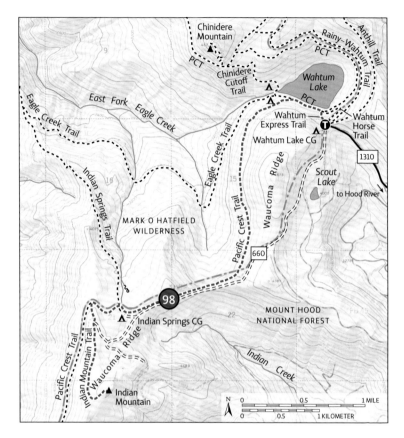

brushy (use caution) Forest Road 13. After 4.3 miles bear right onto paved FR 1310 and continue 5.9 miles to the trailhead at Wahtum Lake Campground (elev. 3950 ft.). Privy available.

ON THE TRAIL

While it's possible to drive to Indian Springs Campground, greatly shortening this hike, the road is rough, and the whole idea is to hike! Start by hiking the Wahtum Express Trail (or taking the adjacent horse trail for a more gradual descent). Immediately enter the Mark O. Hatfield Wilderness, and steeply descend to Wahtum Lake via more than 250 steps, coming to the Pacific Crest Trail (PCT, elev. 3750 ft.) at 0.2 mile. Now turn left and head toward Mexico, traveling along Wahtum Lake's forested shoreline.

At 0.5 mile reach a junction with the Eagle Creek Trail near a popular backcountry camping area. Continue left on the PCT, traveling through beautiful groves of old-growth forest occasionally interrupted with scree slopes providing teaser windows. The way rounds a knoll and gently ascends along Waucoma Ridge. At 2.2 miles leave the wilderness, and parallel FR 1310-660. After briefly brushing against the road, cross a scree slope that provides excellent views of Mount Hood. Then crest a 4260-foot knoll and drop a little, crossing the spur road leading to primitive Indian Springs Campground (elev. 4210 ft.) at 3.2 miles. Here the Indian Springs Trail takes off right, passing the springs and descending 2 miles to the Eagle Creek Trail.

Continue straight on the PCT, soon emerging on an open ridge adorned in showy bear grass, ground-hugging junipers, and blueberry bushes. The view north will leave your mouth agape. From Tanner Butte to Table Mountain, Benson Plateau to Mount Adams, it's one of the finest alpine views in the region.

At 3.5 miles reach a junction with Indian Mountain Trail No. 416 (elev. 4340 ft.). Turn left and follow this lightly traveled, rocky former road past another old road and weather station, then continuing up Indian's open north ridge. Pass through groves of wind-stunted trees before reaching a stand of mature timber just beneath the summit. At 4.5 miles reach the 4892-foot summit, a former fire lookout site with smoking-hot views! Gaze at the horizon from the Columbia Hills to Badger Mountain, Mount St. Helens to Mount Jefferson, and of course Mount Hood, right in your face—practically close enough to feel the cool breezes blowing off its glaciers.

EXTENDING YOUR TRIP
Make a loop to return via the Indian Springs and Eagle Creek Trails through quiet old-growth forest. This variation adds 2.9 miles and 1200 vertical feet to the hike.

99 Green Point Mountain

RATING/ DIFFICULTY	LOOP	ELEV GAIN/ HIGH POINT	SEASON
****/3	3.2 miles	760 feet/ 4736 feet	Mid-June– Oct

Crowds: 2; **Map:** Green Trails Columbia River Gorge West No. 428S; **Contact:** Mount Hood National Forest, Hood River Ranger District; **Notes:** NW Forest Pass or Interagency Pass required. Wilderness rules apply; **GPS:** N 45° 37.459', W 121° 45.556'

Second-highest summit in the Columbia River Gorge, Green Point Mountain is rather unimposing with its long, bulky, forested summit. But clifftops on its eastern slopes grant excellent views over Rainy Lake to towering Mount Defiance and out to Mounts Hood, Rainier, and Adams. Plus, delight in hiking through impressive groves of ancient forest.

GETTING THERE
From I-84 exit 62 in Hood River, travel east on Cascade Avenue (US Highway 30) for 1.2 miles and turn right onto 13th Street (State Route 281). Continue south on Dee Highway (SR 281) for 11.4 miles and turn right in Dee (signed for Dee-Lost Lake). Cross Hood River and immediately bear right onto Punch Bowl Road. After 1.3 miles continue straight on gravel Dead Point Road (Forest Road 2820) toward Rainy Lake. Follow this road for 11.2 miles (last mile is rough, requiring high clearance) to the trailhead (elev. 4025 ft.) located in the Rainy Lake Campground.

Rainy Lake, Mount Defiance, and Mount Adams are all visible from Green Point Mountain.

ON THE TRAIL

Green Point Mountain can be accessed from several approaches, although it's a lightly visited destination. This hike, a loop, is the shortest and easiest approach. The hike is packed with interesting facets, and there are several opportunities to extend it.

Start at the west end of the campground on Rainy-Wahtum Trail No. 409. The walking is easy on this old abandoned-road-turned-trail along Waucoma Ridge. The way travels through gorgeous primeval forest along the Mark O. Hatfield Wilderness boundary. At 0.6 mile cross a creek. At 0.8 mile cross a talus slope and then steadily climb, traversing ledges blasted for the old road.

At 1.2 miles come to a junction. The Rainy-Wahtum Trail continues 4 miles along the ridge to Wahtum Lake, passing viewpoints en route. The Herman Cutoff Trail takes off right, immediately passing an old World War II signal hut before descending in towering ancient forest to reach the Herman Creek Trail in 2.2 miles (Hike 86). You want to make a sharp right onto the Gorton Creek Trail.

Immediately enter wilderness and steadily ascend in open forest along a ridge edge. Expect to hop over a few blowdowns and encounter some brush. And in late summer, expect to munch on a few huckleberries along the way. At 1.9 miles reach a couple of clifftop viewpoints (keep children and dogs near) as you crest Green Point's 4736-foot summit. Savor the view east across Rainy Lake to Mount Defiance. Enjoy views north, too, to Adams and Rainier and south to Hood.

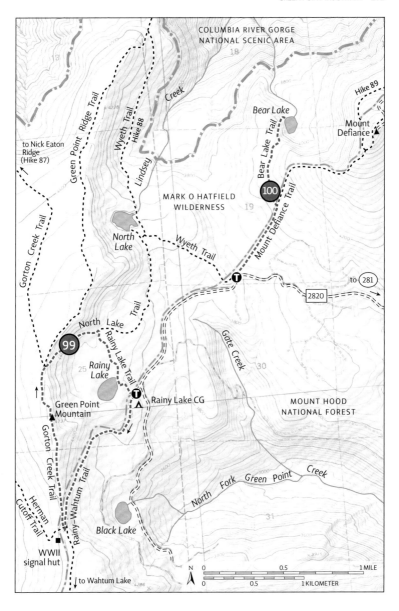

COLUMBIA RIVER GORGE
NATIONAL SCENIC AREA

18

Creek

Bear Lake

Hike 89

Mount
Defiance

to Nick Eaton
Ridge
(Hike 87)

Green Point Ridge Trail

Wyeth Trail

Hike 88

Lindsey

Bear Lake Trail

MARK O HATFIELD
WILDERNESS

19

100

Gorton Creek Trail

North
Lake

Wyeth Trail

Mount Defiance Trail

T

to 281

2820

North Lake Trail

99

Rainy Lake Trail

Rainy
Lake

25

Gate Creek

30

T

Rainy Lake CG

MOUNT HOOD
NATIONAL FOREST

Green Point
Mountain

Gorton Creek Trail

Rainy-Wahtum Trail

North Fork Green Point Creek

Herman
Cutoff Trail

Black Lake

31

WWII
signal hut

to Wahtum Lake

N

0   0.5   1 MILE

0   0.5   1 KILOMETER

Then continue hiking north through pines, descending to a junction (elev. 4550 ft.) at 2.3 miles. The Gorton Creek Trail continues left to Nick Eaton Ridge (Hike 87). The Green Point Ridge Trail continues straight along the ridge. You want to head right on the North Lake Trail, steadily descending. Cross a couple of talus slopes granting good views to Mount Hood and Green Point's ledges. Then enter cool old growth and come to a junction at 2.8 miles.

The trail left continues through primeval forest for 1 mile to North Lake (Hike 88). Head right on the Rainy Lake Trail, soon coming to the shallow manmade lake once used to send logs down a flume. Walk across the dirt dam and enjoy views to Green Point Mountain. Then descend in primeval forest, returning to your start at 3.2 miles.

EXTENDING YOUR TRIP
For a longer loop, follow the forested Green Point Ridge Trail for 2.7 miles to the Wyeth Trail. Then follow the Wyeth Trail to the North Lake Trail to the Rainy Lake Trail 2.8 miles back to your start.

100 Bear Lake

RATING/ DIFFICULTY	ROUNDTRIP	ELEV GAIN/ HIGH POINT	SEASON
***/2	2.4 miles	580 feet/ 4150 feet	Mid-June– Oct

Crowds: 2; **Map:** Green Trails Columbia River Gorge West No. 428S; **Contact:** Mount Hood National Forest, Hood River Ranger District; **Notes:** Wilderness rules apply; **GPS:** N 45° 38.176', W 121° 44.556'

Set in a remote basin beneath the talus fields high on Mount Defiance, the highest summit in the Gorge,

Bear Lake is one of the prettiest subalpine lakes in the Mark O. Hatfield Wilderness. This is an easy hike ideal for children. And if you want more, continue to Mount Defiance's 4960-foot summit via a much shorter and easier path than the steep approach from the Columbia River.

GETTING THERE
From I-84 exit 62 in Hood River, travel east on Cascade Avenue (US Highway 30) for 1.2 miles and turn right onto 13th Street (State Route 281). Continue south on Dee Highway (SR 281) for 11.4 miles and turn right in Dee (signed for Dee-Lost Lake). Cross Hood River and immediately bear right onto Punch Bowl Road. After 1.3 miles continue straight on gravel Dead Point Road (Forest Road 2820) toward Rainy Lake. Follow this road for 10 miles to the trailhead (elev. 3825 ft.) on the right. Parking area on the left.

ON THE TRAIL
From the trailhead the Wyeth Trail (Hike 88) leads left for (the short way to) North Lake. For Bear Lake, bear right and follow Mount Defiance Trail No. 413. Gently ascend in a pleasant forest of mountain hemlock with an understory of huckleberries, a favorite with bears. At 0.5 mile reach a junction (elev. 4050 ft.) with Bear Lake Trail No. 413C. Bear left, immediately entering the Mark O. Hatfield Wilderness and setting out on an easy ramble. After gently climbing to about 4150 feet and crossing a small scree slope, begin descending.

At 1.2 miles come to Bear Lake (elev. 3900 ft.), denned down beneath the rocky upper slopes of Mount Defiance. Cradled in a quiet bowl and surrounded by old forest and shiny talus slopes, Bear is one of the more attractive subalpine lakes in the Hatfield Wilderness.

The clear waters of Bear Lake

Find a good sitting log, soak your feet, and enjoy this placid little backcountry lake.

EXTENDING YOUR TRIP

After staring at Mount Defiance's summit, you may want to tackle it. Retrace your steps to the last junction and head left for 0.9 mile on a moderate grade through a mostly shaded route, reaching a junction (elev. 4800 ft.) in a talus slope. The 4960-foot towered summit lies 0.2 mile to the right. Reach it crossing talus with excellent views of Mount Hood. Head left, skirting the summit, and cross talus for stunning and sweeping views of the Gorge and beyond. You can then loop over the summit for a return. For another approach of Mount Defiance, see Hike 89.

101 Mosier Twin Tunnels

RATING/ DIFFICULTY	ROUNDTRIP	ELEV GAIN/ HIGH POINT	SEASON
***/2	9.4 miles	730 feet/ 540 feet	Year-round

Crowds: 3; **Map:** Green Trails Columbia River Gorge East No. 432S; **Contact:** Historic Columbia River Highway State Trail, Oregon State Parks; **Notes:** $5 day-use fee (pay at entrance, credit cards accepted). Wheelchair accessible. Dogs permitted on-leash. Paved trail is popular with cyclists; **GPS:** N 45° 42.205', W 121° 29.240'

Amble on one of the most scenic stretches

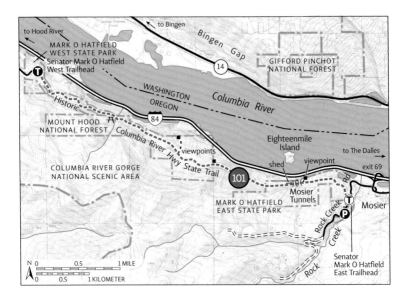

of the old Columbia River Highway that has since been reincarnated as the Historic Columbia River Highway State Trail (HCRHST). Follow this paved path high above the Columbia River, taking in sweeping views, admiring gorgeous wildflowers, and delighting in strolling through two surviving tunnels of the old roadway.

GETTING THERE

From I-84 exit 64 in Hood River turn right onto US Highway 30 and drive 0.4 mile to a stop sign. Turn left onto Old Columbia River Drive (Historic Columbia River Highway) and continue for 1.1 miles to the Senator Mark O. Hatfield West trailhead (elev. 350 ft.). Privy available. To reach the east trailhead, follow I-84 to Mosier at exit 69. Follow US 30 for 0.2 mile and turn left onto Rock Creek Road, following it for 0.7 mile to the parking area just past the trailhead. Privy available.

ON THE TRAIL

Like the sprawling federal wilderness area to the west, this state park trailhead carries the name Hatfield. Oregon's longest serving US senator (for thirty years) and two-term popular governor before that, this progressive Republican and evangelical Christian was a champion of civil rights, human rights, education, and environmental causes, leaving an amazing legacy to his native state, including the Columbia River Gorge National Scenic Area. Perhaps only fellow progressive Republican Tom McCall left a larger legacy as an Oregon political figure.

One of three sections of the HCRHST, this 4.7-mile stretch is the most interesting and scenic. This description starts from the west trailhead and involves traveling out and back. If you're intent on just seeing the tunnels, start from the east trailhead.

Starting on a basalt bench 300 feet above the river, follow the old highway east, transitioning from a wet fir and maple forest clime to a semiarid one punctuated with ponderosa pine. In spring and early summer, showy flowers—poppies, asters, lupines, scarlet gilias, desert parsley, and more—line the way, and lizards scurry back and forth across the warm asphalt.

Gently climb to an elevation of about 440 feet before gently descending 50 feet to a shaded picnic area and seasonal cascade at 1.3 miles. Commence with a long gradual climb, passing original concrete mileposts, handsome stone railings, and basalt pinnacles. At 2.4 miles, just after cresting a ridge (elev. 470 ft.), a short side trail leads left to excellent views across the river of the town of Bingen and the rolling hills and synclines of the Catherine Creek country.

Still gently ascending, skirt beneath a big ledge and arrive at an excellent viewpoint (elev. 540 ft.) of the Coyote Wall and Columbia Hills at 2.9 miles. Now gradually descend, coming to a rather stark-looking concrete shed (elev. 340 ft.) that covers the trail at 3.7 miles. The 700-foot-long shed was constructed to protect trail users from falling rock (notice the big dents in the pavement nearby) and connects to the much more elegantly designed Mosier Twin Tunnels, with their timber supports and windows. Built from 1919 to 1921 and closed and backfilled in the 1950s, the tunnels were reopened and rehabilitated in the late 1990s.

Continue to the Mosier Tunnels, passing through the small one first and then immediately afterward the longer one (288 feet in length), with its two windows granting views out to the Columbia and surrounding rolling

The eastern entrance to one of the Mosier Tunnels

hills in Washington. After emerging from the tunnels, a short side trail (elev. 400 ft.) leads left to a spectacular viewpoint east. The main paved trail descends across a patch of basalt talus, terminating at 4.7 miles at the eastern trailhead (elev. 220 ft.).

102 Mosier Plateau

RATING/ DIFFICULTY	ROUNDTRIP	ELEV GAIN/ HIGH POINT	SEASON
***/2	3 miles	700 feet/ 540 feet	Year-round

Crowds: 4; **Map:** Green Trails Columbia River Gorge East No. 432S; **Contact:** Friends of the Columbia Gorge; **Notes:** Dogs permitted on leash. Stay on the trail to protect wildflowers and respect adjacent private property ownership; **GPS:** N 45° 41.091', W 121° 23.618'

 *Meander along Mosier Creek, passing a pioneer cemetery and a gorgeous waterfall crashing into a basaltic chasm. Then mosey through a meadow shrouded with wildflowers on a plateau once part of an estate. Delight in views of the Coyote Wall across the Columbia and other Gorge landmarks east and west along the river.*

GETTING THERE
From Hood River or The Dalles, follow I-84 to Mosier at exit 69. Then continue 1.2 miles east on the Historic Columbia River Highway (US Highway 30) to parking area on left just before bridge over Mosier Creek. Trailhead (elev. 130 ft.) located on east side of bridge.

ON THE TRAIL
From the trailhead carefully walk east along the Historic Columbia River Highway (US 30), crossing Mosier Creek in a narrow gorge on a beautiful 1920-built bridge. Then hit the trail just after the crossing, climbing up

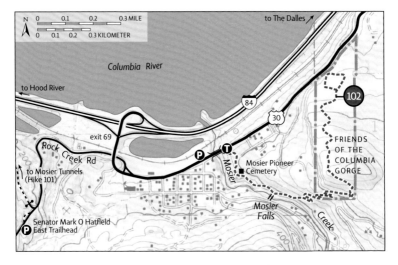

This bridge on the Historic Columbia River Highway was built in 1920.

a bluff of scraggly oaks. At 0.2 mile come to the Mosier Pioneer Cemetery with gravestones dating to the 1860s and to-die-for views of two-tiered Mosier Falls crashing 80 feet in a tight basaltic chasm.

Continue on the trail hiking above the creek and falls. In spring the surrounding pine-oak savanna sports a myriad of gorgeous blossoms (and troves of ticks and fresh leaves of three you best leave be). Soon enter Friends of the Columbia Gorge property. The Friends purchased this prime piece of real estate for its natural and recreational aspects and opened the trail here in 2013. It is part of their Gorge Towns to Trails campaign to ultimately tie together communities and natural areas in the Gorge through a 200-mile trail network.

The way now traverses a steep hillside via switchbacks and a few stairs. It then bends east high on the grassy and flowered plateau, coming to a gorgeous view of the town of Mosier and the Columbia River. Here some large stone seats invite lingering. The trail skirts below some communications towers and continues past windblown pines and sweeping views west of the Gorge. Descend past the foundations of the home and outbuildings that once occupied this prime piece of Gorge heaven.

At 1.4 miles come to the old road access to the home and a junction. Here a small loop trail takes off left (you'll return on the road). Follow the trail through pines and meadows emerging on the edge of basalt cliffs (use caution) rising directly above the historic highway below. Views to the Coyote Wall syncline and the Catherine Creek area across the Columbia are divine. And so too are the bountiful blossoms that grace the plateau. After completing the loop, return the way you came.

103 Memaloose Hills

RATING/ DIFFICULTY	ROUNDTRIP	ELEV GAIN/ HIGH POINT	SEASON
***/2	3.2 miles	750 feet/ 957 feet	Mar–Dec

Crowds: 4; **Map:** Green Trails Columbia River Gorge East No. 432S (trails not shown); **Contact:** Columbia River Gorge National Scenic Area; **Notes:** Dogs permitted on leash. Stay on main trails (described) to protect wildflowers and respect adjacent private property ownership; **GPS:** N 45° 41.625', W 121° 21.053'

One of the Gorge's prime spring wildflower areas, the Memaloose Hills are also home to a healthy rattlesnake population. Follow a rolling path through oaks, pines, and meadows to two small hills granting big views of the surrounding countryside.

GETTING THERE

From Hood River or The Dalles follow I-84 to Mosier at exit 69. Continue 3.8 miles east on US Highway 30 to parking area on left at the Memaloose Overlook Trailhead (elev. 530 ft.) located on right. Parking can be difficult on

Clumps of arrowleaf balsamroot are a highlight of the Memaloose Hills.

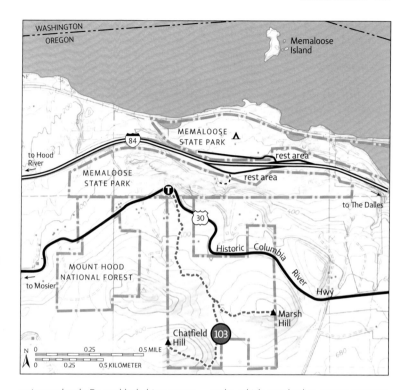

spring weekends. Do not block driveways or park in any manner obstructing traffic. Consider alternative destination if parking is not available.

ON THE TRAIL

Word is out that the Memaloose Hills host one of the best spring floral shows. However, trails were never officially built on this small tract of national forest land. No official trailhead or parking has been constructed either. Hopefully the Forest Service will soon designate an official trail system here. Until then, only hike the trails described here to two of the hills; and do not venture off on side paths, which may lead to private property and/or sensitive habitat.

The well-trodden trail takes off south in pine oak savannah. In spring brilliant blossoms of arrowleaf balsamroot, larkspurs, lupines, shooting stars, and many other flowers paint the forest floor. The way rolls along, gradually gaining elevation. Cross small basalt ledges and pocket meadows. At 0.6 mile the way dips to cross a creek. At 0.7 mile come to a junction. Head left and reach the broad, open 822-foot summit of Marsh Hill at 1 mile. Take in a spectacular view east to Rowena Gap and west to Mounts Defiance and Hood, and the Catherine Creek country. Then retrace your steps 0.3 mile to the junction.

Now head left, skirting a wetland and entering a broad field. Keep hiking south, paralleling fenced pasture to the east and scrappy oaks to the west. The way then begins to climb through oaks and breaks out onto open slopes. The trail angles south and steeply climbs, reaching the 957-foot summit of Chatfield Hill at 0.6 mile from the junction. The views are superb, especially of the Columbia River down to Dog Mountain. Mounts Adams and Hood can be seen too. Contrast the flowered slopes to the adjacent fenced (private) pastureland, where years of grazing have left it denuded of flowers. Return the way you came, reaching the trailhead in 1.3 miles.

Before taking off from the overlook, take in a view of Memaloose Island. Derived from the Chinook Jargon name of *Memaloose Illahee*, it means "land of the dead." The island was one of several used by Native peoples to entomb their dead. Sadly the island was raided and looted by early settlers who had no respect for this sacred place.

104 Rowena Plateau

RATING/ DIFFICULTY	ROUNDTRIP	ELEV GAIN/ HIGH POINT	SEASON
***/2	2.2 miles	300 feet/ 700 feet	Year-round

Crowds: 5; **Map:** Green Trails Columbia River Gorge East No. 432S; **Contact:** Oregon Nature Conservancy The Dalles Office and Mayer State Park; **Notes:** Dogs prohibited. Stay on official trails; **GPS:** N 45° 40.980', W 121° 18.132'

Rowena is a beautiful heroine in Sir Walter Scott's 1819 novel Ivanhoe. *In the Gorge, Rowena is a beautiful gap and a crest renowned for its wildflowers. A land of vernal pools, abrupt cliffs, and incredible biological diversity—from February to June, the Rowena Plateau radiates with blossoms. Saunter on a couple of short and easy trails, and be dazzled by floral and geographic beauty.*

GETTING THERE
From Hood River, follow I-84 east to Mosier at exit 69. Then continue east on Historic Columbia River Highway (US Highway 30) for 6.6 miles to the Rowena Crest Viewpoint. (From The Dalles, take exit 76 off of I-84 and follow US 30 west 2.8 miles to the viewpoint.) The trailhead (elev. 700 ft.) is located on the west side of the road and has limited parking—additional parking is available on the viewpoint loop.

ON THE TRAIL
The Rowena Plateau consists of a mixture of state, federal, and private conservation lands. This hike traverses the Nature Conservancy's 231-acre Tom McCall Preserve. The Nature Conservancy is an international conservation group that has protected millions of acres of natural lands since its inception in the 1950s. Tom McCall, whom this preserve was named for, was a popular Republican governor of Oregon from 1967 to 1975 and was responsible for some of the state's landmark conservation acts, including growth management, the bottle bill, and public access to shorelines.

Follow the wide Plateau Trail across open terrain. Warning signs alert hikers to the eastern Gorge's trifecta of hazards: rattlers, poison oak, and ticks—with poison oak being the one you should be most concerned with. Arrowleaf balsamroot adds its golden touch in the spring, but it isn't profuse here. For a long time this plateau was grazed by cattle

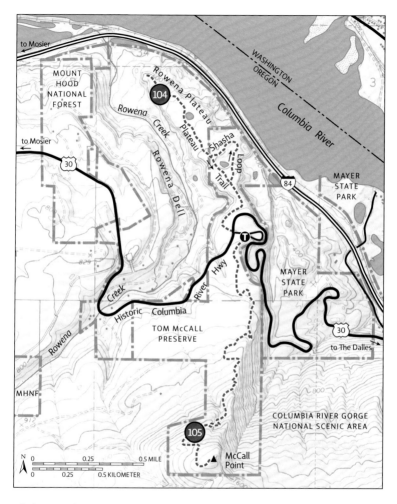

who happen to have a penchant for this leafy member of the sunflower (*Asteraceae*) family. Volunteers have been busy restoring the plateau to its pregrazing glory. Nevertheless, the plateau blossoms with shooting stars, larkspurs, desert stars—the list goes on. The preserve is also home to Thompson's broadleaf lupine, Columbia desert parsley, Thompson's waterleaf, and Hood River milkvetch, all species endemic to the Gorge.

Gently descend on the sloping plateau, reaching a junction at 0.3 mile. Now head right on the Shasha Loop, passing a small pond ringed with oak (both poison and Oregon white). You'll likely hear melodious blackbirds and crooning frogs. The way then passes by a ledge above the Columbia River, directly across from the mouth of the Klickitat River. Avoid an unofficial trail heading right and return to the Plateau Trail at 0.7 mile.

Then head right, continuing across the plateau, traversing a topography of mounds and swales. Look for deer, coyotes, and ground squirrels when not looking out at the river and surrounding golden hills. Pass a small seasonal pond usually teeming with birds. At 1.2 miles the trail comes to a halt at the western edge of the plateau (elev. 440 ft.). Keep children close at hand. Look down. While much of Rowena's windswept plateau is bare of trees, oak groves flourish in the sheltered dales below the rim. Now follow the Plateau Trail 1 mile back to the trailhead.

Wildflowers carpet the Rowena Plateau.

105 Tom McCall Point

RATING/ DIFFICULTY	ROUNDTRIP	ELEV GAIN/ HIGH POINT	SEASON
****/3	3.6 miles	1050 feet/ 1722 feet	Mar–Oct

Crowds: 3; **Map:** Green Trails Columbia River Gorge East No. 432S; **Contact:** Oregon Nature Conservancy The Dalles Office and Mayer State Park; **Notes:** Dogs prohibited. Stay on official trails. Trail closed Nov–Feb to limit tread damage; **GPS:** N 45° 40.965', W 121° 18.042'

Climb to a broad rounded grassy summit honoring one of Oregon's conservation champions. The only thing better than the far-flung views from along this hike are the flowers. They carpet the peak's open slopes, accent its abrupt ridges, and decorate its oak and pine groves in a multitude of brilliant colors. A Nature Conservancy preserve, this land is where more than two hundred species of plants thrive, including several endemic to the Columbia Gorge.

GETTING THERE
From Hood River, follow I-84 east to Mosier at exit 69. Then continue east on the Historic Columbia River Highway (US Highway 30) for 6.6 miles to the Rowena Crest Viewpoint and trailhead (elev. 700 ft.) on your right. (From The Dalles, take exit 76 off of I-84 and follow US 30 west 2.8 miles to the viewpoint and trailhead.)

ON THE TRAIL
The well-maintained trail takes off south across a grassy tableland and along the edge of basalt cliffs. While the Tom McCall Preserve is legendary among wildflower aficionados (May is prime), birders will also

Indian paintbrush on Tom McCall Point

delight here. Look for canyon wrens, horned larks, and western meadowlarks, Oregon's state bird.

At 0.3 mile come to an old road at the base of a talus slope that sports oaks and pines. Turn left to skirt the talus, and travel through big showy plumes of desert parsley. Look below at the snaking Historic Columbia River Highway, an engineering marvel. The trail emerges onto an upper plateau that explodes with blossoms in the spring. Lupines and balsamroot dominate, streaking the countryside in enough purple and gold to make a UW Husky fan blush—and a UO Duck unnerved!

The view gets better as you continue up the sometimes steep trail. Look east to the Columbia Hills, west to hulking Mount Defiance, north to the giant snow cone Mount Adams, and south to snowy cloud-catching Mount Hood. The trail does a short stint switchbacking along a steep ridgeline before weaving back across sun-kissed and wind-whipped grassy slopes. At around 1200 feet pass through a patch of ponderosa pines. In May glacier lilies brighten

the grove. Continue climbing, and continue awestruck at the amazing arrangement of wildflowers: grass widows, prairie stars, shooting stars, Indian paintbrushes, Oregon sunshines—the list goes on!

The way steepens up wide-open slopes and then bends east. At 1.8 miles and after 1050 feet of climbing, crest the round grassy summit of McCall Point. Now soak up as much sun and scenic splendor as your little (and probably now stronger) heart desires. Paths leading south from the summit head to private land. Return the way you came.

106 The Dalles Riverfront Trail

RATING/ DIFFICULTY	ROUNDTRIP	ELEV GAIN/ HIGH POINT	SEASON
***/1	14.8 miles	350 feet/ 200 feet	Year-round

Crowds: 3; **Map:** Green Trails Columbia River Gorge East No. 432S; **Contact:** Northern Wasco County Parks and Recreation; **Notes:** Paved trail open to bicycles and ADA accessible. Dogs permitted on leash. Section through

Riverfront Park is closed Nov–May; **GPS:** N 45° 39.150', W 121° 12.529'

 Follow this delightful paved trail from the *Columbia Gorge Discovery Center along the Columbia River to Riverfront Park near downtown The Dalles. From old farmlands to server farms, the trail takes you through the city's past and to its future. Interpretive displays, historic sites, pockets of natural landscapes, and plenty of good views greet you along the way.*

GETTING THERE

From exit 82 on I-84 in The Dalles, follow River Road west and immediately turn right onto the Historic Columbia River Highway (US Highway 30). Drive 1.4 miles and turn right onto Taylor-Frantz Road, which becomes Discovery Drive. Proceed for 0.4 mile to the large parking lot and trailhead (elev. 200 ft.) at Columbia Gorge Discovery Center & Museum.

ON THE TRAIL

When completed, this wonderful urban trail will run for 10 miles all the way to The Dalles Dam. Currently 8.3 miles are in place, with the westernmost stretch the most interesting and scenic. From the Columbia Gorge Discovery Center & Museum (a must visit) head east and begin descending, switchbacking twice across grassy slopes punctuated with basalt outcroppings and, in springtime, painted with wildflower blossoms. Enjoy excellent views to Washington's Columbia Hills.

The way passes through an old homestead site and patch of locust trees before heading through a railroad underpass. Then on a fairly level grade come to bird-rich Taylor Lake. Continue hiking across a scenic narrow stretch of land between the lake and Rocky Island on the Columbia River. At 1.2 miles reach a junction where a side trail leads right, crossing a lake narrows and coming to an alternative trailhead on River Trail Way in 0.8 mile.

You want to continue straight, coming to a massive Google server farm. As you walk the trail along the river beside the massive building, contemplate how much energy is required to run the internet. The Columbia provides the source here, and like the aluminum industry before, it came at a great cost to the river's salmon and the First Peoples who relied on them.

Continue hiking along the mighty river and bend right to follow alongside Chenoweth Creek in a green inlet. At 2.1 miles come to a trailhead on River Trail Way. It's

The Columbia Gorge sternwheeler docked along the trail

possible here to hike right, following the side trail 0.8 mile back to the riverfront trail for a 4.1-mile lollipop loop. Otherwise keep hiking, crossing the creek and passing an animal shelter. Then return to the Columbia and pass another massive Google Data Center. The trail then continues along the river, passing various businesses and excellent riverfront viewing. At 3.2 miles come to the Kiwanis Pocket Park (privy available) at Klindts Cove, an excellent spot to take a break and turn around for a shorter option.

Beyond, the trail follows alongside Klindt Drive and River Road, passing a large gated

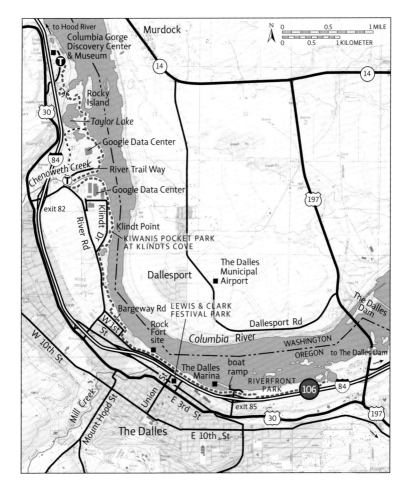

parcel with a pond slated for development, which would make a better greenbelt park. At 4 miles the trail leaves the road and once again travels along the Columbia River, passing some grain silos and a popular pub before reaching Bargeway Road at 4.4 miles.

Now along Bargeway Road, then W. 1st Street, the trail travels through an industrial area with no scenic appeal. At 5.2 miles the way gets interesting again, coming to the Rock Fort site, where Lewis and Clark camped and prepared for an alleged Indian attack. Continue heading east once again along the river. Paralleling W. 1st Street and I-84, expect plenty of highway noise. At 5.5 miles come to a commercial dock where the *Columbia Gorge* sternwheeler docked for years. Just south of the interstate overpass you can access the Lewis & Clark Festival Park and the city's historic downtown.

The trail continues along the river parallel to the interstate, passing wetland coves and forest patches to come to The Dalles Marina at 6.1 miles. Now walk through the large parking lot to the lovely Riverfront Park (closed November 1 through Memorial Day for wildlife protection) and pick up the trail again at 6.6 miles. Then hike through a large natural area of forest and wetlands along the river hemmed in by the interstate. At 7.4 miles the trail ends at a large cove. It will eventually continue east, but for now, return the way you came.

EXTENDING YOUR TRIP

A small 0.9 mile section of trail near the route's eventual eastern terminus is currently in place and can be hiked from Indian Road (off of Bret Clodfelter Way) to The Dalles Dam Visitor Center and almost to the dam itself. There are some nice paths around the visitors center grounds as well.

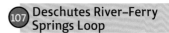

107 Deschutes River–Ferry Springs Loop

RATING/ DIFFICULTY	LOOP	ELEV GAIN/ HIGH POINT	SEASON
****/3	4.4 miles	650 feet/ 750 feet	Year-round

Crowds: 4; **Map:** Green Trails Columbia River Gorge East No. 432S; **Contact:** Deschutes River State Recreation Area; **Notes:** Dogs permitted on-leash. Watch for rattlesnakes; **GPS:** N 45° 37.760', W 120° 54.485'

The Wild and Scenic Deschutes River is one of Oregon's grandest waterways and one of the Columbia's major tributaries. Here at its confluence with the Columbia, at the eastern gateway of the national scenic area, a delightful state park provides several miles of family-friendly trails along the Deschutes to a spring on a high bluff with grand views of the river and its canyon.

GETTING THERE

From The Dalles, follow I-84 east to exit 97 (Celilo Park). Then follow Biggs-Rufus Highway (State Route 206) east for 3 miles, crossing the Deschutes River and turning right into the Deschutes River State Recreation Area. (If coming from the east, take exit 104 at Biggs Junction off of I-84 and follow the Biggs-Rufus Highway west for 3.4 miles to the recreation area entrance.) Proceed 0.4 mile south through the campground to trailhead parking (elev. 170 ft.). Privy available.

ON THE TRAIL

Start by walking south about 0.2 mile across a grassy lawn to a junction. The trail left leads to the Riverview Trail (alternative option for this loop) and the Deschutes River

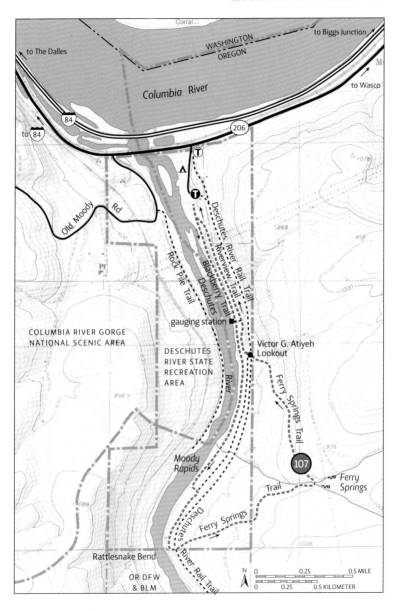

Enjoying an evening run near Ferry Springs

Rail Trail (Hike 108). Continue straight on the Blackberry Trail (also known as the Atiyeh Deschutes River Trail) along the churning river through a swath of riparian greenery. It's quite a contrast from the brown surrounding hills. Named by French Canadian fur traders as Rivière des Chutes (River of Waterfalls), the Deschutes is a popular whitewater run, with its many rapids.

At 0.6 mile pass a gauging station and a connecting trail to the parallel Riverview Trail. Continue straight along the river, passing a cable crossing and a lone big rocky ledge before coming to a small creek crossing and boardwalk. At 1.2 miles pass a privy and nice sandy beach that tempts feet soaking. The trail continues to Moody Rapids and then heads left (an unofficial trail continues straight along the river), making a quick ascent to meet up with the Riverview Trail (elev. 270 ft.) at 1.5 miles.

Now head right, traversing a bluff to a spectacular overlook (elev. 340 ft.) above a series of roiling rapids. At 1.9 miles reach a junction with the rail trail and, just a short distance to the right, the Ferry Springs Trail. Head left on it, steadily ascending

purple- (lupine) and gold- (arrowleaf balsamroot) streaked open slopes in spring, gray sun-scorched open slopes in summer, or barren and cold windblown open slopes in winter. The views grow wider as you continue to climb. Gaze down upon the river's frothy silver streak across a stark landscape—and peer north to the Columbia Hills marred by giant wind turbines. At 2.8 miles reach Ferry Springs in a lush draw (elev. 750 ft.).

Climb over a barbed-wire fence (don't worry, there are stairs), and begin a long descent on an old wagon road constructed in the 1860s to connect isolated eastern Oregon communities with The Dalles. At 3.6 miles once again reach the rail trail. Locate a spur that drops back to the Riverview Trail at the Victor G. Atiyeh Lookout. Governor of Oregon between 1979 and 1987, Atiyeh was responsible for helping to protect the lower 18 miles of the Deschutes River. Now turn right and walk through rolling sage-covered terrain, passing the connector trail to the river and continuing straight, returning to the junction at the grassy lawn at 4.2 miles. Your vehicle is 0.2 mile to the right.

EXTENDING YOUR TRIP

Run, bike, or hike all or a part of the 16-mile rail trail (Hike 108). Or hike the 1.2-mile Rock Pile Trail (accessed at the Heritage Landing boat ramp). Consider spending a night at the park's shaded campground.

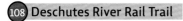

108 Deschutes River Rail Trail

RATING/ DIFFICULTY	ROUNDTRIP	ELEV GAIN/ HIGH POINT	SEASON
****/3	23 miles	700 feet/ 330 feet	Year-round

Crowds: 3; **Map:** Green Trails Columbia River Gorge East No. 432S; **Contact:** Deschutes River State Recreation Area; **Notes:** Dogs permitted on-leash. Watch for rattlesnakes. Fee if parking overnight. Trail open to mountain bikes and horses; **GPS:** N 45° 38.030', W 120° 54.466'

 *Walk along a historic long-abandoned rail line up the wide Deschutes River canyon. The way traverses flowered slopes and cuts across basaltic cliffs high above the Wild and Scenic river. Enjoy views of rapids and watch for big-horn sheep grazing the grassy canyon slopes.*

GETTING THERE

From The Dalles, follow I-84 east to exit 97 (Celilo Park). Then follow Biggs-Rufus Highway (State Route 206) east for 3 miles, crossing the Deschutes River and turning right into the Deschutes River State Recreation Area. (If coming from the east, take exit 104 at Biggs Junction off of I-84 and follow the Biggs-Rufus Highway west for 3.4 miles to the recreation area entrance.) The trailhead (elev. 225 ft.) is on your left just after entering the park. Privy available.

ON THE TRAIL

While appealing more to mountain bikers and equestrians than hikers, the wide graveled Deschutes River Rail Trail makes for some easy and delightful hiking too. Back-country campsites allow for overnight excursions, and while the old Harris Ranch might

TRAIL'S END—ALMOST!

The Columbia River Gorge has long been a busy transportation corridor, and for the thousands of emigrants who came west on the Oregon Trail during the 1840s and 1850s, the Gorge was the last major hurdle before the promised land of the fertile Willamette Valley. After enduring many hardships along the 2000-mile trail, when the settlers arrived at The Dalles they had to float their possessions, livestock, and families on rafts down the treacherous rapids of the Columbia through the Gorge. Some emigrants lost everything at this point—some even lost their lives.

By 1846 some overland routes, such as the Barlow toll road through Lolo Pass, were developed, bypassing the Gorge and offering the pioneers an alternate route. But even these trails were treacherous and harrowing, and the tolls were often steep. Look out at modern I-84 now and try to imagine what travel was like through this beautiful but potentially dangerous landscape before Oregon became a state in 1859. No doubt the pioneers of yesterday would be a bit miffed that we come to the Gorge now to recreate and hike—they had done enough hiking on their trek across America!

Deschutes River

be too far for most day hikers, it makes for a good trail-running adventure.

Start heading south on the wide, well-graded trail traversing sage shrub-steppe above the manicured and shady state park campground lawns. At 0.5 mile pass a trail leading right to the paralleling Riverview and Blackberry Trails (Hike 107) and campground (alternative start). At 1 mile pass the Ferry Springs Trail and Victor G. Atiyeh Lookout.

Next come to a junction with the Riverview and Ferry Springs Trails at 2.2 miles, just before Rattlesnake Bend. The way now leaves state park land to traverse primarily Oregon Department of Fish and Wildlife and Bureau of Land Management terrain. Catch good views of a set of rapids below. Watch the Deschutes River for rafters and the railroad across the river for passing trains. Pass a primitive trail leading right toward the river and connecting with the Blackberry Trail.

At 3.6 miles pass a side trail heading right to campsites (privy available). The main way descends to cross a creek coming out of Gordon Canyon before ascending and skirting beneath strikingly beautiful columnar basalt cliffs (a good turnaround spot for a shorter hike). The way continues traversing steep grassy slopes along the river and below the base of Gordon Ridge. Look for bighorn sheep. At 5.8 miles pass a privy and enter a burn zone from 2018, which unfortunately destroyed an old box car here as well as the structures at the old Harris homestead farther along.

At 6.7 miles pass the supports of the now gone Free Bridge, one of the first to offer toll-free crossings of the Deschutes River. The trail grade is nearly level and the going easy. If you have the energy, keep going. Pass more river rapids and catch views up the Blue Sands Canyon across the river. At 8.1 miles come to the primitive Rattlesnake Grade Road and pass a wash where a trestle once spanned.

Continue past a big bend and traverse the base of steep slopes. Pass old farm equipment and soon come to Fall Canyon Camp (privy) at 10.3 miles. At 11.1 miles reach the old Harris Ranch. Burnt timbers stand where fence lines and structures once stood. The trail runs along a channel that forms Harris Island. At 11.5 miles come to the remains of the old Harris water tower near the mouth of Harris Canyon, where the trail crosses Hays Creek in a thicket of big hackberries. This is a good spot to turn around.

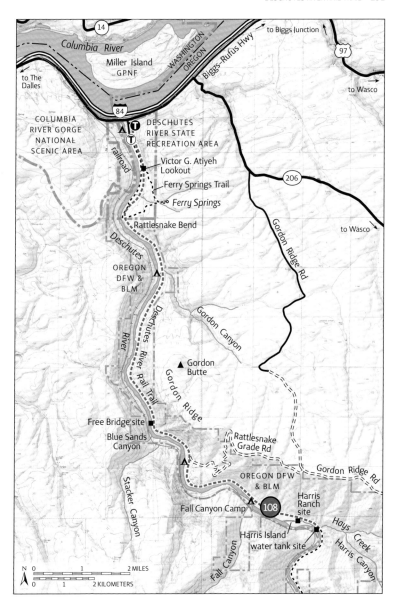

EXTENDING YOUR TRIP

For ultra-runners, mountain bikers, and backpackers, the trail continues through beautiful canyon country on good tread for another 7.6 miles before deteriorating and becoming a rough 4-mile route to Macks Canyon Campground.

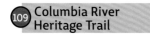

109 Columbia River Heritage Trail

RATING/ DIFFICULTY	ROUNDTRIP	ELEV GAIN/ HIGH POINT	SEASON
**/2	4.6 miles	120 feet/ 300 feet	Year-round

Crowds: 1; **Map:** online; **Contact:** Morrow County; **Notes:** Dogs permitted on-leash. Watch for rattlesnakes; **GPS:** N 45° 54.040', W 119° 29.531'

 *There's no dramatic gorge here in the*

far-eastern reaches of the Columbia's Oregon-Washington border flow. Between the great bend at Wallula Gap and the canyon housing the John Day River, the Columbia languidly (thanks to dams) drifts through a monotonous landscape of sun-parched low-lying hills of sage, wheat, grapevines, and wind turbines. But this area is also ecologically important (and threatened), providing habitat for scores of species. The Columbia River Heritage Trail allows you to get to know it.

GETTING THERE

From The Dalles follow I-84 east to exit 168 (Irrigon). Turn left onto US Highway 730 and proceed east 7.5 miles to the city of Irrigon, turning left onto 10th Street NE, signed for the marina. (From the Tri-Cities, head south on I-82, take exit 1, follow US 730 west for 8.1 miles, and turn right onto 10th Street NE.) Proceed for 0.2 mile to Marina Park and the trailhead (elev. 275 ft.). Privy available.

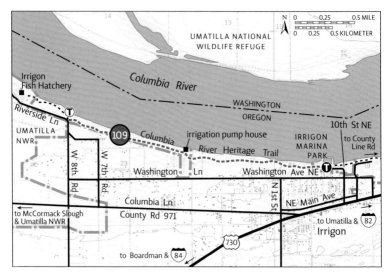

Shrub-steppe along the Columbia River

ON THE TRAIL

The Columbia River Heritage Trail was developed jointly as part of the Lewis and Clark Bicentennial Celebration by Morrow County, the National Park Service, the cities of Boardman and Irrigon, the US Army Corp of Engineers, the US Fish and Wildlife Service, the Oregon Department of Fish and Wildlife, the Confederated Tribes of the Umatilla Indian Reservation, and the Boeing Agri-Industrial Company. While currently touted as 12 miles long (with another 12 miles in the planning stage), much of the trail follows roads.

The 2.5-mile section east from the marina to the County Line Road, which travels mainly through the Irrigon Wildlife Refuge and passes a Lewis and Clark campsite en route, is interesting but pretty rough in places. Your best introduction to this trail is the 2.3-mile section west from the marina to the fish hatchery.

From the boat launch, locate the trail heading west 0.1 mile across a lawn by a nice beach.

After reaching a fence line, enter a more natural environment dominated by antelope bitterbrush and rabbitbrush. At 0.3 mile come to a fishing access road and walk it a short distance west. Cross a dirt road and resume on single track traversing open shrub-steppe on both soft and hard sandy tread.

The trail continues across an undeveloped swath owned by the Army Corps of Engineers. Houses are set back on the left, while there is nothing but Columbia River on the right—and views, too, to the low-lying hills and buttes across the water in Washington.

At 0.7 mile pass the remains of an old estate and at 0.9 mile a boat navigation beacon. Look for deer in the tall grasses. Listen to raucous magpies. In spring, admire showy blossoms. Pass occasional pines and locust trees, and at 1.3 miles pass an irrigation pump house. Walk west a short way on the access road and pick up trail again. Now higher on a bluff (elev. 300 ft.), scan the river—with its muddy, slow-moving water, it almost looks like the Mississippi. At 1.7 miles the trail passes closely to some homes. Continue hiking, reaching at 2.3 miles the W. 8th Road trailhead and lands, now managed by the Irrigon Fish Hatchery. This is a good point to turn around.

EXTENDING YOUR TRIP

You can continue west for 0.5 mile to the hatchery. Or enjoy the western section of the trail in Boardman (access from Boardman Marina), which is paved and runs for about 1.8 miles past a beach, an old tugboat, a campground, resort cabins, and excellent views along the Columbia.

One of the nicest sections of the Columbia River Heritage Trail follows a long-abandoned section of the original Columbia River Highway across bird-rich McCormack Slough in the nearby 23,500-acre Umatilla National Wildlife Refuge. Access the trail from Parking Lot C off of the Auto Route Loop. The 0.5-mile trail is kid-friendly and wheelchair-accessible, and it's closed on Wednesdays, Saturdays, and Sundays from October 1 to January 31. The nearby 0.3-mile McCormack Slough Trail is great for birdwatching.

110 Lewis and Clark Commemorative Trail

RATING/ DIFFICULTY	ROUNDTRIP	ELEV GAIN/ HIGH POINT	SEASON
***/3	14.6 miles	560 feet/ 410 feet	Year-round

Crowds: 2; **Map:** USGS Umatilla, USGS Hat Rock; **Contact:** US Army Corp of Engineers, McNary Lock and Dam; **Notes:** Dogs permitted on-leash. Trail open to horses and bikes; **GPS:** N 45° 55.864', W 119° 16.066'

Hike or run from the McNary Dam alongside a languid Columbia River to a sandy beach just west of Wallula Gap. The way follows a former line of the Union Pacific Railroad, taking you across sage-scented shrub-steppe and atop and beneath basalt cliffs above the river. Pass

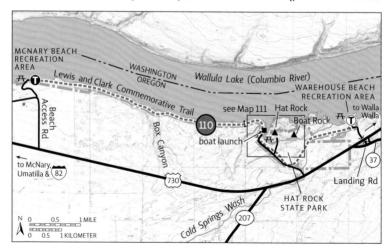

The trail follows a basaltic bench along the Columbia River.

historic sites significant to the Lewis and Clark expedition and to the area's First Peoples.

GETTING THERE

From The Dalles, follow I-84 east for 95 miles, turning north onto I-82. Continue north for 6 miles to the exit signed for Umatilla and McNary. (If coming from Tri-Cities, Washington, follow I-82 south and take the first exit after crossing the Columbia River.) Then head east on US Highway 730 for 2.8 miles, turning left onto Beach Access Road. Continue for 1.7 miles to the trailhead (elev. 375 ft.) at the McNary Beach Recreation Area. Privy available.

ON THE TRAIL

This is a great stretch of rail trail through public land rife with excellent views, historic and culturally significant landmarks, and wildlife-watching opportunities. The terrain can be a little sandy and rocky in places, and heat can be stifling, as there is no shade. So plan your excursions accordingly. The trail can be accessed from three spots, so shorter hiking options are possible.

From the shaded and manicured lawns of the McNary Beach Recreation Area, immediately enter shrub-steppe. The way skirts below and travels along basalt cliffs above the Columbia, here a dammed backwater known as Lake Wallula. At 1.2 miles the trail makes a short steep climb, one of several areas breaking stride from the original rail grade to skirt washouts. The way travels through a wildlife management area. Look for magpies, quails, deer, and coyotes. Snakes are copious, too, including an occasional rattler.

At 2.6 miles cross Box Canyon, near a dramatic spot of big basalt ledges and cliffs. The way then climbs above cliffs where a trestle once stood. Take in good views east to Wallula Gap, an impressive gorge on the Columbia where it bends north into Washington, away from the Washington-Oregon border. At 4.9 miles leave the wildlife area at a gate and pass beneath a bluff sporting homes. At 5.3 miles veer south and leave the river bluffs. Traverse a cut and enter Hat Rock State Park (Hike 111), where it's possible to get some water.

Traverse the park while enjoying views of the basaltic monolith Hat Rock. The trail crosses Marina Drive and continues through the state park on lightly used tread through sandy shrub-steppe. The way then once again follows along on the old rail bed. Cross a wash and pass good viewpoints of the basaltic monolith Boat Rock. Then leave the park and travel across sandy, slow-going terrain, coming to the eastern trailhead (alternative start) at the Warehouse Beach Recreation Area (privy available) at 7.3 miles. Have lunch in the picnic area and take a dip at the sandy beach to enjoy a great view of Wallula Gap before heading 7.3 miles back to your start.

111 Hat Rock

RATING/ DIFFICULTY	LOOP	ELEV GAIN/ HIGH POINT	SEASON
**/1	0.9 mile	80 feet/ 420 feet	Year-round

Crowds: 3; **Map:** USGS Hat Rock; **Contact:** Hat Rock State Park; **Notes:** Dogs permitted on-leash. Watch for rattlesnakes; **GPS:** N 45° 54.926', W 119° 10.208'

A distinctive geological landmark, Hat Rock sits at the mouth of Wallula Gap, a mini yet impressive gorge at a massive bend in the Columbia. It's near here that the river forms the Washington–Oregon border, and it's here that Lewis and Clark first entered what later became the state of Oregon. Enjoy this easy hike rife with natural and human history.

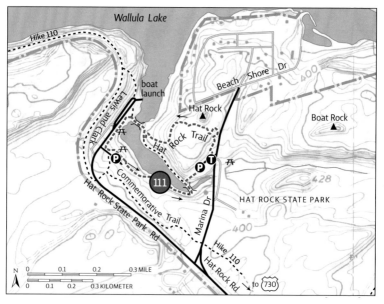

A white pelican glides across a small pond below Hat Rock.

shoreline as well as numerous Native and early American sites and artifacts. Even the vegetation is different—those black locust trees providing much-appreciated shade are transplants from the east.

But this area still possesses great beauty, albeit in a world of contrast between the past and present, natural and modified. Wind your way up the wide and well-manicured trail to the base (elev. 400 ft.) of the hat-shaped landmark, a remnant of the massive lava flows that covered this region more than 12 million years ago. Subsequent ice age floods channeled and scoured the lava flows, leaving behind canyons and outcroppings like 70-foot-high Hat Rock. Good interpretive signs along the trail will give you a better appreciation for the area's natural and human history.

Continue along the trail, passing a good viewpoint looking west to the Columbia River, and then begin a short descent, coming to a junction at a pond (elev. 325 ft.). Left will lead you along the pond back to the trailhead for a short loop. Head right instead, across a dike to a boat launch, parking area, and access to the 7.3-mile Lewis and Clark Commemorative Trail (Hike 110). Then walk the parking lot to another lot on the left and pick up a paved trail traveling east along the pond that trout and ducks (and occasionally pelicans) love. At the far end of the pond, cross a bridge and then turn right at a junction to return to your start. Consider extending this hike with a walk on the Lewis and Clark Commemorative Trail.

Opposite: *The John Day River flows alongside the Hard Stone Trail (Hike 115).*

cottonwood canyon
state park, oregon

One of Oregon's newest state parks and its second largest, Cottonwood Canyon protects more than 8,000 acres of stunning riparian habitat and steep canyon walls along the John Day River. Forty miles southeast of The Dalles, this sprawling former ranch consists of dramatic landscapes similar to the eastern reaches of the Columbia River Gorge but without the urban centers and infrastructure.

Hike on miles of old ranch roads and trails along and above the John Day River, the longest undammed tributary of the Columbia River and a national wild and scenic river. Admire basalt cliffs, sage flats, grasslands, and deep side canyons. Explore old ranch structures and look for grazing bighorn sheep and soaring golden eagles. Cottonwood Canyon is an easy day trip from The Dalles or consider spending a night or two in the state park's beautiful campground.

112 Pinnacles Trail

RATING/ DIFFICULTY	ROUNDTRIP	ELEV GAIN/ HIGH POINT	SEASON
****/2	9.6 miles	120 feet/ 560 feet	Year-round

Crowds: 3; **Map:** online at Cottonwood Canyon State Park site; **Contact:** Cottonwood Canyon State Park; **Notes:** Dogs permitted on-leash. Trail open to mountain bikes. Trail closed at 3.3 miles Feb–Sept to protect nesting golden eagles. Watch for rattlesnakes; **GPS:** N 45° 29.062', W 120° 27.563'

Hike into the heart of Cottonwood Canyon State Park following along the rippling Wild and Scenic John Day River in a deep, wide canyon. Pass old ranch relics, big old hackberry and walnut trees, columnar basalt cliffs, wide gravel bars,

and steep grassy slopes that are home to one of Oregon's largest bighorn sheep herds.

GETTING THERE
From The Dalles, follow I-84 east to exit 97 (Celilo Park). Then follow State Route 206 for 25.5 miles and turn right on Cottonwood Canyon State Park access road. (From the east, take exit 104 [Biggs Junction] on I-84 and drive US Highway 97 south for 8.5 miles. Then follow SR 206 for 16.3 miles south and turn right on Cottonwood Canyon State Park access road.) Follow for 1 mile, passing day-use areas and campground entrance to the trailhead (elev. 550 ft.) at road's end. Privy available.

ON THE TRAIL
The 8000-plus acre Cottonwood Canyon is Oregon's second largest state park. A former cattle ranch owned by the Murtha family, the property was purchased in 2008 by the Western Rivers Conservancy to protect its outstanding wildlife habitat. The land was then sold to Oregon Parks and Recreation Department, which opened it as a state park in 2013. Many of the old ranch buildings have been restored and a new campground developed. But most of this sprawling park remains undeveloped, accessed by a series of trails, many former ranch roads. Winter can be frigid, summer brutally hot. Spring and fall are ideal for visits.

Follow the Pinnacles Trail east, soon bearing right with the Sage Steppe Trail. The trail then skirts campsites (complete with solar chargers) in the Lone Tree Campground and comes to a junction with the Willow Flats Trail at 0.3 mile. Continue straight on an old ranch road past a gate, kiosk, and stand of netleaf hackberry trees. The trail then traverses a narrow bluff above the river along

Columnar basalt along the Pinnacles Trail.

the base of steep and overhanging columnar basalt cliffs. Check out all of the cliff swallow nests in the cliffs.

The trail then traverses a broad flat of sage steppe traveling along the rippling river. Flows vary greatly, as the 284-mile-long John Day River is the fourth longest undammed river in the continental US. At 1.1 miles at a large solo walnut tree, come to a junction with the Lower and Upper Walnut Trails. They both parallel the Pinnacles Trail and reconnect with it—the lower for 0.4 mile near the river, the upper for 0.6 mile along a shelf providing good river views.

Continue hiking downriver. Scan the grassy slopes above you for Rocky Mountain bighorn sheep. The park contains a large herd helped by recent reintroductions. Farther down the trail, the way begins to make a wide bend with the river. Here enjoy good views across the river to towering basalt pinnacles and up Esau Canyon, one of several side canyons in the park. At 3.3 miles reach the seasonal closure point. From October 1 until January 31 you can continue farther, skirting basalt cliffs, pinnacles, and talus.

Look for majestic golden eagles that nest in this area.

The way crosses another sage flat, comes back alongside the river near a wide gravel bar, and passes beneath some basalt towers known as the Pinnacles. The way then continues past cliff bases and talus, ending at a gate in tall sage at 4.8 miles.

EXTENDING YOUR TRIP

From the trailhead, follow the Willow Flats Trail left for 0.8 mile back along the river to restored ranch buildings and interpretive displays. Then cross the park road and return to the trailhead via the 0.4-mile Sage Steppe Trail.

113 Gooseneck Trail

RATING/ DIFFICULTY	ROUNDTRIP	ELEV GAIN/ HIGH POINT	SEASON
****/3	2.2 miles	750 feet/ 1260 feet	Year-round

Crowds: 1; **Map:** online at Cottonwood Canyon State Park site; **Contact:** Cottonwood Canyon State Park; **Notes:** Dogs permitted

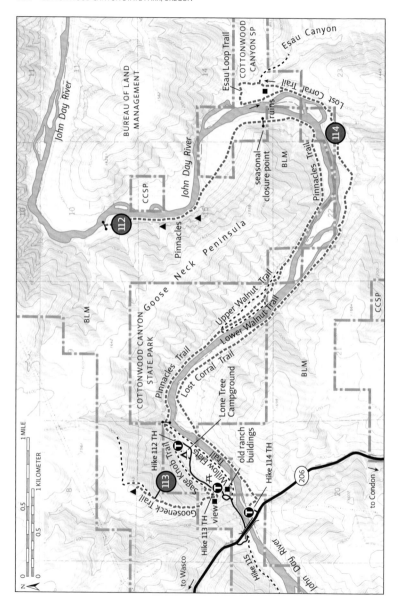

The Gooseneck Trail offers a sweeping view of the John Day River.

on-leash. Watch for rattlesnakes. Trail is primitive and not recommended for novices; **GPS:** N 45° 28.797', W 120° 27.881'

![icons] *Follow a primitive trail climbing steeply up high open slopes for a spectacular view of the John Day River wending below in a deep canyon. Enjoy views, too, of the old Murtha Ranch below. Scan the sage-scented hillsides for bighorn sheep and the oft-blue skies for soaring golden eagles.*

GETTING THERE

From Portland, follow I-84 east to exit 97 (Celilo Park). Then follow State Route 206 for 25.5 miles and turn right on Cottonwood Canyon State Park access road. (From the east, take exit 104 [Biggs Junction] on I-84 and drive US Highway 97 south for 8.5 miles. Then follow SR 206 for 16.3 miles south and turn right on Cottonwood Canyon State Park access road.) Follow it for 0.6 mile to trailhead (elev. 550 ft.) at day-use area. Privy available.

ON THE TRAIL

Start on the Sage Steppe Trail, crossing under a wooden gateway. After 0.1 mile leave the smooth, well-trodden trail left for the Sage Knob Trail. Gently climb through sages via one switchback and reach the viewpoint on Little Sage Knob (elev. 620 ft.) at 0.25 mile. Here take in a limited view of the ranch buildings and park day-use area. The real views are yet to come.

At a wooden gateway frame at the viewpoint, start up the unmarked Gooseeck Trail on light but discernable tread. A primitive path, this trail leads for several miles along a high ridge above a long bend of the John Day River referred to as the Gooseneck. Much of the route is difficult to follow and can be challenging. But the western end (described here) includes some spectacular viewpoints, is fairly well-defined, and can be enjoyed by experienced hikers.

Climb along an open ridge crest following good tread and occasional orange flagging. The way wastes no time ascending. It's a straightforward route with tight switchbacks and an occasional bend to skirt around rocky outcroppings. In spring the way is brightened with wildflowers, notably prairie stars and arrowleaf balsamroot.

At 0.8 mile (elev. 1100 ft.) the trail bends east for a gentle traverse on a broad bench beneath rock outcroppings and ledges. Keep hiking, coming to some large rocks (elev. 1260 ft.) where the trail bends left to skirt a draw at 1.1 miles. This is a good spot to call it quits and collect your visual rewards for your effort. Enjoy jaw-dropping views down to the campground and John Day River and out to its bend at Lost Corral (Hike 114). Enjoy views, too, to Cottonwood Canyon near the road entrance to the park. The trail continues, but the tread gets sketchy past a fence line near a juniper-lined creek gully 0.7 mile farther.

114 Lost Corral

RATING/ DIFFICULTY	ROUNDTRIP	ELEV GAIN/ HIGH POINT	SEASON
***/2	9.2 miles	400 feet/ 570 feet	Year-round

Crowds: 3; **Map:** online at Cottonwood Canyon State Park site; **Contact:** Cottonwood

Canyon State Park; **Notes:** Dogs permitted on-leash. Watch for rattlesnakes. Trail is open to horses and bikes. Area open to hunting; **GPS:** N 45° 28.6158', W 150° 28 .062'

Walk a gentle and quiet old ranch road along the John Day River to an old cattle corral at the base of steep basaltic walls. Admire sage flats, columnar basaltic cliffs, small rapids, tranquil river channels, and plenty of wide canyon views along the way.

GETTING THERE
From The Dalles, follow I-84 east to exit 97 (Celilo Park). Then follow State Route 206 for 25.8 miles and turn left (just after crossing the John Day River) into the J. S. Burres trailhead (elev. 550 ft.). (From the east, take exit 104 [Biggs Junction] on I-84 and drive US Highway 97 south for 8.5 miles. Then follow SR 206 for 16.3 miles south to trailhead.) Privy available.

ON THE TRAIL
The Lost Corral Trail in the sprawling Cottonwood Canyon State Park runs along the opposite bank of the John Day River from the more popular Pinnacles Trail. Start your hike through a fence arch and traverse a sagebrush flat. Catch good views across the river to the old Murtha Ranch and state park structures.

Pass a big lone juniper and come up along the river. Continue downriver along the base of basalt cliffs, soon passing a big outwash area. Then traverse another sage flat and, after passing through a patch of hackberries, resume riverside walking. At 2 miles a bench on a small bluff above the river invites a break. At 2.7 miles walk along quieter waters as the trail follows along a channel beneath basalt ledges. A second bench beckons the weary.

Esau Loop above Lost Corral

The way then follows a bend in the river and canyon and traverses a large sage flat. At 3.8 miles encounter another channel and follow it below big basalt cliffs. At 4.2 miles reach a junction with the Esau Loop Trail at an old fence line. You'll return from the left so continue straight, coming to the Lost Corral tucked along basalt cliffs at 4.3 miles. Check out the ruins (but leave all artifacts in place), including old advertising signs.

Now continue hiking up the old ranch road soon coming to the Esau Loop Trail. Take it left climbing up a small bluff that grants excellent sweeping views of Esau Canyon, the Goose Neck Peninsula bend on the John Day River, and several draws in the big canyon you're hiking in. The trail then meanders through big sagebrush plants and reaches the river. Watch for chukars (small members of the pheasant family introduced from Asia) in the brush, mergansers in the

river, swallows above the river, and eagles high in the sky. At 5 miles return to the Lost Corral Trail. Turn right and head 4.2 miles back to the trailhead.

115 Hard Stone Trail

RATING/ DIFFICULTY	ROUNDTRIP	ELEV GAIN/ HIGH POINT	SEASON
***/2	3.2 miles	240 feet/ 600 feet	Year-round

Crowds: 2; **Map:** online at Cottonwood Canyon State Park site; **Contact:** Cottonwood Canyon State Park; **Notes:** Dogs permitted on-leash. Watch for rattlesnakes. Area open to hunting; **GPS:** N 45° 28.2708', W 120° 28.3378'

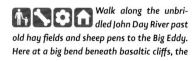 *Walk along the unbridled John Day River past old hay fields and sheep pens to the Big Eddy. Here at a big bend beneath basaltic cliffs, the*

John Day River

river swirls and churns. *Scan the cliffs above for raptors and swallows and the big, broad island at the eddy for resting waterfowl.*

GETTING THERE

From The Dalles, follow I-84 east to exit 97 (Celilo Park). Then follow State Route 206 for 25.5 miles and turn right on Cottonwood Canyon State Park access road. (From the east, take exit 104 [Biggs Junction] on I-84 and drive US Highway 97 south for 8.5 miles. Then follow SR 206 for 16 miles south and turn right on Cottonwood Canyon State Park access road.) Follow it for 0.1 mile. Then turn right for the trailhead (elev. 560 ft.) at day-use area. Privy available at nearby park day-use area.

ON THE TRAIL

Follow an old ranch road past derelict farm equipment while skirting an old hay field that hasn't yet been taken over by sage. The walking is a little rockier here than on the other old ranch roads-turned-trails in the park. At 0.5 mile the road branches left while a paralleling track continues straight. The way left travels close to the river. The way forward climbs a small bluff with a bench granting good views of the river. Hike one route on the way in, the other on the way out.

At 0.7 mile the two tracks meet up near an old rock compound in a thicket of hackberries. The compounds were probably old sheep pens from when this former ranch grazed sheep a century ago. Continue hiking,

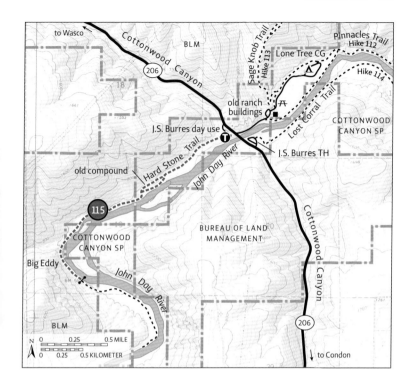

passing junipers and high sagebrush, climbing a tad above the river. Then traverse a talus slope and come to a big bend in the river and the Big Eddy beneath high basaltic cliffs. Stare down at the swirling water and across the river to a large island sporting big juniper trees and often hosting resting flocks of waterfowl.

The trail continues, coming to a fence line and big hackberries at 1.6 miles. This is the official trail ending. Beyond, the path continues for another mile, but it's only open from October 1 to January 31 to protect nesting golden eagles. Look in the sky for their giant silhouettes as you head back to the trailhead.

Acknowledgments

Researching and writing the second edition of *Day Hiking Columbia River Gorge* was fun, exciting, and a lot of hard work. I couldn't have finished this project without the help and support of the following people:

A huge thank you to all the great people at Mountaineers Books, especially publisher Tom Helleberg, project editor Susan Elderkin, and editor in chief Kate Rogers. And another huge thank you to copyeditor Ali Shaw for her attention to detail and thoughtful suggestions to make this book a finer volume.

I want to thank a number of people for accompanying me and supporting me on my research trips. A big thanks to Karl Peterson, Jay Thompson, Wendy Wheeler-Jacobs, Geoffrey Lawrence, and Merill Cray for accompanying me on so many great hikes! Thanks too to Susan Saul and Ryan Ojerio for some terrific tips and trail information. And a big thanks to my in-laws Virginia and Vince Scott for providing me a wonderful base in Vancouver and many delicious meals after long days on the trail.

I want to once again thank God for watching over me while I hiked all over the Columbia River Gorge, keeping me safe and healthy. Most importantly, I want to thank my loving wife, Heather, for supporting me while I worked on yet another guidebook. Thanks also for hiking with me to some of the special places in this book. And finally, thanks to my wonderful son, Giovanni, for hiking with me on so many of these trails. We have so many more miles yet to hike!

Appendix I:
Land Management Agencies

Columbia Land Trust
www.columbialandtrust.org

Columbia River Gorge National Scenic Area
www.fs.usda.gov/crgnsa
(541) 308-1700

Friends of the Columbia Gorge
www.gorgefriends.org
(503) 241-3762

US Army Corps of Engineers
Bonneville Lock and Dam
www.nwp.usace.army.mil/bonneville
(541) 374-8820

McNary Lock and Dam
www.nps.gov/places/lewis-and-clark-commemorative-trail.htm

WASHINGTON
Bonneville Trails Foundation
www.bonnevilletrails.org

City of Goldendale Public Works
www.ci.goldendale.wa.us/public-works/parks-city-parks
(509) 773-3771

Conboy Lake National Wildlife Refuge
www.fws.gov/refuge/conboy-lake
(509) 546-8300

Gifford Pinchot National Forest
www.fs.usda.gov/giffordpinchot

Mount Adams Ranger District, Trout Lake
www.fs.usda.gov/recarea/giffordpinchot/recarea/?recid=31184
(509) 395-3402

Mount St. Helens National Volcanic Monument
www.fs.usda.gov/recarea/giffordpinchot/recarea/?recid=34143
(360) 449-7800

Klickitat Trail Conservancy
www.klickitat-trail.org

Port of Benton (Crow Butte Park)
www.crowbutte.com
(509) 940-7326

Port of Camas-Washougal
www.portcw.com/parks-trails
(360) 835-2196

Steigerwald Lake National Wildlife Refuge
www.fws.gov/refuge/steigerwald-lake
(360) 835-8767

Washington Department of
Fish & Wildlife
www.wdfw.wa.gov

> **Southwest Region (Klickitat Wildlife
> Area)**
> (360) 696-6211

Washington State Department of
Natural Resources
www.dnr.wa.gov

> **Pacific Cascade Region**
> (360) 577-2025

> **Southeast Region**
> (509) 925-8510

Washington State Parks
www.parks.wa.gov
(360) 902-8844

> **Beacon Rock State Park**
> (509) 427-8265

> **Brooks Memorial State Park**
> (509) 773-4611

> **Columbia Hills Historical State Park**
> (509) 773-3145

OREGON
Hood River County Parks & Buildings
www.hoodrivercounty.gov/parksbuildings

Hood River Valley Parks and Recreation
hoodriverparksandrec.org/indian-creek-trail
(541) 386-5720

Morrow County
www.co.morrow.or.us/planning/page/
    columbia-river-heritage-trail
(541) 922-4624

Mount Hood National Forest
www.fs.usda.gov/mthood

> **Hood River Ranger District**
> www.fs.usda.gov/recarea/mthood/
>   recarea/?recid=52776
> (541) 352-6002

**Northern Wasco County Parks &
Recreation**
www.nwprd.org/rivertrail
(541) 296-9533

The Nature Conservancy—Oregon
www.nature.org/en-us
(503) 802-8100

Oregon State Parks
stateparks.oregon.gov
(800) 551-6949

> **Bridal Veil Falls State
> Scenic Viewpoint**
> (503) 695-2261

> **Cottonwood Canyon State Park**
> (541) 739-2322

> **Deschutes River State
> Recreation Area**
> (541) 739-2322

**Guy W. Talbot–Latourell Falls
Trailhead State Park**
(503) 695-2261

Hat Rock State Park
(541) 567-5032

**Historic Columbia River Highway
State Trail**
(541) 387-4010

John B. Yeon Trailhead (Elowah Falls)
(503) 695-2261

Mayer State Park
(541) 478-3008

Rooster Rock State Park
(503) 695-2261

Oxbow Regional Park
www.oregonmetro.gov/parks/
    oxbow-regional-park
(503) 663-4708

Port of Hood River
www.portofhoodriver.com/
    waterfront-recreation
(541) 386-1645

Appendix II: Conservation and Trails Organizations

Bonneville Trails Foundation
www.bonnevilletrails.org

Cape Horn Conservancy
www.capehornconservancy.org

Columbia Gorge Refuge Stewards
www.refugestewards.org

Columbia Land Trust
www.columbialandtrust.org
(360) 696-0131

Friends of the Columbia Gorge
www.gorgefriends.org
(503) 241-3762

Klickitat Trail Conservancy
www.klickitat-trail.org

Mazamas
www.mazamas.org
(503) 227-2345

The Mountaineers
www.mountaineers.org
(206) 521-6000

The Nature Conservancy
Oregon Field Office
www.nature.org
(503) 230-1221

The Nature Conservancy
Washington Field Office
www.nature.org
(206) 343-4344

Pacific Crest Trail Association
www.pcta.org
(916) 285-1846

Trails Club of Oregon
www.trailsclub.org

Trailkeepers of Oregon
www.trailkeepersoforegon.org

Washington Trails Association
www.wta.org
(206) 625-1367

Index

1% for Trails

Where would we be without trails? Not very far into the wilderness. That's why Mountaineers Books designates 1 percent of sales of select guidebooks in our Day

Hiking series toward trail maintenance. Since launching this program, we've contributed more than $34,000 toward improving trails.

For this book, our 1 percent of sales is going to Trailkeepers of Oregon (TKO). Founded in 2007, TKO protects and enhances the Oregon hiking experience through stewardship, advocacy, outreach, and education. Each year, more than three thousand TKO volunteers help design new trails, restore damaged trails, clear fallen logs, and support safe and welcoming experiences on urban and wilderness trails—from the Columbia River Gorge to the Oregon coast and beyond.

Mountaineers Books donates many books to nonprofit recreation and conservation organizations. Our 1% for Trails campaign is one more way we help fellow nonprofit organizations as we work together to get people outside, to both enjoy and protect our wild public lands.

If you'd like to support Mountaineers Books and our nonprofit partnership programs, please visit our website to learn more or contact mbooks@mountaineersbooks.org.

About the Author

Craig Romano grew up in rural New Hampshire where he fell in love with the natural world. He moved to Washington in 1989 and has since hiked more than 32,000 miles in the Evergreen state and several thousand in Oregon. An avid runner as well, Craig has run more than 50 marathons and ultra runs including the Boston Marathon, the White River 50 Mile Endurance Run, and Mount Hood's 41-mile Timberline Trail in a day.

An award-winning author of more than 25 books, Craig was deeply honored when *Columbia Highlands: Exploring Washington's Last Frontier* was recognized in 2010 by Washington Secretary of State Sam Reed and State Librarian Jan Walsh as a Washington Reads book for its contribution to Washington's cultural heritage. Craig also writes for numerous publications, tourism websites, and hikeoftheweek.com.

Craig holds several degrees: an AA in forestry from White Mountains Community College in New Hampshire and a BA in history and a Master of Education from the University of Washington.

When not hiking, running, or writing, he can be found napping with his wife Heather, son Giovanni, and Maine coon kitty Beau at his home in Skagit County, Washington. Visit him at www.craigromano.com and on Facebook at "Craig Romano Guidebook Author."

MOUNTAINEERS BOOKS, including its two imprints, Skipstone and Braided River, is a leading publisher of quality outdoor recreation, sustainability, and conservation titles. As a 501(c)(3) nonprofit, we are committed to supporting the environmental and educational goals of our organization by providing expert information on human-powered adventure, sustainable practices at home and on the trail, and preservation of wilderness.

Our publications are made possible through the generosity of donors, and through sales of more than 700 titles on outdoor recreation, sustainable lifestyle, and conservation. To donate, purchase books, or learn more, visit us online:

MOUNTAINEERS BOOKS
1001 SW Klickitat Way, Suite 201 • Seattle, WA 98134
800-553-4453 • mbooks@mountaineersbooks.org • www.mountaineersbooks.org

An independent nonprofit publisher since 1960

OTHER TITLES YOU MIGHT ENJOY FROM MOUNTAINEERS BOOKS

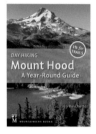

Day Hiking Mount Hood
Eli Boschetto
A year-round guide to the best trails
around this iconic peak

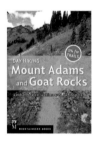

**Day Hiking Mount Adams
and Goat Rocks**
Tami Asars
Featuring Indian Heaven, the
Yakima Area, and White Pass

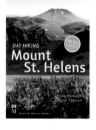

Day Hiking Mount St. Helens
Craig Romano & Aaron Theisen
Featuring the National Volcanic
Monument along with nature
trails, winter routes, and the
St. Helens summit

Urban Trails Portland
Eli Boschetto

Urban Trails Vancouver, WA
Craig Romano
Get outside close to home
with Urban Trails